TUFFERS'
ASHES HEROES

TUFFERS'
ASHES HEROES

Legends & characters
from both sides of cricket's divide

PHIL TUFNELL

with John Woodhouse

HarperCollins*Publishers*

HarperCollins*Publishers*
1 London Bridge Street
London SE1 9GF

www.harpercollins.co.uk

HarperCollins*Publishers*
Macken House, 39/40 Mayor Street Upper
Dublin 1, D01 C9W8, Ireland

First published by HarperCollins*Publishers* 2025

1 3 5 7 9 10 8 6 4 2

A catalogue record of this book is available from the British Library

HB ISBN 978-0-00-875388-7
PB ISBN 978-0-00-879699-0

Illustrations: Shutterstock.com

Printed and bound in the UK using 100% renewable electricity
at CPI Group (UK) Ltd

MIX
Paper | Supporting
responsible forestry
FSC
www.fsc.org
FSC™ C007454

This book contains FSC™ certified paper and other controlled
sources to ensure responsible forest management.

For more information visit: www.harpercollins.co.uk/green

To Dawn – always at my side – and all the
Ashes cricketers, present and departed,
I played with and against.

CONTENTS

CONTENTS

INTRODUCTION

I was just thinking about the launch point for this book when I looked up at the TV and saw an image of perhaps England's greatest Ashes hero – or at least his midriff. Sir Ian Botham, a newsreader revealed, had plunged from a fishing boat into the shark and crocodile infested waters of the Moyle River near Darwin, in northern Australia. Who had rescued him from this unenviable situation? None other than the human moustache, Merv Hughes. The former Aussie paceman reached out a hairy arm and pulled his old Pommie foe from an imminent onslaught of snapping teeth – once word had got round the shark community that there was someone called Beefy in the water the only natural outcome was a scene reminiscent of *Jaws*. Big Merv saw to it that Sir Beef, a few bruised ribs apart, lived to fight another day, although considering his previous exploits Down Under you wouldn't have bet against Beefy taking on a marauding gang of bloodthirsty reptiles and emerging victorious from the water, going on to regain his title as BBC Sports Personality of the Year.

Naturally, I was delighted that Beefy had escaped unscathed. The all-conquering all-rounder was a hero of mine as a kid and even more so when, to my astonishment, I found myself playing alongside him for England. I did wonder why, though, anyone would want to have a day out anywhere infested with sharks and crocodiles. The clue there is the word 'infested'. There's a reason why such breaks don't pop up in many holiday brochures.

As you'll see in this book, I love Australia, but there are things you need to be careful of when travelling out there, most of them beginning with 's'. Spiders, snakes, sharks and Steve Smith to name but a few. On one tour, for some inexplicable reason, several of us were taken on a trip to a saltwater crocodile sanctuary where we were introduced to a vast beast by the name of Mabel. As I watched it launch itself, mouth agape, to consume a dead chicken dangled on a fishing rod, I couldn't help but think that, as leisure activities go, swimming with jellyfish would have been a slightly better choice.

Safe to say then that you would never have found me on that boat with Beefy and Big Merv. At the same time, however, I was warmed that Beefy, nudging his seventies, was still living his best life, and doing so alongside those with whom he'd shared some pretty serious on-field battles. Beefy's the perfect example of how, while the Ashes is one of the biggest rivalries in world sport, an undercurrent of respect between the two sides has led to countless lasting friendships. For example, having on regular occasions seen Merv's facial accoutrement, sprouting, walrus-esque, beneath snorting nostrils as he snarled at me on his follow-through, I still send him a bauble to hang on it every Christmas.

I'll be honest, it took me a little while to work out how the competitive rivalry of the Ashes worked. I made my debut in the landmark Boxing Day Test at the Melbourne Cricket Ground, better known simply as the MCG, a bearpit of an atmosphere on and off the pitch. Nowadays, I'm sure no England player would be thrown into that colosseum without some kind of mental preparation or consultation. They'd be sat down and spoken to, their ability to withstand and manage the occasion assessed. Back in 1990, however, I had to learn to fight and had to do it quickly – because the Aussies were fighting me. When I came on to bowl they weren't holding back. 'I ain't gonna give you my wicket. You're gonna be a one-Test wonder. "Phil Tufnell – never got a Test wicket". That's what it'll say on your gravestone.' I'd be stood there thinking, *What on Earth is going on here? Surely they've got it the wrong way round. Isn't it the bowler who sledges the batsman?*

To find your place amid that degree of hostility isn't easy. It really does take a little bit of doing. I was combative when I was picked for England – there were plenty of batsmen, and umpires, on the county circuit who'd verify that I wasn't averse to giving someone a bit of lip – but there's a big difference between giving a few verbals to Glamorgan's number 11 at Sofia Gardens in front of half a dozen spectators and telling Allan Border and Dean Jones to f*** off in front of 70,000 baying Aussies at the MCG. These weren't friendly people. Aussie skipper Allan Border had decreed that the days of being chummy with the Poms were over when he brought them to England a year earlier. His bonhomie ban had contributed to a steely and single-minded 4–0 thrashing, and so no way was he going to reverse it on home soil. The Aussies sledged as a group, a pack mentality, like wolves bearing down on prey. I actually believe some of them were ordered to shout at me, and I think they quite enjoyed giving it to the new kid on the block.

While, not altogether surprisingly, I went wicketless in that Test, I got five in the second innings of the next encounter at Sydney. At that point I felt that I belonged a little. I was contributing, doing my job. While the Aussies were still coming for me during that game I felt empowered to give a bit back, to show them that they couldn't just take the piss and keep calling me a useless Pommie **** all the time. But that's not to say the first couple of times it doesn't knock you back a little. It's a level of ferocity you're just not used to. At that point you can go one of two ways. You can either buckle under the pressure or use the animosity to build yourself up a bit. In my case, it wasn't long before the sledging I experienced just made me laugh. While at first it felt very real, after a while it seemed more like pantomime. I mean, when you think about it, none of it actually matters. Let's face it, no-one's going to dish out a right-hander on a cricket field. There's never going to be a mass brawl. It's not ice hockey. Once the shock of those first few games was out of the way, I'd look at a player, some bloke in his 60th Test match, trying to impose themselves on me, someone just starting out, and just give it them back. 'What was that, you sweaty old ****? Go on! F*** off back down your own end so I can get you out.' I was quite happy if they wanted to sledge. A bit of argy-bargy kept the proceedings interesting and me fired up. *I'm not going to let you bastards intimidate me or put me off my game. I'm going to try my very best to win this match for England.*

Despite the occasional spot of antagonism, every England player will tell you that Australia is the best tour. The weather, the wine, the restaurants, the bars – it's a very hard place not to have a good time. I mean, come on, it's Australia! You're young, you're playing for England and you're in one of the most incredible countries on Earth. When you've grown up in the drizzle and murk of Britain it's hard to comprehend how dazzlingly different Australia is, quite literally. The light's amazing, the colours so bright – it's as if the world and everything in it has suddenly come to life. Then there's the beaches. Jump in the sea here and you're a block of ice within a minute. Not for nothing did we give the world the woollen swimsuit. Jump in the sea there and it's all lovely and warm. Everywhere you look there's people frolicking in the waves. Get out and the sand is warm and fine under your feet. People are sat on towels tucking into the most sumptuous seafood. Nowhere do you see someone picking seaweed out of a sausage roll behind a windbreak. Before I get any letters, I do of course love the British seaside. After a refreshing dip in the briny, there's nowhere better to get dressed back into five thick layers, under a towel, in fog. I don't know where the flip-flop was invented but I'd put a few quid on it not being Blackpool.

There's just so little not to like about Australia. OK, as England cricketers we'd get a bit of gyp when we were out and about but it always came from the right place, from people who were genuinely pleased to see us, happy that we were there. We heard it all the time. 'G'day mate, how are ya? Great to have you here. Good luck.' Two-second pause. 'Ya bloody idiot.'

Personally, I was fortunate that quite early on the Aussies realised that, rather than the sort of stiff upper lip Pom who traditionally got their backs up, I was a larrikin by nature. The Aussies are partial to a bit of the old larrikin – such a great word and one which should possibly have been the job description on my passport – and because they could see a little bit of me in themselves the reception I received tended to be fun and good-humoured. I don't think it's going too far to say they slightly took me to their hearts. As I did to them. Thing is, when the England team comes over for the Ashes, there's always that sense of them being the posh boys representing the establishment. In the minds of Aussies, cemented over generations, there's an element of the English believing they're superior. It goes a long way to explaining how the rivalry started, and leads to a belief that to win the Ashes is to get one over on the ruling classes, or 'those Pommie bastards' as they're otherwise known.

It's almost as if the Aussies are responding to an innate desire to bring the English down a peg or two, and over the course of the Ashes they'll emerge, bat and ball in hand, from beach and billabong to do so. Weirdly, it's like they're the underdogs, even though for most of England's Ashes tours it's been completely the other way round. Because the Aussies recognised that I wasn't entirely averse to having the odd run-in with the establishment, I seemed to avoid this kind of stereotyping, an element of affection magnified by my appearance. Down the years I've had a few people, English and Australian, say to me, 'I looked at you, Tuffers, and thought "Bloody hell, if he can play for his country, then who's to say I'm not in with a chance?"' Yes, it's a comment that would win Backhanded Compliment of the Year nine times out of ten, but I took it in the way it was intended.

I mean, think about it, most of us have a crack at a bit of sport at one time or another. More than anything, we do so because we love it. We never really think we're going to make the big time. That's a rarefied world reserved for only the most committed individuals. And then I came along, with my long hair, shirt hanging off my shoulder, grass stains all over my trousers, bowling at the MCG, without – how shall I put this? – the most meticulous preparation. Forget endless nets, hours in the gym, eating the right foods and going to bed at half past nine; I was more, 'Right, come on you bastards, I'll try to get you out, you try to smack me out the ground, let's see what happens!' I just didn't fit that traditional bill. In some ways I was like a little schoolboy who'd somehow achieved his greatest goal. *Roy of the Rovers* stuff, except Roy always looked immaculate and never called the ref a w*****. Obviously, I'd played well enough to deserve my spot on the plane, but inside it didn't seem two minutes since I'd been messing about playing cricket with my mates. To continue the football analogy, I was more Jamie Vardy than James Milner. One minute playing non-league, the next at the top table.

That's not to say dealing with the Aussie crowds was plain sailing all the way (see the chapter I've devoted to the subject), but while the treatment they dished out could get a little rough at times it was pretty much always good-natured and never aggressive. As a player, it was part and parcel of touring Australia and for me was 100 per cent something I wanted to experience, in a funny sort of way even more than the cricket. I didn't want to feel like I'd missed out on anything. No disrespect to the other Test-playing nations, but I knew the Australia tour was the pinnacle, and I was going to be right in there at the deep end. I was never going to be someone sat quietly in the background.

For a few seasons prior to that 1990 tour I'd been playing with internationals at Middlesex. They'd have a bit of something extra about them, a presence that came from playing for their country. I'd look at them and think, *OK, that's 100 per cent where I want to be.* Angus Fraser, for instance, had been on England's tour of the West Indies the previous winter. He'd tell me these fabulous stories about going out on fishing boats catching marlin and playing golf at Sandy Lane, one of the world's most breathtaking courses, winding through an ancient mahogany grove. Then there was Wayne Daniel, our West Indies quick. Once he took me to one side in the dressing room and, in his hushed Barbadian tone, told me, 'Hey Tuffers, you know where the real cricket is? The World Series in Australia. That's where you want to be. That's the best life you can ever have.' No two ways about it, international cricketers were having the most wonderful, wonderful time.

It wasn't *only* the off-field stuff that appealed. I might hear John Emburey saying, 'The MCG is incredible – you really do need to experience it.' But if I'm honest a lot of the chat was about wineries and snorkelling and flying around in helicopters. It seemed pretty obvious to me that touring Oz was about having brilliant times with your pals – with a bit of cricket thrown in here and there. You'd be all over the place, playing state games, up-country matches, Tests, one-dayers, flying here, there, and everywhere for four months.

Playing warm-up games got us into the swing of the tour. It was part and parcel of it. But times have changed. It's like bats. It wasn't that long ago that when you got a new bat you had to oil it and knock it in. Nowadays you pull off the wrapper and there it is, ready to go. But for sheer fun value, I loved those longer tours. That's not the same for everyone – some of the boys found them really tough. But I loved going round the country, seeing all these places. For me, it was part and parcel of playing for England. I get that these days the cricket calendar is a lot more packed, and so tours are shorter by necessity, but modern players miss out on so much. When I was touring, people would disappear into the Blue Mountains for a few days living in their underpants in a hut, or they'd go off on fishing adventures. Between games, you'd go down to breakfast in the hotel and there'd only be a couple of players there. People would have taken themselves away on safari to see some amazing wildlife spectacle, or gone off with an easel to paint a big rock. There'd always be a few who liked sitting round the pool but plenty of others saw playing for England as a chance to live their best life and took every opportunity to do just that. If you weren't too sure what a place had to offer there were always a couple of tour liaison officers around to fill you in. 'Well,' one of them would say, 'my Aunty Maude keeps water buffalo in her backyard. She puts on a lovely spread too. Do you want me to give her a call?' And that was it, half an hour later a minibus would arrive and off you'd go to Aunty Maude's. After ten minutes admiring a few horns, a barbie would be lit, the wine would be flowing and at the end of the night you'd bed down in a lovely little cottage in the grounds.

'OK,' I hear you say, 'that all sounds very nice, but what about keeping yourself ticking over before the next game?' Good question. I wouldn't want you to think it was all rest and relaxation. On winery trips, it wasn't uncommon to have a quick net between the vines. You'd send a few down between the Chardonnay and the Pinot Noir and one of the batting boys would pat a few back. Cross bat shots into the grapes were strictly forbidden. Do that and you were out.

People say, 'You're there to do a job,' – and you are. But you can't keep that level of intensity up all the time. At the end of a Test match against any opponent, let alone Australia, you're mentally gone, much more so than you are physically. Living in that competitive bubble is exhausting, so when a bit of time came to switch off, I, and a lot of the other boys, always grabbed it with both hands. Five Test matches is a marathon stretch. Add in the epic nature of the battle – the crowds, the stadium, the media frenzy, the trash talking – and it's like going 15 rounds with Mike Tyson over and over again. It's another reason why I enjoyed the up-country games because compared to the Test matches you could have a bit of a laugh. It was all a bit more 'white picket fence' and you might wander round signing autographs, chatting to the locals and what have you. It was like playing cricket with your mates. You could take your foot off the gas and play your natural game. Compare that to walking into the MCG or the Wacca for the first day of a Test match. At that point you were right back in it. Without those mental breaks in between, it would have been incredibly difficult to manage. A three-day game in Ballarat against Victoria could be demanding, but it was nowhere near like five days against Australia at the SCG.

If I'd not made it in cricket, chances are I'd have spent my life silversmithing, the family business. Long hours in a bloody hard environment. Instead I was on an Ashes tour and I was going to enjoy it. The way I saw it, touring Australia was an epic opportunity to see the whole country, the England tracksuit opening every door along the way. I don't think I ever changed out of my gear, because it was just easier to be in it. There I was with a suitcase stuffed full of all my going-out stuff, posh shoes, best shirts, mohair socks, the works, only to discover that no matter where I found myself – cricket ground, winery, boat trip, nightclub – trainers and tracksuit sufficed for every occasion.

From pretty much minute one, it was everything I thought it was going to be, with some of my absolute sporting idols thrown in along the way, one or two of whom, like David Gower and Allan Lamb, really did understand how to enjoy themselves. Wherever he went, Lamby, for instance, seemed to know every-one. At every hotel, he received an 'Allan, me old mate!' from the bloke on the door. In every city, he knew the best wine merchant. In every harbour, he knew the bloke with the best lobsters. If there was anything you needed, you gave Lamby a call and he'd sort it out. In a different life he'd have been a fixer, snaffling escape kit for the chaps in Colditz Castle. 'Eh, Lamby, we need a guard's uniform, some false passports and 30 feet of rope.' 'No bother. I'll have it with you by 6 p.m. I'll give you a wink, and it'll all fall out the right leg of my trou-sers.' I'd find myself in casinos with these more experienced boys all the time. They were open 24 hours and you could get yourself a drink and have a bit of a laugh without it being quite as conspicuous or unpredictable as wandering into the nearest bar. When I first started going I didn't realise they pumped in oxygen to keep everyone awake and spending more money. I'd come out of those places feeling better, and poorer, than I ever had in my life.

Nothing will ever beat being in the thick of it as an England cricketer, but commentating comes close. Australia is such a wonderful place. You get up in the morning and nine times out of ten the sun is shining. Jump in your yellow cab and it whizzes you off to the ground, the crowds, the buzz, growing as you get closer. Sometimes I'll walk to the stadium, the same excited punter as everyone else, and it's then you really do get a taste of the anticipation, the atmosphere. People are laughing and joking, others predicting what's going to happen, each bit of chatter, in a funny sort of way, re-igniting what you felt as a player. The difference is you can relax into the day instead of being 'on' all the time. At no point are you scrabbling around for a helmet, trying to stem Matthew Hayden in full flow, or re-attaching a toe. You can take a stroll out to the middle without someone shouting unpleasantries from the boundary, or squashing a meat pie on your head (signing autographs can be particularly perilous when touring Australia). None of that in the commentary box. Even Glenn McGrath has restrained himself on the pie front. It's just a case of enjoying a very lovely time having a little chat about the cricket.

While in recent times Australia v India has established itself as one of the biggest Test series in the world, the element of history means it will never rival what we have with the Ashes. However, the fact that the India series has grown in importance does reflect how rarely in the past 40 years England have gone Down Under and actually competed, to the extent I genuinely believe there have been times that Aussie fans have tired of the domination. They want to see a tight battle, not a rout. As a player, once or twice I got the feeling they were willing us on, as if the Aussies' winning ways had made them just that little bit too cocky for the supporters' liking. 'They're walking round like they're the bee's bloody knees, mate. Someone needs to take them down a peg or two!' We did that on occasion, but the vast majority of the time they were just too good. It's very, very hard to win in Australia. The very best England players, desperate for that career-defining away Ashes win, have found it incredibly difficult to leave even the slightest mark on the Aussies on their home turf. The fact it's the Ashes, in Australia, shouldn't make a difference to who wins and who loses. When all's said and done, the game itself hasn't changed. It's still one person bowling at another from 22 yards, three sticks at each end. The leading players should come out on top and that's that. And yet there's many an England legend with a blank in the win column Down Under.

Thankfully, for the past 20 years England have at least turned the win ratio round at this end. For a good while, which included my entire international career, the Aussies would routinely turn up and do us over. Coming to England didn't worry them at all. If anything it was a bit of a treat. They'd have a lovely time. Top hotels, good grub, hardly any travelling between games. When they stepped on the plane in Sydney, they weren't filled with trepidation, they couldn't wait to get over here and grind us into the dirt. In between doing that they could have a wander round the shops, get their golf handicap down, find themselves a wife. The fact the series was in England didn't seem to matter one jot to them, whereas for us the 'away' element felt so much more significant. I'd hear footballers complaining about travelling down to Plymouth Argyle for a 90-minute away fixture and be thinking, *You what? You're moaning about going a couple of hundred miles to Devon? Try 10,000 miles to Australia mate. For four months!* Olympians were the same. 'Two weeks in the Olympic Village is going to take a bit of getting used to.' Again, I'd be incredulous. *Two weeks? In a village full of the most incredible human specimens on Earth? How about 16 weeks being called a 'Pommie bastard' by several thousand pissed-up blokes with mullets?*

At least we didn't have to travel three weeks to the other side of the world by boat – the last time that happened was 1958–59 – but it did still take the best part of a day to get there. It's no secret that I'm not the best flyer in the world and at Heathrow in 1990 nerves were getting hold of me big time. Not only was this an epic flight but I'd be sharing cabin space with a load of blokes who were pretty much my childhood heroes. I explained this to the England physio Laurie Brown before we took off. 'Look,' I said, 'I've been watching some of these people since I was a kid. The last thing I want is to make a fool of myself, to show any weakness. I don't want to be hanging on to an air hostess weeping as we're taking off and then sat there a gibbering wreck for the next 20 hours.

'Don't worry,' Laurie said, and reached into his bag of tricks from where he produced a few pills, as I recall a couple of little green ones and a pink one. 'These will do the trick,' he told me. And then he looked me in the eye. 'But whatever you do, don't have a drink with them.'

Over time, my preferred pre-flight drink would become a Bloody Mary. Right now, Laurie's words were pitched into a sudden, and ultimately losing, battle with an overbearing urge for that classic whisky and Drambuie combination, the Rusty Nail. With a couple of those inside me, any nerves were left on the tarmac. Problem was, I'd also been transported to an entirely different mental state. In my head, I was no longer a promising left-arm spinner heading out to Australia, I was the baby Jesus in a nativity play. The newspaper I'd picked up was my blanket. My club class seat was my manger. And at one point, as I hallucinated wildly, when he came over to say hello, Graham Gooch was one of the wise men. Tour manager Peter Lush was the donkey.

I only wish I could remember who was the Virgin Mary. A few hours later, after a nap and a couple of beers I found myself walking down the aeroplane steps in Perth. I really do need to check the footage. I've got a horrible feeling I greeted the civic dignitary waiting on the tarmac with a small bow and a whispered, 'God bless you my child.'

I'm sure England trips Down Under now are more professional in every way. I mean, for crying out loud, I only found out I was going because I had a look on Ceefax. Every England cricketer of that generation has the number 340 imprinted on their brain, because that was the 'cricket headlines' page where you found out whether you'd been picked or not. The selection process itself was utterly unfathomable, essentially a forerunner of the National Lottery. You'd be sitting there waiting to see if you were playing and somewhere a couple of hundred miles away there'd be a shout of 'Spin the balls!' There'd be a pause – 'and first out this week . . . Robin Smith!' There was no such thing as forward-planning. No 'Let's have a right and left-handed opening partnership.' It was just, 'And the next ball – Mark Lathwell!' Mad now to think that was how international sportsmen discovered if they were spending four months away in the winter. The first person to actually call me wasn't any of the England hierarchy, it was the lady who sorted out the players' official blazer and trousers. Instead of, 'Hi Phil, I'm delighted to tell you you've been picked for the tour of Australia,' it was, 'Good afternoon, can I have your inside leg measurement?' It was a good job I'd looked on Ceefax, otherwise my first reaction would have been to think it was a heavy breather.

You can only hope things have changed. After all, nowadays if someone rings you up asking for personal details you can't put the phone down quickly enough. I dread to think how many players have missed out on touring spots because they mistook the England tailor for someone trying to discover their online bank login. A few days after the trousers call I received an embossed card through the post. 'You are cordially invited by the MCC to tour Australia with the England cricket team.' *Ah, right*, I thought, *then it really is happening*. I'm sure someone with some kind of authority in the England set-up must have phoned me eventually but I don't remember who. All I can say is that I'm pretty sure it wasn't Graham Gooch, because, for reasons that will become clear, he didn't particularly like me!

Of course, the main element of playing for England that's changed since my time is central contracts. Prior to their introduction in 2000, we'd be playing for our county one day and our country the next. There was no job security and even less continuity, whereas nowadays, not only do players have a very good idea if they're touring or not, but they're pretty much sure to know one another when they get on the plane. In that 1990 England squad, the only person I really knew was Angus Fraser, because him and his vast sweaty feet were plonked next to me in the dressing room at Lord's. While I'd played a fair bit of county cricket, quite a few of the more established England boys tried to avoid it so I hadn't really bumped into Allan Lamb, David Gower and the like. The rest of us were pretty wet behind the ears – only five members of the 16-man squad had toured Down Under before – and so were hardly well-acquainted either. Basically, most of us were rocking up to the airport with a bunch of strangers.

Over the next 11 years I'd play with dozens of other similarly uncontracted players, all trying, despite the Aussies' clear superiority and the inefficiencies of the selection system, to bring the Ashes back to Blighty. Someone had to take the hit of facing that great Australian side in their pomp, to get them to the point where they were slightly on the decline, and that someone was us lot who played them in the 1990s. We did the preparation work for what happened later. We were, if you like, the fluffers. Someone else then came in and finished the job.

After so much pain, to watch England finally come out on top in that incredible series of 2005 was just amazing. For England not merely to win, but to actually dictate, was unbelievable for cricketers of my generation. Playing for England against Australia in the 1990s, with the chance of a series victory virtually nil, the best we could realistically hope for was the joy of a great individual effort, be it a teammate's or one of our own. Believing that could happen was the only way we could keep going. Because they so stifled our ability to perform as a team, without the possibility of occasional outstanding personal performances the experience would have been both suffocating and utterly demoralising.

A team performance means an opener getting a hundred, a couple of others getting 50 plus, the bottom order adding another few dozen, and then one bowler getting a five-fer and two or three more causing difficulties or tying up an end. When it came to Australia, they simply never allowed that to happen. Look at the games we won against them between the end of the 1980s and 2005 and there's always an outstanding individual performance. It was as if the ship was sinking and there was only one of us going to get out alive; only one of us could ever make it to the hatch. You could only hope that at some point during the series it would be you. Against that top seven in the Australian order – including the likes of Matthew Hayden, Justin Langer, Ricky Ponting, the Waugh twins, David Boon, Michael Slater, Mark Taylor, Damien Martyn, Allan Border and Adam Gilchrist – you'd have to work your socks off for a two-fer. The chance of them giving you a four-fer was pretty remote. So to get a five-fer, or more, then you had to be the dog and it had to be your day. When I got my eleven-fer at The Oval in 1997, I must briefly have been the personification of an entire kennel's worth of hounds of various descriptions.

It's the biggest disappointment of my career that I never managed to be part of an Ashes-winning side. Ultimately, as an England cricketer, a lot of how you're judged is down to how you get on against the Aussies. Look at Joe Root. The guy's a genius, England's record run-scorer, but because by the time England were heading out for the 2025–26 series he still hadn't notched a ton Down Under there was always a little question mark against him. On the other hand, he is on the honours board at Lord's for scoring 180 in a winning cause against the Aussies aged just 22, so, you know, swings and roundabouts! I wouldn't know, but I expect making a hundred against the old enemy at Lord's gets the heart beating just that little bit quicker than were it to happen against another team. Again, no disrespect, but when Joe's an old gent, sat flat-capped in his rocking-chair with his grandkids on his knee, it's more likely that he'll be waxing lyrical about that single Lord's century against the Aussies than the three he's made there against Sri Lanka. It's the same in football. Every Barcelona player wants to score against Real Madrid. Every England player wants to score against Germany.

To come out on top in an Ashes series must just be amazing. The teams I played in never did anything other than win the odd game here and there, and even then pretty much always once the urn was gone. England had a problem in the 1990s. The Australians were better than them. Not a bit. A lot. All you can ever do in that situation is pray, either for a tin of Duckham's Hypergrade to be poured on a length by a campaigner against wrongful imprisonment, or a bit of luck. Except, of course, luck very rarely sets up home with an habitually losing side. While they played and missed our good balls, we always nicked theirs. They'd hit the stumps on a run out, we'd have a shy and it would go for four overthrows. They'd pull off an amazing catch at slip while ours went to ground.

Not only weren't we as good as them, but we made it hard for ourselves. And of course all the time they were far from backwards in letting us know they were absolutely smashing us to pieces. Their batsmen would be having a great laugh in the middle while we trudged past on our way to oblivion. It was like constantly running uphill. We just weren't at the races. In those circumstances all you can do is fight. But against that kind of firepower, scrapping just isn't enough. In the five Ashes series I played in we lost 3–0, 4–1, 3–1, 3–2 and 4–1. They destroyed us, turning each series into a real test of mental and physical endurance. Today's Ashes series are condensed down to the bare minimum of days. In 2023, they completed an entire five-Test series in six weeks. When I was playing, the Ashes was spread out over the entire summer. In 1993, the teams played six Tests across 12 weeks. As tended to be the way in times of zero continuity I was dropped after the first two, but for the guys involved in every clash it was brutal. Some players can switch off between games, but there's plenty who can't.

No longer available for selection, these days I tend to find a bit of winter sun in Tenerife rather than Tasmania – the flight's just that little bit shorter – but my memories still burn as strongly as the Melbourne sun. In this book I've focused those golden rays on a half-century of the greatest players and biggest characters to have entered my Ashes orbit. Some I played with, others I partied with, others simply amazed me and became my childhood idols, inspiring me to have a pop at living my own Ashes dream. Celebrated also are those who I've admired from my post-playing perch in the commentary box. The Ashes is unique for throwing up incredible spine-tingling drama – the gift that keeps on giving – and more than once my fellow pundits have had to pin my excitable self to the seat to stop me disappearing through the roof.

In many ways, in writing this book I've come to realise that inside I'm still that little kid who watched the Ashes on TV. I still find the whole England/Australia thing *that* exciting. I hope that by revealing my Ashes heroes, I'll transport you on your own memorable journey into this most glorious of sporting contests which I'm happy to say has formed such a wonderful part of my life. I loved playing for England, but I'm more than happy to admit there's a big part of me that adores Australia too. The country and the people that is – I'm not issuing an invitation for Big Merv to stay in my spare bedroom for three months. Although, should the situation arise, he is very welcome to pluck me from the shark-infested waters of deepest Surrey.

I'll be honest; if I could be anyone else, I'd be an Australian. I know all the terminology – 'tinny' (can of beer), 'barbie' (barbecue), 'mental disintegration' (traditional welcome for England cricketers). The name's Tuffers, me old cobber, and here's my 50 Ashes heroes.

1.

DAVID GOWER

*An absolute one-off, David did things
his way. Be it in the heat of a Test match
or the cockpit of a Tiger Moth.*

Until you've seen David Gower sabre the top off a Champagne bottle, you really haven't lived. If I'd been in charge of Sky Sports I'd have had him do it as the introduction to every day's play. It was a truly magnificent sight, first witnessed by myself at a winery in South Australia. A few England players had been invited down there on the 1990–91 tour. There were established wine connoisseurs like David and Allan Lamb, and myself, who, at a push, could tell the vintage of a pint of Skol – '1989, bartender, am I correct?'

I spent the first hour or so wandering round with my jaw hanging open – and not just in the hope that someone would tip something in it. Everywhere I looked there were tables groaning with seafood and steaks, like it must have been if Cleopatra had you round for a barbecue in the old days. The only thing missing was the bath of ass's milk and those women in togas lowering grapes into your mouth. It was as if I'd been parachuted into another world. For years I'd been perfectly happy with a KFC.

Eventually, someone appeared with a sabre. For once it wasn't Graham Gooch at a disciplinary hearing. Immediately, David perked up. To him, the weapon was akin to a call to arms, although at this stage I had no idea what was going on. 'Why've they given him a bloody great sword?' And then all of a sudden he picked up a bottle of Champers, drew the sabre back along the neck, and *Schudoom!*, sliced the top away. I was waiting for someone to say 'Careful, you'll have somebody's eye out', but nobody did. Like me, they were reeling from being present at such an impressive feat. I imagined it to be the sort of thing a high-ranking general would do after a good day in the Napoleonic Wars. 'We gave those Prussians a damned good pasting! Fetch my sabre and a jeroboam of Veuve Clicquot!' In this case, however, David was ceremonially opening the afternoon. Everyone clapped before turning round and getting stuck into a load of lobsters and booze.

David's little trick really was a hell of an introduction to the world of wine. Until then the only time I'd drunk the stuff was when the beer ran out at a barbecue and there was half a bottle of Blue Nun kicking around, possibly the dregs of a Paul Masson California carafe. The South Australia jaunt was my first taste of really good wine, to which I then became quite partial. I'd listen to the more experienced boys chatting about how, with a plate of seafood, it would be beneficial to have a Sauvignon Blanc, or how with a good steak it's always worth investing in a grippy Shiraz. In fact it wasn't long before these older boys began to warm to me as I started dropping in a few little comments of my own. 'Oh David, I've just tried that Chardonnay – nutty, with a caramel aftertaste, like a Marathon.' I started reading up on the stuff; the best drop to have with a couple of prawns, that kind of thing. If anything, I was doing more preparation for my wine drinking than I was for my cricket. 'Oh Graham, glad I caught you, I won't be netting this morning, I'm afraid I have a tasting at Alfredo's swordfish restaurant in town.' I was even receiving tips from David himself. 'If you fancy a slightly smoother grape, Tuffers, try the Tempranillo.' All I needed now was to stop drinking it from a pint pot.

I'm in two minds as to whether David Gower qualifies as a larrikin. He certainly wasn't one in the larger-than-life manner of a Freddie Flintoff or a Beefy. David was more suave, assured, the sort of person able to wreak mayhem in a foreign land while stood leaning on a mantelpiece in Marylebone in a smoking jacket. Essentially, he was one-step removed from a larrikin. A larrikin with staff. Who would then go out and larrikin on his behalf. But then again David was responsible for perhaps the all-time greatest piece of larrikin behaviour, divebombing an England cricket match – in which he was playing – in a Tiger Moth, so maybe actually he's the biggest larrikin of the lot.

We were playing a state match against Queensland when David spotted biplanes in the sky near the ground in Carrara. With England going along nicely in their first innings, and himself back in the hutch, he grasped the opportunity for a bit of fun. At lunch, he and the Derbyshire batsman John Morris, who'd just hit a fantastic ton, sneaked out to the airfield. Next thing the rest of us knew a Tiger Moth appeared low over the ground. From the dressing room, we watched Allan Lamb, at the wicket at the time, raise his bat and feign using it as a gun to shoot them down. He knew who the begoggled pair grinning down at him were even if the England hierarchy didn't. When they found out, the captain, Graham Gooch, along with team and tour managers Micky Stewart and Peter Lush, were apoplectic and fined David and John the maximum £1,000. David saw the Tiger Moth ride as just a bit of fun, which it was, but the management took the whole thing so seriously that all sense of context was lost.

It was a huge overreaction. Flying a Tiger Moth over a cricket ground didn't all of a sudden make David a bad tourist. When, during the bollocking, Graham asked David what his motivation was, David pointed out that of the three Test matches so far he'd top scored in both innings of one and made a hundred in the others. His motivation was the same as it had always been, to do the best he could for England, but because of the way he went about it, like so many other flair players, he was constantly having to defend himself. So often, cricketers like David become a victim of their own success. They make everything look so easy that on the days when they don't get a hundred, or a five-fer, or take a one-handed over-the-shoulder catch on the boundary, people think they're not trying. 'Can't you do that every day of the week?' It's as if the easier you make something look, the more trouble you get in. Even more so if, in your spare time, you're partial to slicing corks off bottles of Champagne.

Admittedly, David was slightly prone to getting in situations that might not always be looked upon kindly by the management. On that same 1990 tour, after the second day's play in Brisbane, he and Allan Lamb accepted an invite from Aussie media tycoon Kerry Packer for a meal in a restaurant followed by a trip to a casino. It turned into something of a late night, which might not have drawn criticism had Lamby not been not out overnight and stand-in captain for the injured Gooch. In the morning he added just four to his score prompting an England collapse. You can imagine the reaction. A great big roulette wheel on the back of one of the Aussie papers with Lamby's head in the middle.

Personally, however, I loved this adventurous side of David. Hanging around in his circle was the first time I'd ever been shown a little bit of culture. I was used to knocking about with all the boys who used to go down the pub, get stuck into ten pints, sing some rowdy songs and knock a couple of cows over on the walk home. David, on the other hand, was more into renting World War I Tiger Moths and drinking the output of fine wineries. It was him who introduced me to seafood, showed me how to eat an oyster without causing offence.

In every cricket team there are different types of personalities. With Beefy you could see the steely determination. He'd run in to bowl with his hair all over the place, sweat flying everywhere, and then with the bat he'd be trying to smash it out the ground. But with David that same competitiveness was done at a much more leisurely pace. He was never going to scream and shout in a dressing room, he was more of a cajoler. 'Come on, let's see what we can do out there.' Laidback was what worked for him. Waiting to bat was water off a duck's back. He'd be sat there in his pads with his feet up doing the cryptic crossword, there'd be a shout of 'Owzat?', down his paper would go and off he'd mooch out to the middle. Sometime later he'd mooch back, take his gloves off, and ask, 'Anyone had any luck with 14 down?' If he ever chucked his bat against the wall, I never saw it. He was always measured. But none of that means he wasn't a hugely determined character.

I never played with anyone else remotely like David Gower. Funny as it sounds for people who outwardly seemed miles apart, we did have our similarities. If he lost a game, he wasn't going to sit and wallow in misery for hours and neither was I. Then again, I don't know what he got up to in the depths of his bedroom. He might have been in there sticking pins in effigies of umpires, for all I knew. However, in my experience, he was much more likely to say, 'Well, that's not gone our way, but if anyone's interested I've organised a catamaran to take us to this lovely little island where they've laid on a beautiful lunch.'

'Well, if you insist, David,' I'd say. Like him, I wasn't going to retire to a dark corner and rap myself on the bottom with a spatula for the rest of the afternoon.

David felt positivity, not opprobrium, was the way to lift performance. In the previous Test at Sydney, Graham had given us a bit of stick for our fielding and bowling not being up to scratch. Then Micky Stewart did exactly the same. David said something about getting a bit of positive input and for me that was fair enough. You can't just be hammering people all the time. But it felt to me that the management saw David's comment as somehow flippant. That wasn't the case at all. He was just saying, 'Yes, we've been smashed, but can we have something a little more upbeat to work with? Something to take us forward?'

Unsurprisingly, that 1990–91 Ashes was the series where Graham and David, who'd always been good mates down the years, started to go their separate ways, not helped when, soon after the Tiger Moth, in the fourth Test at Adelaide, right on lunch on the third day, the final ball of the session, David fell hook, line and sinker for the trap that had been set for him and flicked a ball from Craig McDermott straight into Merv Hughes' sizeable bread basket. I hid under a towel in the dressing room as another piece of cement in the old pals' relationship crumbled away. But again, it's sport, we all make mistakes. David had been playing Test cricket for 13 years at that point. He didn't need treating like a naughty schoolboy. The PA announcer at the Adelaide Oval certainly didn't think so. As David came out to bat he'd played 'Those Magnificent Men In Their Flying Machines'. Perfect! It showed David's Tiger Moth trip for exactly what it was – an idle jape, something to make people smile, which it did. I distinctly remember that, while the hierarchy were absolutely seething about it, me and a couple of the other younger lads were sat in the dressing room cracking up, trying not to show it, but with our shoulders going up and down, maybe putting a helmet on back to front so no-one could see our faces.

Instead, the flight marked the beginning of the end of David's England career. The Lamb/Botham/Gower era disappeared and everything became more pressurised and intense. What had previously been fun became more like hard work. Graham believed that was the way forward, for everyone, but it is possible to move a culture too far the other way. All of a sudden it felt like if you got a duck or didn't bag a few wickets then you should spend half an hour whipping yourself in a cold shower. Or if you lost you should go home and not surface for 48 hours, most definitely not be seen in a pub. It was as if, unless you felt bad about it, you didn't care. But of course that's not how everyone operates. People care in all kinds of different ways. The England kit was plenty adequate without a hair shirt being added.

For me, it was an absolute privilege to tour Australia with David, not least because up to that point I'd never actually seen him bat for any length of time. I'd heard all the stories about his elegance and grace, and seen him on TV as a kid, but in the flesh it had never really happened. If the chance came in Australia I vowed to actually watch him in action. That chance came early on. David made a hundred in the second Test at Melbourne, and I was blown away by how easy he made it look. Just thinking about it has got my mouth watering.

Only one way to celebrate David Gower's prowess and character – with a king prawn and a Tempranillo.

42 ASHES TESTS

Runs: 3,269
Highest Score: 215
Avg: 44.78
Hundreds: 9
Fifties: 12

2.

GLENN McGRATH

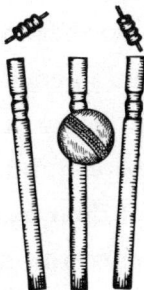

Forget the corridor of uncertainty, Glenn's unerring accuracy lulled countless England batsmen into the passageway of oblivion.

Everyone remembers Gary Pratt as having the ultimate walk-on role in the 2005 Ashes. I, however, would like to nominate someone else – whoever rolled the ball across to where Glenn McGrath trod on it during the warm-up for the Edgbaston Test. If Paul Collingwood could get an MBE for appearing in the fifth Test of the series, then surely the bloke who rolled that ball should have got one too. Collingwood only helped to draw that final Test. At Edgbaston, the mystery ball-roller was very possibly the matchwinner. Glenn had taken a man-of-the-match-winning 9–82 in Australia's victory in the first Test at Lord's, including a wrecking-ball spell of 5–2. Safe to say that without that little accident his presence at Edgbaston would have been worth more than the two runs by which England eventually crept over the line. The accepted version of events surrounding the ball-stepping incident is that, while the Aussies were messing about with a rugby ball, Brad Haddin threw Glenn a dodgy pass. In reaching for it, he then trod on the ball. However, if I was a conspiracy theorist, I'd say there was more to Glenn's little accident than met the eye. Can anyone account for the whereabouts of the great English bowls maestro David Bryant that morning? Is it entirely in the realms of fantasy to suggest that, unseen behind a sightscreen, he propelled the most beautifully weighted ball in Glenn's direction?

Inarguably, Glenn's absence was a huge boost to England's confidence, same as it was in the fourth Test at Trent Bridge which he missed with an elbow problem, England creeping over the line in Nottingham by just three wickets. A metronomically accurate bowler, wonderful, skilful, Glenn gave the opposition precisely nothing. Always there or thereabouts, top of off stump, he constantly had the best batsmen in the world doubting themselves. If you didn't know to the millimetre where that off stump was, he'd have you. And even if you did know, there were a million and one other questions to answer. Is he going to bring one back? Is he going to nick me off? Is he going to do this, do that?

With a bowler like Glenn there's only one thing to look forward to – the moment he collects his cap off the umpire and clears off down to fine leg for a rest. Except with Glenn that never happened. He was always bowling! Or at least that's how it felt. I'd talk to our batsmen and they'd explain just how big a headache Glenn's presence was. The Aussies were an attacking side. With the riches of talent at their disposal they could afford to be. A central part of that front-foot mantra was, 'Always start a session with your best bowlers.' When your best bowlers are Glenn McGrath and Shane Warne that means only one thing – a tough examination for the batting side. More often than not, no matter how the previous session ended, when the next one started our batsmen were straightaway back under the cosh. It felt like every time we steadied the ship, there, waiting to stir up the waters, were Glenn and Shane. So often they'd get a wicket or two. It was properly daunting. The bell ringing for the start of a session essentially became a reminder that the torture was about to start again. It was like walking out to a bed of nails at one end and a thumbscrew at the other. There was just no respite and it was impossible to build momentum from one session to another. Glenn was a massive part of that. He ended up with 157 Test wickets against England out of a career total of 563. He never had the express pace of Thommo, Lillee or Brett Lee but his insistent accuracy and ability to bowl long spells meant he could cause a massive amount of damage. Like the West Indies equivalent, Curtly Ambrose, he wore you down. Every ball was a battle.

When I was playing for England, I didn't speak much to Glenn. I could have asked where he wanted me to edge it – second or third slip – but what was the point? In the absence of any meaningful dialogue, I formed an impression of him based predominantly on his footwear. Aussie through and through, he always seemed to be wearing Blundstones. If you're not familiar, these boots, brown leather, ankle high, are much-loved by Outback cattlemen. And yet Glenn, and more than a few of the other Aussies, would wear them with trousers and a blazer. I'd look at this get-up and think, *Well, hang on a minute, that doesn't really go. You can't be wandering round St John's Wood looking like some sort of rancher. There's no sheep round here. Would it hurt to put some shoes on?* It's no better over there. You can be in Brisbane on a scorching hot day, trotting round in flop-flops, only to find yourself surrounded by people in massive boots. The only concession they make is not to wear the ones with steel toecaps.

In retirement, I've got to know Glenn from the ankle up. Every home Ashes series he joins us in the *Test Match Special* box as a pundit. Naturally, he still wears the Blundstones – my guess is he sleeps in them – but I have discovered other sides to him, not least his dry and mischievous sense of humour. In all honesty, this came as a bit of a surprise to me because I'd always thought of Glenn as a little shy and reserved. Even with the ball in his hand he was more chunterer than sledger. It's one of the pities of Ashes cricket that you're in such a competitive bubble, so aligned with your own camp, that you rarely get a chance to find out who the opposition really are as people. For years they're either a pain in the arse or a thorn in the side. After six hours of torment, the last thing you want is to have a spot of dinner with them, prodding a meatball round your plate while discussing the testicle they trapped against your inner thigh. Work with one of those blokes in retirement, when the on-field stuff is all done and dusted, however, and so often you find you've got so much in common. More than once I've looked at an Australian batsman and thought, *If you hadn't kept punting me into the crowd at long-off, we really could have been very good pals.* I've mourned the boat trips, theatre outings and pie and mash evenings we could have had together. Glenn is just that sort of bloke. I'm delighted to report that these days we get on like a house on fire.

Glenn is, of course, famous not just for filling Michael Atherton's life with misery, but for rubbing English noses in the dirt with his constant predictions of 5–0 Ashes hammerings. While every England fan has, I'm sure, a deep respect for Glenn's soothsaying abilities, and his pride in being an Australian, it would be dishonest to deny that at TMS any Ashes-based occurrence that upsets him is generally greeted with glee. Take Lord's 2023, when Mitchell Starc caught Ben Duckett on the boundary only to mistake the ball for a handbrake, dragging it along the turf to stop his slide. When the catch was ruled out as not being under control, Glenn was seething. 'If that's not out, then every other catch that's ever been taken shouldn't be out,' he told the listeners. This soon morphed into spurious claims of unfair treatment. 'If that's England taking that catch, that's out!' Glenn's not a person who generally gets outraged. He's more of a simmerer. So it was good fun to see him so irate, something I'd never witnessed on the field. We never gave each other much grief as players. Fellow number 11s, there wasn't much point in giving one another a send-off. Neither of us ever threatened to cause much damage with the bat. Glenn's dismissal of me in my final Test innings, at The Oval in 2001, when I wafted one to Warney at slip, is a case in point. We lost by an innings and 25 runs. That was what usually happened against the Aussies. When I arrived at the crease in the second innings we'd generally need another 400 to win. Even Marsh and Lillee wouldn't have bet on that. Glenn did have a slightly higher batting average than me – 7.36 to my 5.1 – and actually had a famous Ashes moment with the bat when, at Old Trafford in 2005, he survived nine balls as he and Brett Lee somehow managed to see out the last four overs to secure a draw. But before he starts gloating in the commentary box, I'd like to point one thing out. Glenn, you never had to bat against yourself.

No doubt Glenn will continue to make his Ashes whitewash predictions. I don't see the Aussies having it quite so easy in our next few clashes. My view is that Glenn should back his words with actions. If Australia don't win 5–0 again before the end of the decade he should sit down, grab a knife and fork, and eat one of his Blundstones.

30 ASHES TESTS

Wickets: 157
Best Bowling: 8–38
Avg: 20.92
Five-wicket Innings: 10
Ten-wicket Matches: 0

Runs: 105
Highest Score: 20 not out
Avg: 6.17

3.

PHILLIP DeFREITAS

*As underrated as he was unconventional, Daffy
played one of the great counterattacking innings
to deliver a brilliant win in Adelaide.*

I was freezing my nuts off. It was the winter of 1986–87 and I was stuck in a dingy little place in Sidcup. Nursing my hot water bottle one night, I stuck the telly on. And there he was on the Ashes highlights, my mate, Phil DeFreitas, smashing Merv Hughes round the Gabba while Beefy was piling up a big ton at the other end.

I was sat in this little house, remote control in fingerless glove, mice throwing themselves on the traps, and right in front of me was my pal having the time of his life, playing in the biggest series in world cricket, in front of a full house, in brilliant sunshine. I looked at my own surroundings. Instead of the start-ling colours of the Gabba, I had four grey walls. My green grass was a balding grey carpet, my sun a three-bar electric fire. As I sat huddled under a blanket, toes turning blue, like a peculiarly unfortunate character in a particularly grim Charles Dickens novel, a thought struck me. *Hang on! If my mate can do it, so can I!*

That, quite honestly, was my catalyst to make it as a Test crick-eter; the fact that me and Daffy were cut from the same cloth only making the idea that I could emulate him even more real. I'd met Daffy on the MCC Young Cricketers programme, a pathway for youthful players looking to make it in the profes-sional game. Both being a little bit unorthodox, rebellious even, we'd soon become close friends. Daffy's elevation to the England ranks showed me that, for all you might be seen as a bit hard to handle, if you put in the hard yards and got your wickets, then playing for your country remained achievable. Whereas before I saw the England cricket team as something that happened to other people, suddenly I really did feel like I could be part of it, that the next step was as open to me as it was to everyone else. I was so much nearer than I'd ever thought. *Hang on! I play for Middlesex. There's one more rung to the top of the ladder, and I can take it.* My eyes were opened to what was possible. I'd played club cricket out in Oz, and done well, but what I was seeing in front of me now was the big time. Not only could I play in Australia but I could do so playing for England, on the biggest tour there is by miles. The absolute pinnacle. The history, the rivalry, the arenas, the crowds, the buzz. Something incredible happened in that dark little lounge that night. The dawn of realisation.

Fast forward to the end of summer 1990 and after a decent county season there was a little bit of a buzz around me. It was almost four years since I'd seen Daffy on the telly and that big Ashes tour was coming around again. With the chill of Sidcup forever in my bones, I'd concentrated quite hard on my game that year. England manager Micky Stewart came to have a little look at me and I started to think that if the selectors were thinking of taking two spinners Down Under then I was in with a chance. I wasn't expecting anything to be handed to me on a plate, but I did feel I'd put in a few hard yards. You don't get to be sunning yourself on Bondi Beach without spending a few days standing in a cloudy nine degrees on the outfield at Northampton, and I'd done exactly that. My optimism turned out to be well-placed, with me and Eddie Hemmings on the plane. At that point, Eddie was in his forties while I was a spritely-ish 24. He was also an off-spinner while I was slow left-arm orthodox. While it wasn't unusual for a new kid to go on tour predominantly to experience the England set-up, there was enough difference between me and Eddie to make me think I'd get a go. In fact, I had my eye on him from ball one because I so wanted to play. I wasn't there to make up the numbers. I had every expectation of being involved. And that's what happened. No longer was I sitting at home watching my mate Daffy on the telly. I was with him on the field. A victory, maybe not for England, but for nonconformists everywhere.

I'll never forget the bus ride from the hotel to the MCG. As a kid I'd always loved FA Cup Final day, especially the bit where they had cameras on the team buses and showed them driving through the crowds as they neared Wembley. Streams of supporters with flags parting to let them through. The players peering out through the windows, thousands of fans waving back at them. And now, as we approached this great cricketing amphitheatre, it felt like the same was happening to me. This wasn't a few dozen people emerging from St John's Wood tube station, there were hordes of fans all flocking to the 'G', as the Aussies call it. And in the middle of all this madness, sitting on this bus, there I was in my England tracksuit. I was right there experiencing precisely what had kept me glued to those iconic sporting events. Glued to the Ashes highlights in the winter of '86. *Bloody hell!* I thought to myself. *This is a big old game!*

I learned a lot from Daffy during that trip, not just about the on-field stuff, but how to click with the older blokes for whom this was just the latest of several rodeos. But I haven't just stuck Daffy in this list because he was my mate. On the next Ashes tour, I saw him play one of the finest counterattacking innings I've ever seen in the flesh to win us the Adelaide Test. Daffy could bat, and when it was his day he could really make a difference. At Adelaide in 1995 it was his second-innings 88, at almost a run a ball, which just about gave us something to defend when the Aussies batted again. We were 181–6, a lead of just 115, heading for yet another defeat when Daffy arrived at the crease. I then watched from the balcony as he crashed 22 runs off a single Craig McDermott over while rocketing England to 328 all out. His heroics deserved a century, something which eluded him in Test cricket, but for some reason he deemed it unlikely that myself and Devon Malcolm would stay with him for any length of time and so threw caution to the wind. Even so, his rout was enough to set the Aussies a testing 263 for victory, just enough scoreboard pressure to prompt a collapse. In the end we won easily by 106 runs.

As Daffy was awarded man-of-the-match, I looked on, delighted for my old pal. Even in a period when pretty much every England player suffered the whims of the selectors, he was treated particularly shabbily. Hard to think of any other England cricketer dropped three times in one summer, as happened to Daffy against the West Indies and Sri Lanka in 1988. He really did deserve his moment in the spotlight.

A quick mention also for another little Daffy stat. He's one of the few England bowlers – in fact, very possibly the only one – to vomit during his run-up. To be fair, he was performing in the intense heat of Pakistan at the time. I didn't have the same excuse when, with Middlesex, I hurled over an all-weather pitch after a late night on a pre-season 'fitness training' camp in Portugal. Breakfast the next morning probably hadn't been the best idea. Scrambled eggs, bacon and orange juice is tricky to get out of any matting-based facility. In my defence, I had slipped in my run-up and dislocated a finger. It was the pain that made me sick. Honest.

Something we don't have in common is that Daffy played in an Ashes-winning side. That sunny Brisbane Test I'd watched on TV was the first in a series which England, against all odds, won 2–1. The clouds then moved in for the best part of 20 years. In Adelaide, that one golden afternoon in 1995, Daffy did his very best to blow them away.

I think of him every time I switch on my electric blanket.

13 ASHES TESTS

Wickets: 37
Best Bowling: 4–56
Avg: 44.97

Runs: 329
Highest Score: 88
Avg: 15.66
Hundreds: 0
Fifties: 1

4.

STEVE WAUGH

*The nuggetiest of a very nuggety bunch, coming up
against Steve Waugh was like trying to contain a
hungry tiger with a small packet of sliced ham.*

It should have been the greatest Ashes hat-trick. The Sydney Test
of 1991 was just my second for England. In their second innings,
I had Allan Border caught on the sweep by Graham Gooch
before, next ball, Dean Jones came down the wicket and clipped
the ball head-high straight back to me. Two wickets in two balls! I
was flying and so were the rest of the boys. And then in he came
– Steve Waugh. We stuck the whole team round the bat. It was
like a medieval siege. We'd have catapulted a diseased cow on to
the wicket if we could. In I hopped, Steve pushed a little too
hard, and the ball flew towards David Gower's outstretched hand

at second silly point. This hand, this thing of grace, of delicate beauty, from which silken runs had flowed, grasped at the orb. And yet nought but a single digit made contact. Steve escaped. My dream was no more. Instead, that hat-trick of Allan Border, Dean Jones and Steve Waugh – no mere tailenders for me – lives only in my imagination.

Perhaps that's just as well. If my celebration after Dean's wicket is anything to go by, I'd have last been seen somewhere west of Venus. Look carefully at that footage and you'll see how hard I am trying not to whip my top off and twirl it around my head. In fact, forget the top, given half a chance I'd have had the whole lot off, my full pastiness revealed to the world, complete with one-pack and slight beer belly. As it was, it took a while for everyone to catch me. I'm pretty sure all exit gates were locked as a precaution. Such a reaction sounds mad, I know, but being new to the side I desperately wanted to show the rest of the England boys – some of whom were my heroes – what I could do. Starting out, when you try something and it comes off, it's massive. In fact, throughout my career, I considered a big wicket the equivalent of scoring a goal. I wasn't going to stand there and shake hands with a couple of teammates like they did in the old days. I was experiencing a great release of pent-up emotion, especially if I'd got myself worked up before I went out there in the first place, and I was more than happy to show it.

As it was, I got a five-fer in that innings, which went a long way to establishing me as an international cricketer, but it would have been nice to have that one little thing to chuck back at the Aussies, Steve Waugh in particular, because, when it comes to Australian cricketers, he's surely the nuggetiest, the steeliest, the most utterly uncompromising, of them all. Believe me, just one look from Steve could have you questioning your entire raison d'être. Do you carry on playing cricket or retire in disgrace to a small Himalayan hermitage? I'll give you an example of just how withering Steve could be. One time Robin Smith and I were having a few throwdowns on the outfield before play, the usual kind of half-arsed stuff that England did in warm-up sessions back then, with precisely zero relevance to anything that would happen when the game started. We'd moved on to lobbing a ball to one another, basically like having a game of catch in the garden with a seven-year-old, when Steve walked past with his brother. The look he gave us was one of absolute disdain. It came with a sort of half-laugh, half-sigh. I did actually say, 'What does that mean?' He didn't reply. He didn't need to. The Waughs were masters of the sneer, but Steve especially seemed to have a permanent bearing of 'F*** off mate, who the f*** are you anyway?' He carried that countenance with him in Ashes Tests for years. I'm assuming he switched it off at home. It's not something you'd want to see over the breakfast table on a regular basis.

Steve was exactly the same with a bat in his hand. Style-wise, he was far from a Brian Lara or a Sachin Tendulkar. There was never a flourish. Instead he relied on a granite temperament, accumulating via a series of stabbed shots, each a wound to England's confidence. If it's possible to ooze grit, then Steve Waugh did. It was like he represented his country on a broader field than just cricket. He might as well have been the Prime Minister and, in a lot of Aussies' eyes, more or less was. Like Allan Border before him, he was a true leader. I'm certain Steve looked at what his predecessor did in turning Australia into an uncompromising cricketing machine – and then took it to another level. 'Mental disintegration' he so poetically described his methodology of crushing the opposition. The only surprise with Steve was that his autobiography was called *Out Of My Comfort Zone* and not *What The F*** Are You Looking At?*

If you want your team to buy into that kind of ethos you have to lead from the front. Steve relied on no-one else. Like every other member of the England team, I could only look on in bemusement as he scored a century on one leg at The Oval in 2001. His Ashes should have been done and dusted when he tore his calf muscle halfway through the third Test of that series. But this was Steve Waugh. The restrictions of human biology meant nothing to him. With typical iron will, he reduced the usual recovery time from three months to ten days. It was like he was a robot, gone in for a minor repair, and now back out doing his job. I tell you, Steve Waugh just wasn't normal. He could plummet 17 floors in a hotel lift and emerge into the lobby like nothing had happened. Even when, at The Oval, the calf injury recurred, with a buttock strain (Ow!) to boot, it didn't stop him. He was on 30 when he started hobbling. At that point, most players would have a quick slog and get out. Not Steve. He notched an unbeaten 157 including – get this! – a dive into the crease to reach three figures. He didn't need to bat again. His heroics went a long way to the tourists winning easily by an innings.

I don't know why, but back then it seemed like every international cricketer played better with a key part of themselves either shattered or torn. As a kid, I remember watching the late great Malcolm Marshall bat one-handed against England at Headingley after breaking his thumb in the field. With his lower arm in plaster, he then skittled England with 7–53. Seven years earlier, in the Centenary Test at Melbourne, Aussie opener Rick McCosker was bowled by Bob Willis *off his chin*. Batting number ten, second time round, McCosker appeared from the pavilion with what can only be described as a 'comedy bandage' round his head to hold his shattered jaw together. It was like something you'd see on *Tom and Jerry* with a big bow tied on the top. You half-expected to see a small cluster of cartoon birds tweeting round his head. In that state, he scored 25 runs and lasted 85 minutes. Like I say, this is what cricket was like. Blokes with broken arms, hopping on one leg, or missing half a dozen teeth, would routinely play an absolute blinder. There was a definite element of, 'Be careful of him – he's injured.' I clearly remember someone saying to me, 'The last thing you want to do is play against Gordon Greenidge on one leg. It'll just make him even better.' And they were right. Once or twice I even considered throwing myself down the stairs on the way to breakfast, or asking Angus Fraser to kick me in the bollocks on the way out to bat. Sadly, I very rarely got injured. My own maladies were usually of the dehydration variety. Short of dragging my drip out on to the field of play there wasn't a lot I could do.

Mere mortals might write themselves into cricketing folklore once. Steve Waugh is no mere mortal. Two years after his Oval heroics, he was back at it. While he'd already skippered the Aussies to a convincing Ashes win, equalling Allan Border's record of securing victory within 11 days, and with his team 4–0 up with one to play, his own form was suffering. Well, by Australian standards anyway. With fifties in his two previous Tests, he wasn't exactly crawling around the carpet looking for crumbs. Whatever, it looked to all intents and purposes that the final

Test of the series, at Sydney, would be his last. A fellow Aussie, Russell Crowe, played the gladiator in Ridley Scott's Oscar-winning epic, but only, one assumes, because Steve Waugh was unavailable. With his home ground of the SCG as his Colosseum, Steve repelled every attack his opponents could throw at him. As the second day neared its end, having already passed 10,000 Test runs, there he was, closing in on not just another Test hundred but the one that would put him on a par with Sir Don Bradman's 29. The only opponent Steve had in creating one of Australian sport's greatest moments was time. Just as *Gladiator* wouldn't have been the same had the big fight between Maximus and Commodus been brought to a halt during the final blows and resumed at 10.30 a.m. the next morning, Steve really needed to reach the milestone that evening. With one over remaining, he needed five more runs. When he could only pat off-spinner Richard Dawson's first three balls back down the pitch, everyone assumed that was that. Even more so when, after taking three off the fourth ball, he found himself stranded down the wrong end. Fortunately, he was batting with a genius. Adam Gilchrist manoeuvred a single and Steve was back on strike for the last ball of the day. England skipper Nasser Hussain wasn't going to make it easy. By the time he'd finished conversing with Dawson, the entire stadium could have fetched another beer. When, finally, Dawson delivered a quicker one outside off stump, Steve promptly dispatched it to the cover boundary. The eruption of emotion in the SCG as he punched the air was incredible. From the minute he'd walked out to bat, also to a standing ovation, everyone had been willing him to reach a century. When he got there, even the England players admitted the hairs on the back of their necks were on end.

Aggers counts it as one of the most extraordinary cricketing spectacles he's ever seen, and considering Aggers has been present at more Test matches than most midwives have births that really is saying something.

By the time Steve finished tormenting England, 17 years, 46 Test matches, and 10 centuries after he'd first done so in 1986, I was no longer a cricketer. By then I was eating witchetty grubs in the Australian jungle, which was still preferable to meeting Steve on a flat pitch in Adelaide. Then, blow me, when my punditry career took off, if he didn't start looming up again. That's the thing with commentating – previous tormentors lurk around every corner. You look up in the media centre and there's Steve Waugh. 'For f***'s sake, not you again!' I try to stop myself saying it, but it's no use! The difference is, of course, that now he'll greet me with a smile rather than a snarl. Although, for all that they're friendly, old foes like Steve can never resist reminding you of past scorelines and are always insistent that the same thing is going to happen again. It's hard for the likes of me in the media centres of the great Australian grounds. No sooner have I nipped off for a cup of tea than there's a voice behind me, 'Eh, Tuffers, remember that double hundred I got against you?' Or 'Eh, Tuffers, remember that time I got seven-fer and knocked your middle stick out?' You start to wonder where it's going to end. Wake up at 3 a.m. one night and there's Merv Hughes at the end of your bed – 'Eh, Tuffers, remember when I speared one right into your box at the Wacca? Bloody bonzer mate, wasn't it?' Genuinely, though, it is great to bump into these blokes, especially knowing you then don't have to go out there and take them on from 22 yards.

Steve, by the way, commentates better on one leg.

46 ASHES TESTS

Runs: 3,200
Highest Score: 177 not out
Avg: 58.18
Hundreds: 10
Fifties: 14

Wickets: 22
Best Bowling: 5–69
Avg: 41.54
Five-wicket Innings: 1
Ten-wicket Matches: 0

5.

GRAHAM GOOCH

*Zapata moustache he might have had, but he was
no fan of my revolutionary ways. Myself and Goochy
had more than a few legendary fallouts. And yet
he's the England batsman I admire the most.*

It's 7 a.m. and I'm about to have an exceptionally violent encounter with a rubber plant.

I've just come in from a night out, still in my civvy gear, and am legging it across the hotel lobby towards the lifts, desperate not to be seen, only to slip on the marble floor. Within seconds I'm enmeshed in several pots of ornamental greenery. A few feet away a silver arrow shows the hotel lift's descent through the floors. I see my utter disarray reflected in the polished elevator doors. I'm just disentangling myself from some Triffid-esque tendrils when *Ding!*, the doors open. To mark our trip Down Under, a benevolent sponsor has provided the England touring party with intense, brightly coloured running shoes (an irony which isn't lost on a few of us). They're a combination of white, pink and pale blue. Even now, 35 years on, I can picture them distinctly. Lying on the floor, I raise my head to see three pairs of those very trainers. I have only one thought. *Please let it be Lamby, Smithy and Gower.* But it isn't Lamby, Smithy and Gower. As my eyes travel upwards I recognise team manager Micky Stewart's ankles, tour manager Peter Lush's legs, and, most cata-strophically of all, the knees, tanned, knobbly, of Graham Gooch, the captain. It's the worst possible scenario – the hier-archy coming down for breakfast. Micky, bless him, doesn't quite compute what's going on. Peter's similarly thrown by the scene in front of him. The only words, abrupt, straight to the point, come from Goochy. 'Phil, what the f*** are you doing?'

'Sorry skipper,' I splutter, blowing an errant frond from my lips.

To be fair to Goochy, he doesn't go ballistic there and then. He tells me he'll address the situation that evening. As he points out, eating breakfast, getting ready, travelling to the ground and then preparing to face whatever barbaric paceman the opposi-tion has lined up for the day, is quite enough to be going on with at that point in time, without a spinner in a rubber plant as well.

'Get upstairs, get changed, get on the coach and we'll deal with this later.'

Thankfully, I'm not playing. I spend all day sitting in a corner of the dressing room hiding behind my sunglasses.

The bollocking duly comes, but it's a fair bollocking. Goochy points out that the managerial set-up is trying to build something with this England team, and that also, while he's having to think about me, perhaps I should think about him. 'I've got to captain and open the innings,' he points out. 'I don't need to pick you up and throw you in the shower as well.'

His words resonate. 'Sorry, Goochy. Next time I'll come in the tradesman's.'

And then, me being me, I have a slight chip back at him. 'I have been bowling well, you know. Had I been picked for the game I'd have been in bed at 10 p.m. with a cup of tea.'

Basically, I was telling him, 'You made me go out!'. It was a valiant, foolish and ultimately fruitless effort.

I'd sometimes wonder if me and Goochy banged heads so much because of the rivalry between our counties, Middlesex and Essex, at the time constantly battling it out for the domestic silverware, the Liverpool and Arsenal of cricket. Goochy would later be joined in the England set-up by another big Essex character, Keith Fletcher, who came in as coach. I wondered if sometimes they looked at me and my shenanigans and thought, *It's that lot from Middlesex – and he's the worst one of them!* I'm sure it wasn't actually like that, but I felt it a little bit.

In reality, however, we clashed predominantly because he was so wedded to the idea of hard graft being the best way to get the most out of players. I, and a few others, didn't operate that way. We'd always give our utmost on the pitch but we were going to enjoy ourselves along the way. There's something very easily forgotten when playing professional sport for your country – this is the best time of your life. You've done all the hard work, done all the practice to maximise your skills. Now isn't the time to sit in your hotel room. Now is the time to get out there and enjoy it. You're playing for England. Don't walk on to the pitch like you've got a bag of coal on your back. Walk out there as light as a feather with a smile on your face. And enjoy it while it lasts. Hang around up there as long as you can. Enjoy the view. It's a bit like climbing Everest and then, the second you get to the summit, starting back down. The descent will come soon enough without you encouraging it.

Too often back then, however, playing for England felt like being beaten with a big stick. 'This is how we do it! Fall in!' The aim was to make us better. But it's guidance that improves your game, your skillset. Doing 25 laps of a cricket ground isn't going to affect anything. Any player wants to make themselves better but you need people, systems, to make that happen. It's all very well trying to change the culture but if there's nothing in place to drive that change then what's the point? Goochy was a head-master with no teachers. He simply didn't have the staff. In their absence, he wanted people like Gower, Lamb and Robin Smith to be his prefects. But Gower, Lamb and Robin Smith really weren't the prefecting kind. They were the ones pointing out how to find the back door of the hotel.

Goochy's was a thankless task. The early 1990s was a transi-tional time. He was trying to ease out the proper old party types only to find that a good few of the new boys were even worse. He could be forgiven for thinking, *For crying out loud, when will there be someone who actually wants to do a bit of running!* I'm sure I remember him once actually saying, 'The trouble with England cricketers is that no-one actually wants to play cricket.' And he had a point. We were all looking out the dressing room window hoping it would rain. If we'd had the weather apps they have now, we'd have never been off them. All too often rain was what stopped us getting beat.

Gooch, Mike Atherton, Alec Stewart, Nasser Hussain – the way they all captained was dictated by a desperation to be successful, particularly in the Ashes. Work-ethic was big for them because in terms of talent alone they just didn't have teams that could compete. It's funny how, to some degree, the culture has now gone full-circle. Under Brendon McCullum it's gone back to, 'Well, if we lose, let's go and have a game of golf and not worry about it.' Ben Stokes is the same – really into just allowing people to express themselves. But they have the system, support-ive, nurturing, to allow them to do that.

I'd talk about mine and Goochy's fallouts with John Emburey, because he was a big mate of Graham's. He and Mike Gatting were trying to point me in the right direction when I was playing up a bit, and it might well have been due to their input that Goochy stuck with me for as long as he did. In fact, I wonder now if it was following a chat with Goochy about my being on the selectors' radar that Gatt marched me into a barbers at Uxbridge and made me have a slightly more respectable haircut and my earrings taken out, because it was straight afterwards that I got picked for England. However, I was still going to push back against a regime if it felt overly disciplined. It was just I didn't always do it in a way that was particularly Gooch-friendly. The Christmas party on that 1990 tour is a case in point. Away from home for the festivities, it was traditional for the players to cheer one another up by sticking on a bit of fancy dress, or perhaps getting up on stage and doing a turn. In my case, I thought it would be a terrific idea to do a fitness class – Keep Fit with Graham Gooch – complete with impressions of the skipper. As I implored my audience to go through a series of push-ups and star-jumps, I could see Graham trying his very best to smile.

In retrospect, I expect he'd have liked to club me round the head with the turkey.

For all we might have been very different people, and had our various run-ins, Goochy was 100 per cent the best batsman I ever played with. Throughout my England career, it was a case of, 'If Goochy don't get any, then we don't get any.' The Aussies knew that as well – he was very much the talisman. Get him out early and they were halfway there. Bear in mind that in those days we had rabbits coming in at number eight, and Goochy was walking out to bat dragging the tail – the likes of Andy Caddick, Devon Malcom and me – behind him. I can well imagine what he was thinking. *If I don't get any, you can bet your life they won't.* Goochy led from the front.

I'd have loved to have played with him when he was a younger fella, when he was unburdened from responsibility. He was a good laugh by all accounts. Embers was forever telling me what a character he was, and I'd think, *Well, how come I never see this funny lively bloke? Where is he? Where's this bloke I've heard so much about?* But the run-ins we had weren't relentless, and no matter how bad they felt at the time, one thing never changed when it came to me and Graham Gooch. The minute he put those pads on I was clinging to his leg. 'Please Graham! Please go and get some runs! Don't let them get to me, skip.'

At a time when England were sliding one way and the Aussies heading in entirely the opposite direction there was only so much Graham Gooch could do. But I, and every other England cricket fan, was massively grateful.

42 ASHES TESTS

Runs: 2,632
Highest Score: 196
Avg: 33.31
Hundreds: 4
Fifties: 16

Wickets: 8
Best Bowling: 2–16
Avg: 59.75

6.

ALEX CAREY

Aussie wicketkeeper who showed he wasn't quite as meek and mild as he looked.

The man who caused the biggest controversy in recent Ashes history might be a strange choice as a 'hero', especially for an Englishman. But for me, Alex Carey has to make the list. I owe him a huge thank you. The Aussie wicketkeeper gave me my greatest ever day at Lord's.

I have never commentated on a game like the Lord's Test in 2023. This most serene of places, this little slice of St John's Wood, where aged colonels fall asleep beneath trilbies, the home of the maiden aunt, was suddenly an absolute bearpit. I'd never seen anything like it. It was like walking past a Women's

Institute meeting, glancing through the window, and there being a full-on riot going on inside.

The catalyst? A certain Alex Carey, actually one of the more anonymous members of that touring squad. Had it been David Warner who'd sparked the uproar, possibly after taking an industrial sander to the ball, then few would have been surprised, but Alex had a real butter-wouldn't-melt look about him. In another life, he could have had a career in kids' television, although he had been an Aussie Rules footballer before he plumped for a cricket career and those blokes are proper tough. They have to be to tolerate those tiny shorts. Now keeping wicket for his country, the South Australian might not have shared the gnarled and leathery look of Rodney Marsh, but, as Lord's was about to find out, he was just as uncompromising.

England were chasing 371 to win that second Test and level the series 1–1. In the old days, any thought of reaching that kind of fourth innings target was an absolute pipedream. But this was peak Bazball. No score was deemed out of reach for captain Ben Stokes and coach Brendon McCullum. Even at 45–4, England carried on believing, recovering to 177–4 before the dismissal of Ben Duckett brought Jonny Bairstow to the crease alongside the skipper. With the best part of 200 still to get, the home side was very much in the last chance saloon. But if anyone could do it, it was these two. Ben had broken Aussie hearts in the most spectacular of ways at Headingley when chasing a similar target four years earlier, sharing a partnership of 86 with the Yorkshireman along the way. Jonny, meanwhile, had turned into a human firework when battering 136 from 92 balls against New Zealand to snatch victory from the jaws of defeat at Trent Bridge the previous summer. The Aussies understood the stakes. Break the partnership and win. Allow this pair 20 overs together and lose.

Jonny really did look in the mood, cracking a couple of early fours, when, at the end of an over from Cameron Green, having touched his bat down in his crease, and with the ball in Alex's gloves, he set off for a chat with Ben. Spying his chance, Alex then rolled the ball along the ground and broke the wicket. The Aussies appealed and, with the decision referred to the third umpire, Jonny was given out stumped. Several ex-England players, including Athers and Nasser Hussain, said the Aussies were perfectly entitled to claim the dismissal – 'you don't leave your crease, it's something you learn as a kid'. But for me it was poor form. OK, it's in the laws of the game, and if it had been, say, the third or fourth ball of the over, I'd have said fair enough. But this was the last ball and Bairstow had tapped his bat down a couple of times before starting to walk down the wicket. No way was he trying to gain an advantage. It wasn't like he was going to sidle up to Ben and whisper, 'Quick! Run!' Everything pointed to that over being done and dusted. Even the umpire was getting the bowler's cap out of his pocket. And that's why it felt so wrong. I thought it was out of order, and so did pretty much everyone else in the ground.

That included Ben Stokes. And this is why that day at Lord's will, I'm sure, never be beaten. From that point on, in an attempt to win the game before he ran out of partners, England's captain went absolutely ballistic. From the next 16 balls alone he smashed 38 runs. He brought up his century by hitting Cameron Green for three consecutive sixes. The effect on that Lord's crowd, riled by what they saw as blatant cheating by the

Aussies, was absolutely electrifying. From the minute Jonny was out, no-one sat down. It basically became a standing game of cricket. Add in Ben's pyrotechnics and the last thing anyone was interested in was resting their backside. It was like the old Kop at Liverpool, everyone stood there hollering and cheering.

Only the Ashes could see an injection of such energy into the home of cricket. People were delighting in shouting and scream-ing because in any other circumstances it would have been deemed unseemly. Right there and then, though, they felt like they had every right. A complete injustice had happened before their eyes and now Ben Stokes was going to put it right.

There was an hour where it really did look like, in true super-hero style, Ben would see off the 'baddies' and get us over the line, and in that hour all those years of restraint, of suffering at the hands of the Aussies, came pouring out. When Steve Smith dropped the England captain on 114, I looked across at the pavilion and spotted some ancient, double-barrelled lord, a man who'd slept through every minute of every day's play he'd ever been to, shouting, 'Serves you right, you ****ing b******!' Just fabulous. Everywhere I looked people were storming around. 'This is a ****ing disgrace!' Of course, that extended to MCC members actually confronting opposition players in the Long Room. Again, unbelievable. Totally unheard of. I'd assumed nothing short of the four-minute warning could get these fellas out of their seats. And even then they'd have to finish *The Times* cryptic crossword first. And yet here they were, frothing at the mouth, berating the baggie greens. It made me laugh the next day when I saw the MCC's statement in the paper, along the lines of 'Quentin Bartholomew Archibald Snettersham-Smythe the Third and Zebedee Xavier Mahogany Wilberforce-Fotheringay have forthwith had their membership suspended while investigations into the events in the Long Room take place.' It took half the front page just to print their names.

The World Cup Final against New Zealand in 2019 is the only other time I've seen Lord's so animated, but that was a different kind of energy, a gradual build-up of anticipation and nervous excitement erupting into a crescendo of celebration. In 2023 the explosion was immediate – an unforgiveable sporting wrong inflicted by our oldest cricketing enemy. Had it been the Sri Lanka wicketkeeper who'd thrown the wicket down the uproar wouldn't have happened. It had to be the Ashes. Without that history, there'd have been a few shrugged shoulders, England would have slumped to a routine loss, and that would have been that.

As a commentator, it was one of those days when I never found the off switch. Even at midnight I was still buzzing, almost as if I'd been involved myself. I couldn't help thinking how amazing it is that while these controversies can happen at any time, in any game, they always seem to happen in the Ashes. Huge talking points popping up all the time. I'm sure they will again. Alex Carey was asked if he'd ever repeat the stumping trick. 'If there was an opportunity,' he replied, 'I definitely would.'

Please not while I'm on *TMS* duty, Alex. I don't think I could survive it.

What. A. Day.

10 ASHES TESTS
(TO OCT 2025)

Runs: 383
Highest Score: 66
Avg: 21.27
Hundreds: 0
Fifties: 2

Wicketkeeping dismissals: 49

7.

SIR ALASTAIR COOK

It's not always the mongrel, the down-in-the-earth battler, who has the real iron will. Sometimes it's these other fellows. Fellows like Alastair Cook.

Andrew Strauss, Alastair Cook, Alec Stewart, these kinds of people, always remind me a little bit of that series of *Blackadder* set in World War I. Stiff upper lip generals who'd order the complete bombardment of the opposition lines and then put a hand up. 'OK chaps, let's stop for tea.' The difference is that these blokes would also be first over the top, whistle in mouth, with their men. Just because you like your collar starched doesn't mean you haven't got inner strength. These blokes can fight it out with the best of them. They just give you a posh kicking instead of a normal one.

The Ashes win Down Under in 2010–11 is a case in point. It was built on a phenomenal level of run-scoring, most notably by Alastair Cook. Across that five-match series Cooky scored 766 runs, almost 200 more than his nearest rival, with one double-hundred, two hundreds, and two fifties, finishing with a not inconsiderable average of 127.66. Ultimately, you win a Test match by taking 20 wickets, but without runs on the board you haven't got a chance. I remember getting up one morning during the first Test and seeing England had declared on 517–1. Cooky had made 235 not out backed up by centuries from Andrew Strauss and Jonathan Trott. Bearing in mind that England fans are long used to waking to news of overnight annihilation in Australia, I was utterly dumbfounded. I was sticking pins in myself to make sure I was awake.

Ultimately, however, one big score doesn't win a series. You've got to do it again and again. And that's exactly what happened. In the second Test, at Adelaide, England declared on 620–5, with Cooky again a century maker with 148, backed up by Kevin Pietersen's 227. After a blip in the third Test at Perth, England then racked up 513 at Melbourne and 644 at Sydney, where Cooky filled his boots once more with 189. On that tour, Cooky made life-changing, career-making, scores. Now a *TMS* pundit, he often talks about 'daddy' hundreds, and for good reason. When it comes to winning Test matches against average opposition, one bloke getting 110 and a couple of others getting fifty, might be enough. Against the really strong teams, like Australia, you need people getting big, big totals. When I played the Aussies, one player getting a score in the low hundreds didn't really mean anything. It just signalled that three of theirs would do the same. To defeat the Aussies, 'doing well' doesn't mean getting 105, or 3–60, it means getting 190 or 7–45. If you want to beat the Aussies you've got to properly wipe them out. Give them even the slightest glimpse of a way back and they'll have you.

That counts double on their home turf. Remember, in Australia, conditions very rarely help you out. Pitches are hard, the ball doesn't do much, the weather's hot, the sky's cloudless. To win is very hard work. So don't go down there and feel pleased with yourself for getting 70, because 70 isn't going to get you over the line, or anywhere near it. The same goes for team scores. Normally, scoring 340 and having the opposition at 180–5 would be seen as a decent position. But not against Australia, who more often than not will summon up a maverick, such as Adam Gilchrist or Andrew Symonds, who can blast a hundred out of nowhere, or a Ian Healy-type figure who'll grind you into the dirt for a gritty 85. Suddenly you're 150 behind on first innings wondering what the hell just happened. When I played it was very hard to ever feel relaxed against Australia.

As a teammate, I imagine Cooky was the perfect antidote to that pressure. He was straight up about how he played the game. 'I've got my method, I've got my shots, I like my daddy hundreds, I'm going to wear you down, and I'm going to get them.' I'm convinced Cooky was an assassin in a former life. The bloke is just so clinical with the way he goes about things. I look at him in the *TMS* box and it's like butter wouldn't melt, he's such a nice chap, but I know as well that as a player he must have been absolute nails. To go out and open the batting against the fastest in the world, and yet be totally unperturbed at all times, that really is quite something.

In some ways Cooky was our version of Steve Smith, a man who just loved batting, and was quite happy to do so until the opposition were absolutely and utterly sick of the sight of him.

The difference is Cooky was rather more manicured, possibly even conjuring up his inner Denis Compton with a dash of Brylcreem. Alec Stewart was the same, the sort of person who could be pursued several miles by a wild boar and arrive back at camp with not a hair out of place. Cooky batted for hour after hour on that 2010–11 tour in blistering heat. In such conditions it's not uncommon to see a player pressing the top of their helmet down and releasing several gallons of sweat on to the pitch. Not Cooky. Off it would come at the end of the day and there he'd be, pristine. He could have stepped straight on to a theatre stage as the debonair star of a West End show, the Essex Hercule Poirot, and no-one would have batted an eyelid.

Never a rolled-up shirt sleeve out of place, there's no mere dog in Cooky. He never looks anything less than a thoroughbred spaniel about to make a Best in Show appearance at Crufts. And yet he could scrap and fight with the best of them. A character of absolute steel, but a trait you only ever saw when he had a bat in his hand. In real life, Alastair's the nicest guy you could ever meet. You can't ever imagine him sticking the old knife in. But then again he's a farmer. He sees stuff the rest of us don't. He's used to getting his hands dirty, delivering lambs, sticking his arm up cows' backsides, dispatching vermin. He's done it all. And with such a lovely soft pair of hands. He's also very funny. The more I see of Cooky in the *TMS* studio the better he gets. That little bit of distance from his playing time has allowed him to open up and be this person who's not only very knowledgeable but great fun as well. And no matter how hot it gets in that commentary box he still doesn't sweat. There must be something about opening batsmen. First there was Athers and his inability to smell, and then there was Cooky with his inability to sweat. Clearly, to open the innings you need some deep-seated physical unusualness.

I still feel that someone somewhere needs to make a film about England's assault on the 2010–11 Ashes. I see it as being a bit like *The Wild Geese*, except instead of Richard Burton and Roger Moore you've got Cooky and Straussy.

'Righto chaps,' the Essex stalwart would pipe up, 'we're in a predicament here. We're a long way from home and there's a lot of fellows round here who'd like nothing more than to send us home with a bullet between the ears. I'll be honest boys, we've been given a bit of a suicide mission. But we're going to fight tooth and nail to bring that booty back to Blighty.'

The final scene would see the victors back in their London club. 'We did it chaps,' Cooky would say, cigar hovering above pristine white tablecloth. 'Yes,' Straussy would reply, 'and I'll tell you what, one day we'll ruddy well go back over there and do it all again.'

Cue brandy glasses being clinked. Credits roll to *Soul Limbo*.

35 ASHES TESTS

Runs: 2,493
Highest Score: 244 not out
Avg: 40.20
Hundreds: 5
Fifties: 11

8.

THE UMPS

You expect to be called a 'Pommie bastard' in
Australia – just not by the officials.

It's not uncommon as a bowler to enquire of the umpire how many balls are left in an over. You might think counting to six isn't that hard but when you're fuming at an lbw decision being denied or have waited five minutes while the sphere's retrieved from the Trent, it's easy to lose count.

The MCG offers a particular set of distractions. The fact the stadium holds 100,000 people for a start. Also, the unerring knowledge that the vast majority of them are willing you to make a complete arse of yourself. Subsequently, during my Test debut, I didn't think it anything out of the normal to ask umpire Peter McConnell how many balls to go. His response, however, was extraordinary. McConnell looked at me. 'Count 'em yourself you Pommie bastard.' I couldn't believe what I was hearing. I mean, I was expecting a bit of grief off the Aussie crowd, and clearly their players wouldn't be holding back, but the umps?

'Sorry?' I asked as I picked my jaw up off the floor. 'I only asked how many balls were left!' It was a proper *Is this actually happening?* moment. I looked around. Everything appeared to be real. There was Alec Stewart's starched collar, Jack Russell's battered sunhat, David Gower's remarkable golden curls. I definitely wasn't Bobby Ewing in the shower. Good job, because Graham Gooch was about to join me.

'You can't talk to my player like that,' he told McConnell. But actually he could. He was the umpire. Who was going to stop him? He let the skipper say his piece, bided his time and then showed exactly who was running the show by ignoring a nick behind by David Boon so obvious it was almost like the slip-catching practice that coaches would put us through at the start of the day.

'Not out,' he responded to my ever-more desperate appeals. It was unbelievable, and no way was I going to stand there, be all 'Yes sir, no sir', and meekly accept the injustice.

'You f***ing bastard,' I told him.

Not my default reaction to a decision going against me, but on this occasion I simply couldn't believe what I was hearing. A top-quality batsman can take a game away from you with one life. The last thing you need is them being gifted two. Boony, who'd come to the wicket with his team 10–2 chasing a victory target of 197, went on to make 94 not out. On such calls, an entire match can turn. And it did. His stay of execution condemned us to defeat. I don't blame Boony for any of what happened, by the way. He was just trying to win the game for Australia. It wasn't up to him to walk. If the shoe had been on the other foot, pretty much every England batsman would have stood their ground as well. But it does show just how 'wild west' umpiring could be before neutral officials began to be introduced in 1992.

After going so unjustly wicketless at Melbourne, eventually my first Test scalp came in the following game at Sydney. Greg Matthews skied one and Eddie Hemmings swallowed an indisputably high catch at mid-off. Immediately I turned to McConnell's fellow umpire Tony Crafter. 'I suppose you're going to tell me that's not out either.'

But the joy was short-lived. Fed up with my continual appeals for plumb lbws against tailender Carl Rackemann, who'd taken root after very quickly realising he had free rein to use his legs to deflect my every delivery, Crafter informed me, 'OK, that's it – I'm not even going to look at lbw from now on.' I was incredulous. 'Really? You're seriously saying that we're playing a game with no lbw.' I was bemused going on apoplectic.

'Just checking, are caught and bowled still OK?'

I was being facetious, but not long afterwards Alec Stewart clung on to a tricky chance at short leg and that was deemed not out as well. In the end, Rackemann hung around for a 100-ball, near two-hour nine, before Devon Malcolm bowled him, one of the few remaining acceptable forms of dismissal. Instead of a reasonable run chase, we were left seeking 255 at ten an over. David Gower was promoted to open alongside Goochy, and they did their best to right the injustice, belting along for the first few overs, but once they were gone, and Wayne Larkins and Stewie fell quickly, all we could do was hunker down for the draw.

To be fair, it wasn't just Aussie officials; all through my career umpires either wilfully ignored the truth or looked the other way when it came to lbw decisions. That's not me being bitter. The evidence backs me up all the way. Just nine of my 121 Test wickets were lbw. Monty Panesar and Graeme Swann, who played in the era of the Decision Review System, snaffled a quarter of their victims that way. What I'd have given for technology. DRS totally confirmed what I'd been saying all those years. I really should have been compensated. Although in Australia in the early 1990s, who's to say even the tech wouldn't have been biased? 'Can we have ball-tracker please?' Cue image of yorker bouncing three feet over the stumps.

There were times I'd actually get umpires asking me to stop appealing, like I was being tiresome. I mean, 'Sorry for interrupting your sunbathe. Would you like me to rub some factor-40 on your back? Nip up and fetch your Len Deighton from your hotel room?'

I was in that team to get wickets. It's unlikely that at the next selection meeting anyone would be going, 'Well, you know, if the umpire hadn't ruled out lbw, Phil would have had a five-fer, not none for 145.' What the 1990s was missing was some sort of cricketing ombudsman, a higher power who could overrule all dodgy umpiring decisions. *In the case of Tufnell v McConnell, the office of the Cricket Ombudsman rules that David Boon did indeed practically take the leather off the ball when edging behind to Jack Russell. A wicket shall henceforth be added to Mr Tufnell's statistics.*

Of course, there was one thing I appreciated about the home umpires when playing Australia. An unpleasant ball from Merv Hughes didn't actually have to break my fingers on the way through to the keeper to be given caught behind. Three inches of fresh air between glove and ball and up the finger would go. Bat under the arm and back to the pavilion.

Lovely jubbly!

9.

DEREK RANDALL

*Absolute lunatic. As a kid I couldn't take
my eyes off him. Watching Derek on TV
made me want to be a cricketer.*

'Come on Rags! Watch the ball Rags! Ragsy! Watch the ball!'

The first time I encountered Derek Randall he got a fabulous hundred on a turning pitch against myself and Embers at the top of our game. Other players had warned me Derek was a bit 'out there' when batting, but even so I couldn't believe what he was like when I actually played against him. He was rattling away to himself all the time – 'Ragsy! Keep watching the ball! Ragsy! Come on Ragsy! Concentrate!' He was doing this at volume. It wasn't just the players, the crowd could hear him too. The first time I bowled at him I did actually stop halfway up to my mark. 'What's going on here?' I asked the ump. 'Is he all right?'

He looked at Derek, geeing himself up, twitching all over the place, playing with his pads, and then looked at me. 'That's just what Derek does.'

'Well, I don't know if I can bowl at him then. I mean, could you tell him to shut up?'

'Oh no, Phil, I'm sorry, but he can do what he wants.'

I glanced down the wicket. 'Come on! Bowl the ball! Rag-or! Rag-or! Watch it, Rag-or!'

Bloody hell, here goes . . .

Whether he hit it or not didn't matter. 'That's it, Rags! You know what to do! Come on Rag-or!' Although hitting it for runs did spark a whole new conversation. 'That's two Rag-or! Come on, Rag-or! Push for two, Rag-or!'

I'm standing there thinking, 'Please just shut up!'

Faced with this madness, it was easy to tell myself that this bloke Randall hadn't got a clue. A couple of hours later when he'd peeled off a magnificent ton I was telling myself something different. Derek Randall could really play. I'd just encountered one of the finest and most entertaining batsmen of his generation. Heading for the bar that evening I assured myself that no way could he be the same off the pitch as on it. But of course there he was, not so much with ants in his pants as eels down his trousers and scorpions up his shirt. He literally couldn't stand still. It was a mystery how any of his drink actually reached his mouth.

Thinking about it now, I'd have been disappointed if Derek had been any different. As a 10-year-old I'd sat and watched highlights of Derek's most glorious match, when, in 1977, he almost dragged England to a very unlikely victory in the Centenary Test at Melbourne. In the first innings, Dennis Lillee whizzed a 90 mph bouncer past Derek's forehead, at which point Derek stood bolt upright in front of his stumps, doffed his cap to the paceman, and told him, 'No good hitting me there mate, nothing to damage.' You can just see the smile on Dennis's face as he heads back to his mark. I love the way Aussies respect character and personality. If anyone else had doffed their cap to him, DK would have ripped his head off. Not Derek. It was one of the greatest sporting moments I'd ever seen in my short life, and actually I still consider that to be the case. There was no-one else in cricket doing that kind of stuff. I knew nothing about Derek Randall, but I knew for sure he was an absolute one-off.

In the second innings, DK did actually test Derek's 'nothing to damage' theory, pinging one off his cap straight to cover. As the Aussie fielders rushed in to check he was OK, Derek performed a backward roll and sprung straight back to his feet. Again, DK, a man not generally lost for words, could only stand there in open-mouthed astonishment.

Watching Derek and DK in this wonderful duel definitely stirred something in me. Minus being hit on the head (something I never favoured), I wanted to be part of this battle between old foes, yes pushing one another to the limit, but also clearly having the best of times along the way.

Derek went on to make 174 that day, a score I've never forgotten because a Nottinghamshire butcher vowed to give him the same number of lamb chops on his return. I can still remember seeing this bloke, in full butcher's garb, and thinking, *Blimey, 174 lamb chops! I wouldn't mind a bit of that!* Fast forward 13 years to my own first Ashes trip and David Gower was the recipient of a (naturally) slightly more upmarket offer. For every century he scored on that 1990–91 tour – two as it turned out – he was handed a bottle of pre-World War I vintage port. I still think the lamb chops was the better deal.

Just a few months after Derek's heroics in Melbourne, thousands packed into Trent Bridge in the hope of seeing the Nottinghamshire maestro repeat the feat in his home Test. And then Geoffrey Boycott ran him out. Watching it on the telly, Derek's walk back to the pavilion, Gunn & Moore in hand, pads flapping all over the place, shaking his head, on the verge of tears, seemed to take forever, the silence broken only by the occasional volley aimed by a spectator towards the Yorkshireman, stood head in hand, in the middle. So upset were the faithful that it felt for a minute as if the authorities might have a riot to deal with. People were seriously unhappy with Boycott and how he'd sold short the local hero. Quite unusual for an English cricket crowd of that era, but that just shows how much people loved Derek. It was fortunate for Boycott that he went on to get a hundred, otherwise he might not have got out alive. There was a very real chance that he might have had to be dressed as a waitress and squirreled away through a back door.

Derek might not have made the big score he desired, but he was always 20 runs in credit in any match because of his unbelievable prowess in the field. Known to all and sundry on the cricket circuit as Arkle, after the three-time Cheltenham Gold Cup winner, his speed across the turf was second to none. Derek was the first person to really make fielding a feature of the game. While the rest of us just used to stand there and make a vague attempt to stop or catch the ball if we were unfortunate enough for it to enter our vicinity, Derek made it a discipline all of its own. Traditionally, fielders would trudge in as the bowler began his run-up, but Derek would prowl, on the balls of his feet, ready to sprint in any direction. At the point of delivery, he'd already be running in anticipation of the trajectory of the shot, scooping up the ball like a monkey while some poor devil floundered to make his ground. It really did seem like Derek's arms were twice the length of everyone else's. It was like Nottinghamshire had Mr Tickle in the team.

It was a massive loss to the game when Derek hung up his boots in 1993. I admired him so much as a player but even more so as a character. For a while in retirement he was the coach at Cambridge University and one of my favourite cricketing memories is strolling round the boundary at Fenner's having a lovely conversation and laugh with him. As we walked, I couldn't help thinking back to myself as that kid on the settee, watching that Centenary Test, in awe of the man now at my side as he took on DK Lillee.

I mean, even when he was out he was still unmistakeably Derek, getting lost on the way back to the dressing room and ending up on the Queen's balcony. 'She was very nice about it,' he reported. There are 'bigger' names in this book but I'm not sure any had quite the effect that Derek had on me.

There's a suite at Trent Bridge named in Derek's honour. If ever you find yourself in there, don't mention Geoffrey Boycott. Do, however, behave like you've got eels in your pants.

18 ASHES TESTS

Runs: 1,161
Highest Score: 174
Avg: 38.70
Hundreds: 3
Fifties: 6

10.

DENNIS LILLEE

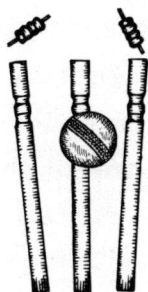

A beautiful hostility. To see him run up to the wicket was to watch poetry in motion. No-one, before or since, has ever looked better in a set of whites.

'G'day Tuffers!'

I looked up and there he was. Top few buttons still undone on that big white dinner shirt. Medallion swinging against hairy chest. Moustache. Sharply creased trousers with flares. No, Tom Jones hadn't come to watch the Test match. This was one of the greatest fast bowlers the game had ever seen. I looked at him with only one thought. *This is fantastic!* DK Lillee! Even his name was bloody great!

To play on the same pitch as Dennis Lillee in the traditional Ashes tour opener at Lilac Hill in 1990 was a dream come true.

Growing up watching cricket on the box there were players I really did like the look of. Players who had that indefinable X factor. I'll be honest, more often than not they were Australians. And none more so than Dennis Lillee. OK, he had a few miles on the clock by the time I encountered him in the flesh but to me he still looked exactly the same. Everything about him was perfection. The whole day was just the most ridiculous thrill.

I'm not sure what it says about me that, as a kid, the Aussies appealed to me more than a lot of England players, but my dad was the same. Yes, he loved Denis Compton – handsome, talented, debonair – but he had massive respect for a lot of Australian players, as did many of his generation. I put it down to them having a certain magnetism. No disrespect, but once you'd flicked the TV on and witnessed Dennis Lillee cruise in and put the frighteners on some poor sod on a lightning-fast wicket in Perth, seeing Chris Old turn his arm over in a Sunday League game at Derby just wasn't the same. Dennis was definitely my cup of tea. I didn't know the bloke, obviously, but it was clear to me that here was someone who lived life to the full. You knew that at the end of a hard day he'd sit down, take his boots off, crack open a beer and have a laugh. He, and most other Aussies, just seemed to do things differently. They were beer, barbecues and beaches while we were big coats, balaclavas and boots. They had the life the rest of us wanted. They could express themselves while we were wrapped up in 15 layers from the Edinburgh Woollen Mill.

More than anything they weren't consumed with that old-fashioned English view that everything has to be done in a certain way. Dennis was the absolute symbolisation of the Aussie 'just go with it' attitude. When the teams were introduced to the Queen at the Centenary Test, while the England blokes were bowing and curtseying, Dennis took the opportunity to whip out pen and paper and ask for her autograph. I can imagine it now – 'C'mon Liz, how about sticking your name on here?' In fact, when introduced to the monarch on receiving his MBE in 1981, Dennis did actually offer the truly unforgettable greeting, 'G'day, Queen!' Not quite as bad as fellow paceman Rodney Hogg's infamous 'Nice legs for an old Sheila!' as the monarch made her way down the line of Australian players at Lord's, but unorthodox nevertheless.

This sort of stuff had the old colonels in the pavilion at Lord's choking on their brandy. 'How dare that man insult our Queen and country? This chap can't be allowed to play at Lord's, he's an absolute savage. He's never put a tie on in his life.' There'd be a hullaballoo, questions asked in the House. Next thing you knew Dennis would be on the back pages of the tabloids, a mock-up of his head on the block beneath a glowering executioner.

And that was what made Dennis unmissable. In any situation there was no saying what he'd do next, his striding out to the wicket with an aluminium bat in the first Test at the WACA in Perth in 1979 being a case in point. Personally, I found it virtually impossible to score runs with any sort of bat, aluminium or otherwise, but Dennis seemed sure that metal not willow was the way to go, perhaps spurred on by the fact he had several hundred of the things in his garage to get rid of. England captain Mike Brearley didn't notice at first, only alerted to the situation by the rather unusual 'Clang!' Dennis's bat made when it hit the ball, a bit like the gong at the start of the J Arthur Rank films. Brears complained and in the end the umpires decided

Dennis couldn't use the bat because it was damaging the ball. Even then he wouldn't let it go, claiming there was nothing in the rules to say he couldn't use it. Only when his skipper Greg Chappell marched out to the middle with a face like thunder did he make the switch, hurling the bat a good 20 metres across the turf before carrying on. Looking back I'm disappointed Dennis didn't get away with his metal bat. As a fellow innovator, once eyeing up the arm of a settee as a thigh pad when things turned nasty at Sabina Park, Jamaica, I'd have enjoyed expanding the theme to a full suit of armour. Certainly, Brears held no grudge. Typical Lillee, at the denouement of the series, he asked the England skipper to sign the offending item. Brears took the felt-tip. 'Good luck with the sales,' he wrote.

I'm glad to say that, while I admire Dennis immensely, I never actually faced him in that match at Lilac Hill. Even at the age of 41 he was pretty lively. In fact, four years later, in the exact same fixture, he was still motoring in, claiming the not inconsiderable scalps of Mike Atherton and Graeme Hick. He also hadn't forgotten his way with words. 'Move out the way Gatt,' he told our portly batsman, 'I can't see the stumps.' Thankfully, I wasn't in the side that day, happy to watch DK from the comfort of the dressing room while a few others got an up-close glimpse of what he was like in his pomp.

DK Lillee, what a bloke. I wonder if I'd made an effort I could have looked a bit more like him. Probably not. I never ironed my trousers (if I could find them I was happy) and my chest was never quite hairy enough.

Anyway, everyone knows you can't be a spinner and wear a medallion.

29 ASHES TESTS

Wickets: 167
Best Bowling: 7–89
Avg: 21.00
Five-wicket Innings: 11
Ten-wicket Matches: 4

Runs: 469
Highest Score: 73 not out
Avg: 18.03
Hundreds: 0
Fifties: 1

11

MIKE ATHERTON

*Athers was England's rock but even he could
never quite stem the onslaught of the Aussies.*

When Mike Atherton, on 97, clipped a ball from Allan Border off his pads down towards the legside boundary at Lord's, we all gravitated towards the balcony to applaud yet another of his gargantuan efforts in concentration and determination. What happened next was one of the most horrible things I've ever seen on a cricket pitch. It was like it was happening in slow motion. As Merv Hughes came round and gathered the ball, Athers turned and set off for the third run that would bring up his century. It was then that he saw Gatt, hand up, sending him back. Aghast, he turned, lost his footing and was left scrabbling on all fours as Ian Healy smashed down the stumps. Up on the balcony, after the second run, a couple of us had already started clapping. What should have been a great moment of celebration very quickly turned into a hushed 'Oh.' No-one could quite believe what had happened. It just didn't seem real. There was almost a cartoonish element – like when a character's legs are moving but they're not getting anywhere. I watched the footage back on video recently. On the BBC TV commentary, Tony Lewis was as dumbfounded as the rest of us – 'He's fallen! He's slipped down! Oh tragedy, tragedy!' That's how it felt. Everyone was just so gutted for Athers. Instead of one of the greatest moments of his life he was down there scrabbling about in the mud, dirty gloves, dirty knees, bat flapping round his head.

Looking back, running three with Gatt was always going to present a problem. It was as he finished the second run that he thought, *Hang on a minute. I don't do threes!* Gatt, a rotund figure, had a big turning circle at the time. Athers was running 22 yards while he was doing 25. Either way, I learned a valuable lesson that day. Don't start clapping before the batsman has actually got that hundredth run. All we could do now was wait for the poor bloke to come through the dressing room door. In that situation, there's nothing anyone can say to make it better. When some players get out, you're ducking out the way of flying bats in the dressing room. Athers was a more low-key character but his disappointment was tangible. You never play for personal milestones, and Athers would have been hoping to have put in a Herculean effort to save the match, but hundreds against Australia at Lord's don't come around very often. As it was, he would always remain one run, one slip, short of making it on to the honours boards at the home of cricket.

England had actually been putting up some good resistance in that second innings and then, yet again, the mood was punctured and it was back to 'Here we go again.' The way it happened only emphasised that 'For f***'s sake' feeling. Allan Border, a bit-part slow left-armer had bowled the ball. Merv Hughes, basically a Sherman tank with a moustache, had fielded it, and yet somehow the result was our opener sat like a burst ballon back in the pavilion. For Athers, unless someone had shot him, I don't think it could have got any worse. For the rest of us, having just stood and watched the Aussies get 600, nothing going our way at all, we could have been forgiven for thinking, *Someone upstairs really isn't looking after us here.* Every moment of suffering against Australia in the 1990s was encapsulated in that Athers run-out moment.

By the time the 1994–95 Ashes tour came around, Athers was captain, and it was another batsman closing in on a century. Graeme Hick was 98 not out at Sydney when Athers, concerned that England were running out of time to bowl Australia out in their second innings, declared. Again, we were out on the balcony waiting to mark the achievement when all of a sudden Athers got up and waved Hick in. I'll admit that, unlike the other players, who were scattering to all corners of the pavilion, I didn't quite see the bust-up potential of Athers' actions. My only thought was to head back inside the dressing room to get ready to field. There followed a very awkward exchange between Athers and Hick while I suddenly took a very deep interest in the pattern on my socks.

To be fair to Athers, by the time of the Sydney Test, England were already two down in the series. He was a young captain under an immense amount of pressure. In fact, looking back recently at some pictures of that trip I was struck by just how young he looked. The contrast between this shiny-cheeked Cambridge graduate and typically gnarled Aussie captain Mark Taylor couldn't have been greater. When it came to the toss, Taylor must have been thinking, *Hang on, they've sent the mascot out!* A Cambridge alumni was a bit of an old-school look for England, especially compared to many in the opposition team who, hard-faced and unshaven, wouldn't have looked massively out of place in an ageing photo of the Australian gold rush 140 years earlier. They all seemed to have big hands, hardened with calluses, and looked like they could live on rats for a fortnight. A few of us Poms, on the other hand, looked like page boys. They must have thought, *We'll just growl at this lot and they'll s*** themselves.*

Athers, though, could justifiably have hoped that a youthful England could give Australia a run for their money in terms of athleticism if nothing else. However, the selectors had kyboshed that dream by insisting that Gatting and Gooch be part of the squad. Without wishing to be unkind, it had been a while since either had been mistaken for a whippet. Their selection was, in hindsight, a mistake. The last thing any England team heading Down Under wants to do is give the impression they're coming across with players who are on their way out. The Australian players, media and fans seized on that and never let up. Gatting and Gooch's selection was a double whammy for Athers. Having the previous two Ashes tour captains along was only ever going to cramp his style. At least Glenn McGrath took his mind off the situation. Throughout Athers' career, Glenn had him on a piece of string. Like a pissed-off pike pulled repeatedly from a fishing lake, Athers was netted a remarkable 19 times, still the highest batsman/bowler combination in Test history. By the end of his career it was almost as if he had a neon sign over his head – BOWLED MCGRATH. Athers was desperately unfortunate to play in an era of great opening bowlers. Along with McGrath, West Indies' Curtly Ambrose and Courtney Walsh both hooked him 17 times apiece.

I played a lot of cricket with Athers. We actually shared our last Test match, albeit in slightly different circumstances – I got jettisoned and he retired. After the Aussies won the toss on a flat Oval wicket I disappeared after taking 1–174 from 39 overs in my single appearance of the 2001 series. Athers, on the other hand, was bowing out after 115 Test matches and 7,728 runs. I knew this was the end of my Test career, and, last man out, for a duck, as I got halfway up the steps to the dressing room I did allow myself a brief moment to turn round and look at the crowd. Not that they were clapping me – they were too busy applauding another dominant performance by the Australians – but nevertheless I wanted to take in the moment. I knew that in all probability that was my lot.

Athers' retirement, meanwhile, was typically understated. It was almost as if the news slipped from his lips by mistake. 'Oh, by the way everyone,' he told us, 'I'm retiring.' We all went, 'Oh!' and that was that. He didn't want to be that player who announces their departure with a couple of matches to go and has that final wave of the bat as they disappear from view. He wanted to come back into the dressing room, sit down, and reflect, 'Well, that's it.'

Athers was only 33 when he retired but had been plagued by a bad back for years, and like a few others, was a little weatherbeaten from playing in an era low on success for English cricket. He deserved better than never to play in an Ashes-winning side.

A century at Lord's would have been some consolation but he was denied even that. Former Aussie coach John Buchanan said it all when he described Athers in that 1990s period as 'the face of the English spirit'. He's an Ashes hero precisely because he was always trying, always believing.

I always got on very well with Athers, and, having been in neighbouring commentary boxes for the past 20 years, still do. In some ways we might seem like opposites, but actually we've spent some interesting times together, not least when we were both abandoned in Bangalore for a week after the plane to Jamshedpur for a one-day international was deemed two seats too small for the whole squad. Seen as the least likely to play, we spent seven solid days solely in each other's company. With Radio 4 unavailable, he quite happily chatted away to me and I pretended to know what the hell he was on about. It wasn't the first time we'd been forced together on an England tour. Early in his career, Athers was often put down to room with me because, the management thought, his lack of a sense of smell meant he wouldn't mind stinking of Benson & Hedges. It's this shared past of closeness which makes me wonder if at some point we might go caravanning together. Do pop round to the *TMS* box, Athers, if you're interested.

33 ASHES TESTS

Runs: 1,900
Highest Score: 105
Avg: 29.68
Hundreds: 1
Fifties: 15

12.

SHANE WARNE

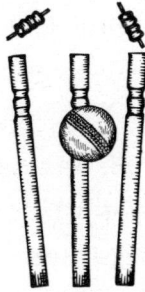

The larrikin to end all larrikins. An absolute superstar who transcended cricket like nobody in the history of the sport.

Fair to say we were feeling quite chipper. We were going OK, bowling the Aussies out for 289 on a greenish damp wicket at Old Trafford was a pretty good effort, especially as we proceeded without too many headaches to 80–1 in our first innings. I was just having a nice cup of tea, sizing up a Bourbon, when someone said Shane Warne was coming on to bowl. No-one knew much about him other than visually he was quite striking. Peroxide blond hair and an earring marked him out among Ashes cricketers. If Geoffrey Boycott ever considered the look, he never took it up.

This was 1993. No YouTube videos or acres of analysis. If you wanted to see what someone was like you had no choice but to see them in the flesh. However, watching from the balcony at Old Trafford was pointless. Back then it was side-on to the wicket. You couldn't see if a spinner was turning the ball. When a quick was on you couldn't see the ball at all. If Wasim Akram was bowling for Lancashire, you'd see him run up to the wicket and then 0.3 seconds later, as if by magic, the stumps would explode. We duly gathered round the little telly in the dressing room.

As Allan Border tossed Warney the leather, the general view around that TV set was, 'Well, this bloke with the dyed hair and the earring won't be very good. He's a leggie so he'll bowl us a few gimmes and we can smash him about.' Up he trotted. We watched as the ball drifted to leg, gripped, turned about three feet and crashed into the top of Mike Gatting's off stump. Complete silence. Gatt was a fantastic player of spin. All my life at Middlesex I'd watched him destroy spinners. And there he was, stood in the middle, utterly perplexed. He didn't know how it had bowled him. We didn't know how it had bowled him. I'm not sure even the Aussies knew how it had bowled him. It was jaw-dropping. Eventually from one of the England boys there was an awestruck 'Bloody hell!', followed quickly by a whispered 'What the f***?', and a barely stifled 'Christ on a bike!'

I'm sure they were using slightly different language but the TV boys clearly couldn't get their heads round what they'd just seen either. They were showing the replay again and again. No matter how many times you saw it, the delivery just didn't make sense. 'And that was his loosener!' someone pointed out. Amid all the disbelief at what we'd just witnessed, we'd clean forgotten that was Warney's first ball in Ashes cricket. Not the fourth, or the fifth – the first! Forget a couple of Tests to get used to English conditions. Ball one! But, as we'd come to see over the next 14 years, Warney's sense of performance was second to none. If we'd known then what we know now, we'd have said the 'ball of the century', as it came to be called, was never in doubt.

Next morning, Gatt remained so perplexed by the delivery that when we went out to do our fielding practice he stood on the pitch trying to work out the mechanics of how the thing had bowled him. You could see the cogs whirring – 'It pitched here, my foot was there, I had my bat just here – how the hell did it happen?!' He really did have to verify in his own mind that it was possible. I wondered if while the rest of us had been tucking into our evening meal he'd nipped down to B&Q and got himself a slide rule. For a short while he was basically Pythagoras in whites.

Robin Smith was the next man in after Gatt. On his way out the door, he detoured over to me. 'Hey, Tuffers,' he said, 'what have you been doing for the last couple of years?'

'Oh f***ing hell,' I thought, 'here we go.'

I must admit I was jealous when Warney turned up. I was making my way, like him a spin bowler, doing all right, getting a few wickets, going out enjoying myself, living the larrikin life, and then all of a sudden this über-larrikin burst into the picture. I felt a little bit knocked off my perch.

Thing is, how do you compete with Warney, a born entertainer who, quite literally, made every ball an event? Usually it's when a batsman – Beefy, KP, the likes of them – comes out to bat that people exit the bars, but very swiftly Warney – well, you can't get much quicker than his first ball – became the one who everybody wanted to see. From that point on he had players, spectators, the lot, in the palm of his hand. I was a little bit envious of his ability to do that, let alone his ability with the ball.

There was something else I coveted. Warney was doing what he was doing on the *winning* side. There were a few sniffs of disapproval when he did his famous shimmy dance with the stump on the balcony at Trent Bridge to celebrate the Aussies retaining the Ashes in 1997, but they weren't coming from me. In those days you celebrated your victories. That went especially for England for whom wins didn't come often, but the Aussies were no different. My wins against Australia always came in a losing cause. Making it 3–1 instead of 3–0 can never match the overwhelming euphoria of securing a series. Had I been on a victorious Ashes team I'd have done exactly what Warney did. Possibly worse!

No-one has taken more Ashes wickets than Warney. Across 36 Tests he claimed 195 victims at an average of 23.25 including four ten-wicket and 11 five-wicket innings. I make several appearances on his list but did at least deny him one record – an Ashes quadruple. At Melbourne, in 1994, I slunk out to the wicket with Warney having already seen off Phil DeFreitas, Darren Gough and Devon Malcolm. It was Warney's misfortune that he'd done so off the fourth, fifth and sixth balls of his over. He never got a chance to have a crack at me because I was caught behind off Craig McDermott the next over having not troubled the scorers. Having been run out for nought in the first innings, I thought it was much better to plump for a pair. It was the second time in as many matches I'd denied Warney a landmark. In the first Test, at Brisbane, he'd snared Daffy and Martin McCague. Milking the build-up for all it was worth, tossing the ball in the air, moving the close fielders around, finally he decided, reasonably enough, that his best bet was to send me down a googly. I could no more pick Warney's googly than I could identify the wading birds of the Thames estuary. I saw it as an inviting half volley, had a gargantuan heave, missed and then watched helplessly as it veered violently towards middle and leg stump. I was mentally preparing to be a footnote in another chapter of Shane Warne folklore when it fizzed over the bails by an inch. With Warney seen off, I motored along serenely to a not-out innings of two.

While I – or anyone else for that matter – couldn't match Warney's bowling prowess, we did share a similar attitude to the game. Being in a gym 24 hours a day and running 25 laps of the outfield wasn't for him any more than it was for me. After being forced by coach John Buchanan to endure a military-style boot camp ahead of the 2006–07 Ashes, Warney famously revealed his disdain for such methodology by declaring that 'the coach is something you travel in to get to the game'. He was speaking from a position of strength. Australia might have lost the previous series in England, but Warney still took 40 wickets and was a real thorn in the hosts' side with the bat. He very nearly dragged Australia over the line at Edgbaston and went a long way to denying England victory at Old Trafford with a stubborn 90.

Like Beefy before him, Warney was a deadly Ashes combination – a brilliant player with a boundless will to win. Look at what he did at Adelaide in 2006. Both teams had scored 500-plus in their first innings, using up the best part of four days in the process. On day five, England were looking more than comfortable on 69–1. They were 107 runs ahead in the game with the clock ticking down. Everyone in that stadium believed it was a nailed-on draw. Everyone, that is, apart from Shane Warne. He bowled 27 overs on the trot and took 4–49. He strangled the life out of England and served them up on a plate as the Aussies made short work of the winning target.

With the whitewash completed a month later in Sydney, Warney and his old pal Glenn McGrath slung their arms round one another's shoulders and walked off into the distance. Between them they had 352 Ashes victims. Five of those were me. But I did put up some resistance. In my last Test, I actually smacked Warney over mid-off for four. Not easy since he had a habit of making much better batsmen than me feel like they'd never picked a bat up before.

'Great shot Tuffers!' shouted Adam Gilchrist behind the stumps. I didn't tell him it was an accident.

It's hard to believe Shane's not still around. People say no-one can ever be bigger than the game, but if ever anyone got close to doing so it was the genius that was him. And yet one of my favourite memories of Warney isn't in his pomp on the grand global stage, it's at Southampton's Ageas Bowl when he was among a group of TV and radio broadcasters who'd formed a behind-closed-doors lockdown 'bubble' to cover a Test match at the ground. In this eerily deserted space we were having a game of 'concourse cricket', and out he came to join us, bowling a few deliveries at *TMS* producer Adam Mountford. It was just the best thing ever. The greatest bowler the world has ever seen, messing about with the rest of us. I don't think Adam has ever got over either the shock or the privilege.

Doesn't matter where you are, Warney, you'll always be cricket's ultimate showman.

36 ASHES TESTS

Wickets: 195
Best Bowling: 8–71
Avg: 21.00
Five-wicket Innings: 11
Ten-wicket Matches: 4

Runs: 946
Highest Score: 90
Avg: 22.00
Hundreds: 0
Fifties: 4

13.

MICHAEL VAUGHAN

Ice-cool skipper whose steel provided the ideal support for England's team of 2005 to bring the Ashes home after a long and painful absence.

I'll be honest, I thought Australia had won the Edgbaston Test of 2005. Steve Harmison bowled a full toss outside off stump, Brett Lee's eyes lit up, and *wallop!*, out it sped towards deep extra cover. I was just about to slump to my knees with a pained cry of, 'Same old bloody England!' when Simon Jones appeared out of nowhere to save the boundary. Even so, with just two runs now needed, I couldn't see England winning. It looked like the all-time classic case of England snatching defeat from the jaws of victory. It was like one of those Wile E Coyote cartoons where it looks like the much put-upon canine is finally about to catch the roadrunner. He's got the anvil set up perfectly on the edge of the cliff, the birdseed is spread on the road below, and yet somehow it's him who ends up with half a ton of metal on his head. Michael Vaughan has told me since that he was having exactly the same thoughts. At that point England were a single hit away from losing the entire series. You didn't go 2–0 down to that Australian team and come back. But of course Michael couldn't be standing out there with head in hands muttering, 'For f***'s sake, how have we lost this?' He had to maintain that purposeful look on his face. 'Nothing to see here! We know exactly what we're doing!' Not for a single second did he look flustered. England won the Ashes that year but Michael really should have won the BAFTA for Best Actor as well.

A few balls later and my emotions, and his, had flipped 180 degrees. Harmy fired one down the legside, Michael Kasprowicz gloved it, and Geraint Jones dived to take a brilliant catch. The fact that Kasprowicz's glove wasn't on the bat handle at the time, and so he shouldn't actually have been given out, has been lost in the mists of time. You can only thank goodness there was no DRS in 2005. Imagine being that third umpire, puncturing one of the biggest Ashes celebrations of all time. You'd have to go and live in a hermitage deep in the Tibetan mountains.

I initially encountered Michael on what was his first and my last tour, to South Africa, in 1999, when, with England 2–4 in the first innings of the first Test, and Mark Butcher, Mike Atheron, Nasser Hussain and Alec Stewart all back in the hutch, he showed massive mental fortitude in making a hard-fought 33 against a rampant Allan Donald and Shaun Pollock to save England from what, even by our 1990s standards, would have been total humiliation. Michael was clearly a class act with a bat in his hand but what struck me more than anything was his immense calmness, born, I felt, of an innate confidence. Unlike me, who would constantly ask others whether I'd performed well – a habit I then took with me into broadcasting – he had self-belief by the bucketload. There are some people in life who don't need someone to pat them on the back, and I saw early on that he was one of them. He had a steely trust in his own actions. He knew what he was doing. But that shouldn't be mistaken for arrogance. Look at the Ashes in 2005. The first thing he says when people talk about his captaincy of that side is that it's always a lot easier if you have a great set of bowlers. I think he's being a little bit modest there. Even with a good team he still had to get the very best out of them if they were to beat the powerhouse that was Australia. What Michael was very good at was striking a balance. The finest captains get the best out of players without being aloof. They command while still being part of the team like everyone else. It's a tricky combination and not many can pull it off, but because he was right in the thick of it he instilled a togetherness in the boys and a belief that they could really pull it off. It was that, more than any kind of tactical masterclass, which made him the perfect skipper for the job.

Michael could also soak up pressure to an incredible degree; brilliant at deflecting the expectation that built as pretty much the entire nation began to believe that this really could be the summer that England finally stuck one on the Aussies. As captain, the non-playing side of the job is massive. The media is constantly wanting a slice of you and, for a few weeks in 2005, the England cricket team became the biggest story around. The media wanted to know everything. What time the players got up in the morning, where they were training, whether they preferred prawn cocktail or cheese 'n' onion. He was a master at all that stuff, a real ambassador for the game and the team. No matter what the situation, he was never distant or flippant.

As a competitor, however, he was a different animal. In the heat of the battle, the 'dog' in him was a bit more apparent. There was that definite Yorkshire element of getting stuck in, wanting to rough the opposition up. He'd have been great turning out for Sheffield Wednesday on a cold February night in Stoke. 'It's f***ing cold! And I f***ing love it! Come near me and I'll kick you up in the air!'

Michael took a more measured version of that hostility into the Test series, Harmy catching Justin Langer a nasty blow on the arm that first morning at Lord's and cutting Ricky Ponting's cheek with a nasty bouncer. While England had the Aussies on the ropes, bowling them out for 190, ultimately their own batting let them down and they lost the match. However, they'd seen that by playing positive and aggressive cricket it was possible to put the tourists on the back foot. They'd found a chink in the Aussies' armour which they'd try their very best to exploit. In the past, such an idea would have been just so much hot air, but for once England knew they had the personnel to match words with action. And that's exactly what happened at Edgbaston where, looking back now, it really does feel like we were offered an embryonic glimpse of Bazball. Batting first, England made a conscious decision to score quickly. They knew that to do so offered a chance to take the game to the Aussies. By the end of the first day they'd made 407 all out off 79 overs. In the context of Test cricket, against the best team in the world, that wasn't so much fast as supersonic. It was the first occasion that England, as a unit, said, 'Listen, we're not going to leave it and block it, we're going to go out there and absolutely smash it.' Well, the coach Duncan Fletcher might have put it slightly differently, but you get what I'm saying. For those of us brought up on Boycott and Tavaré, it was a wonderful, wonderful thing. Don't get me wrong, I admire the skill, technique and mental fortitude required to bat like that pair, I just don't particularly want to sit in front of the TV all day watching it. Marcus Trescothick smacking it around, that's a different matter entirely.

While the last day at Edgbaston is the one that will always be remembered, it's the first that told the bigger story – of the evolution of the England team since the dawn of a new and far more professional age under central contracts. Three of the top six got fifties and the last four wickets added 114. No longer were England relying on a bits and pieces approach. Now they could make a concerted assault on the Ashes, with the added bonus of a skipper unscarred by previous mission impossibles. While Australia had comfortably won the previous Ashes series Down Under 4–1, Vaughany had notched up magnificent centuries at Adelaide, Melbourne and Sydney to confirm himself as a truly class act, for a while becoming the number one ranked batsman in the world. The biggest shame for Michael was that his knee gave up and so he never got to captain England in Australia for the return series in 2006–07. If ever you need a skipper who can eat up pressure, it's down there.

While Michael's England captaincy was slightly curtailed, he has of course gone on to forge a very successful career in the media, including as one half of *The Vaughany and Tuffers Cricket Club* podcast. Sometimes as I hear us deliver our incredibly pertinent and well-informed opinions on the sport, I can't help but wonder just what England missed out on in not making us captain and vice-captain. Vaughany really would have been a great assistant.

10 ASHES TESTS

Runs: 959
Highest Score: 183
Avg: 47.95
Hundreds: 4
Fifties: 1

14.

RICKY PONTING

*'Punter' was a streetfighter, yes, but a classy one.
More like a well-groomed Tasmanian devil.*

Ricky Ponting had always been in such a dominant side – and then the 2005 Ashes came along. It was almost as if, after all the years of English hurt, the gods had convened for a chat. 'You know what? Let's have Ricky suck it up for once.'

When he was run out by England's substitute fielder, half-man-half-hare Gary Pratt, at Trent Bridge, and started mouthing off at England coach Duncan Fletcher as he walked back up the pavilion steps, I really did think he'd been pushed over the edge. I was expecting bats, pads, possibly even Duncan himself, to come flying over the balcony. I saw the same red mist descend at Cardiff in 2009 as the Aussies desperately tried to crack

England's barnacle-esque last-wicket pairing of Jimmy Anderson and Monty Panesar. The home side were again pushing the rules to the limit, an endless conveyor belt of gloves coming out from the dressing room, consuming valuable seconds as the clock ticked down. Every time the Aussie skipper looked up there was some little lad from Glamorgan stood with two pairs of batting gloves in hand. I could only imagine the conversation. 'You again? What the f***? This is the fourth time I've seen your face in the last 15 minutes. You'd better f*** off right now mate.'

While Ricky would have provided the perfect cover illustration for the *Ladybird Book of Exasperation*, never did he actually completely lose it. There were times in the 2005 series especially when he really could have exploded. From the commentary box you could see he was like a pressure cooker, teetering on the edge of boiling over. And yet he never did. I have huge respect for Ricky for the way he handled himself during that encounter. He was dignified. Simmering, but dignified.

Ricky never knew when he was beaten, a fact which was best illustrated by the third Test at Old Trafford. Famously, the final day's play – where England needed 10 wickets and Australia to bat 'til the close – began with more than 10,000 people locked out of the ground. There were times when I was playing the Aussies that they'd have been pushing them in! England took wickets steadily throughout. All except one. Ricky didn't just bat the best part of the day, but did so with such grit and skill that at one stage it looked like he might carry his team to the most unlikely of wins. It says everything of his character that when finally he was out for a near seven-hour 156 his only reaction was anger at himself for leaving Australia's last-wicket pair with 24 balls to survive. Ricky didn't deserve to be on the losing side, and, after a nail-biting climax, he wasn't. Of the 287 innings he played for Australia, that innings at Manchester is the one he's most proud of. Not only did he survive 275 balls, under extreme pressure, with an entire Ashes series at stake, but there were times when he actually took the attack to England. Truly remarkable.

But that was Ricky. Throughout his Ashes career, he was like a boxer who didn't know how to give up. England would have him against the ropes but he'd always fight back, often delivering a knockout blow. He was an incredible competitor, so mentally tough. He took a lot of stick during that 2005 series, be it being cut on the face by Steve Harmison's vicious bouncer at Lord's, boisterous crowds constantly on his back, or the opprobrium heaped on him after putting England in to bat in the first Test at Edgbaston despite Glenn McGrath damaging his ankle in the warm-up. In defence of the pundit community, that was a little bit blasé. 'Our premier fast bowler has gone down, but we'll still knock you over.' It was a touch of arrogance which came back to bite the Aussies, a decision based perhaps on the past rather than the now. Ricky had played in Ashes series where the entire team could have played on one leg and still won. But on this occasion it didn't quite pan out like that. Instead, Australia were reduced to the team we'd once been. They were the ones chasing the ball 50 yards to the boundary only to lose the chase by six inches. They were the ones watching balls flash past grasping hands in the gully. They were the ones switching the bowlers around to no effect. And of course it had to happen at Edgbaston. The Hollies Stand on their feet, going absolutely nuts. Wave after wave of chanting and cheering. The ball seeming to gravitate to the boundary. Four. Six. Four. The Ashes on steroids. The cricketing version of the tornado that had hit the city just days before. And that's what it took to beat Australia. Not only did you need top-drawer performances from everyone, but also that little bit of luck, which for the Aussies, first with Glenn standing on the ball at Edgbaston, and then the Gary Pratt run out at Trent Bridge, must have looked like it was never going to turn their way. The pressure Ricky was under was immense. He faced becoming the first Aussie skipper to lose an Ashes series in 18 years. He was also leading a team containing some big and very successful characters, not least Shane Warne, the greatest skipper the Aussies never had. And yet all the time he kept fighting, putting in the performances, never taking a step backwards.

Ricky's immovability was no surprise to me. While I did actually get him out a couple of times in my career, he was so, so hard to bowl against. He was never going to slog one up in the air. You had to be on the absolute top of your game – as in the over Fred bowled at him at Edgbaston – to send him packing. It was always very difficult for England's seamers to find the right length to bowl at Ricky. He was so switched-on, so technical. Send down some pretty little away swingers and he'd maul you. Drop the ball short and he'd pull you to death – that incredible signature shot of his that was almost impossible to counter. Our lads would be perplexed. Ricky didn't seem to play by the same rules as other batsmen. He'd pull a ball that could never be defined as short. Pitch it up another inch and he'd drive through the offside. Hold it back half an inch and out came that pull shot again. You'd hear someone at lunch say 'I've got a quarter of an inch to play with otherwise I'm f***ed.' He had so much time to play that pull. Read the paper, light the cigar, *Bang!*

I always thought Ricky looked like he should be in a black and white photo from the 1930s, baggy cap, unloading a cargo ship at the docks. That kind of tough, tough character, someone you'd want on your side 100 per cent. Of course, having met him a few times now as a commentator, I've been astonished to find that the hard-faced and smileless bloke who I used to encounter from 22 yards is actually a friendly cove who loves a laugh – although, admittedly, there was one occasion when he wasn't hugely impressed with my own sense of humour. In the wake of England's Ashes victory of 2005 I was asked to make a video reflecting playfully on some of the key moments of the summer. Naturally I majored on Ricky's decision to insert England at Edgbaston, with a couple of other bits and pieces thrown in for good measure. I thought no more about it until a few weeks later when, lying in bed early one morning, my phone lit up like Blackpool Illuminations. While I'd thought the video was a little bit of fun to be shown at a corporate dinner or something, it had actually been screened at one of the most prestigious nights in the Australian cricket calendar, the dinner marking the award of the Allan Border Medal, recognising the most outstanding Aussie cricketer of the past season as voted by peers, media and umpires. Ricky had sat stony-faced through the whole recording, naturally not hugely impressed at the spectacle of an impish me taking the mick out of his team's performance. My phone was going nuts as various media outlets sought my reaction to this rather unexpected turn of events. That reaction was to hide under the duvet and vow never to find myself alone in a lift with the Tasmanian. Thankfully, all was forgiven when, at the following year's ceremony, another video was shown, this time of me making light of something entirely different – England's very recent 5–0 thrashing.

Subsequently, there are no hard feelings between me and Punter. Although, just to be on the safe side, I still don't mention substitute fielders.

35 ASHES TESTS

Runs: 2,476
Highest Score: 196
Avg: 44.21
Hundreds: 8
Fifties: 9

Wickets: 1
Best Bowling: 1–9
Avg: 27.00

15.

ALAN MULLALLY

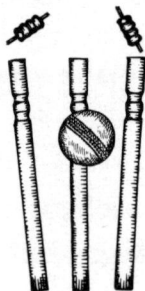

A big bloke and an even bigger character, Alan Mullally played one of the shortest, yet most significant, Ashes innings ever.

It's not often an innings of 16 would gain you entry to an Ashes hall of fame, but when it comes to big Alan Mullally (tall not wide) I can't help feeling it's entirely deserved.

Let me explain. This is a bloke who, by his own admission, could not bat. Once, believing there must be some reason for his grotesque inability with the willow, he went for an eye test, only to be told he had perfect vision. 'Have you ever thought,' the expert pondered, 'that you might just be s*** at batting?' So for me, Alan Mullally getting 16, and a 16 that meant the difference between winning and losing, is akin to a real batsman getting 150.

The great event came to pass during the Boxing Day Test of 1998. In their second innings, as was often the case, England were scrabbling to set the Aussies an at least slightly challenging target. When 'Big Al Mullall' strode to the wicket – I'm assuming in the right direction – England were 221–9, a lead of a mere 151.

By memory, whenever Al left the dressing room with a bat in his hand, pretty much everyone else used the 60 seconds before he reappeared to either change into their bowling gear or pack their bags. Only once, two years earlier against Pakistan at The Oval, had he shone in the lower order. Before he set off down the steps, then England coach David Lloyd had offered to buy him 30 pints of Guinness if he reached the same number of runs. When Al got to 20, he turned to the dressing room and mimed pulling a pint. By the time he got to 24, Bumble was dusting off the old wallet. And then Waqar Younis did him with a slower ball and that was the end of that. Those 30 pints of Irish stout stayed firmly in the barrel. Nothing since had suggested Al was going to recapture that brief glory. In fact, prior to the second innings in Melbourne he'd recorded seven ducks in his last nine outings. The chances of him hitting a game-changing knock were slightly less likely than Eddie the Eagle winning that year's Winter Olympics.

And yet it happened. And it wasn't just that it happened, it was the way that it happened. Al actually had the temerity, on three occasions, to smash Glenn McGrath to the boundary, a scenario not particularly well-received by an Aussie legend who saw England's tailenders as little more than toast-topping. The Aussies always gave Al a bit of extra gyp because, while he was born in Southend, he'd grown up Down Under and actually played for the Australians at Under-19 level, although he was always desperate to play for England. Glenn dished out the verbals but it was water off a duck's back to Al. What did he care? He was having the time of his life. He gave Glenn a nice little smile, made the universal hand signal for 'You talk too much pal!' and carried on doing what he was doing. Glenn did eventually snaffle his prey caught and bowled, but potentially at a price, later fined 30 per cent of his match fee, suspended depending on his future conduct. According to Al, the match referee felt it took two to tango and so he was in line for a fine too. Only coach David Lloyd rescued him, with a Sarah Lancashire-esque performance, claiming that Big Al was a much-misunderstood character who in fact was virtually in tears about the whole thing.

For once, Al walked back into the England dressing room to a barrage of backslapping, like they do with a horse when it's won the Grand National. I think they might have chucked a bucket of water over him and everything. Morale had been lifted tremendously by his cameo. England now had a lead of 174. Not much, but potentially enough against a side whose Achilles heel was a habit of tripping up in the pursuit of low scores.

Despite Al doing some damage, removing Mark Taylor and Justin Langer cheaply, Australia looked to be cruising at 140–4. But Dean Headley and Darren Gough then ripped through the lower order to leave the home side 12 runs short. Those three boundaries Al smote off Glenn McGrath were, in the end, the difference. To Glenn's credit, he was the first to buy his tormentor a pint afterwards. Meanwhile, England built on the momentum generated by Al's heroics by dropping him for the next match at Sydney.

I was delighted that Al had his time in the sun. He was a terrific cricketer and always great fun to be around. I once found myself on a fishing boat with him in New Zealand. I'm not a man of rod and line, but Al mentioned the excursion to me, and it sounded fun. After all, I could pass a bit of time lounging around with a beer while everyone else pulled strange-looking creatures from the ocean. I had of course forgotten about the motion of the boat, and was just about to be sick over the side when, blow me, if Al didn't heave a shark on to the deck. I was astonished. It wasn't quite that one off *Jaws* but it must have been six foot. Naturally, it wasn't too happy to find itself plonked in the midst of a party of England cricketers, making its feelings known by thrashing around the boards. Eventually, the bloke who'd taken us out brought it under control, and it was during this short period of wrestling that Al came up with a plan, the core details of which involved the fish and Athers' bed. I mean, all you can do in a situation like that is bow to the man's sheer inventiveness. A shark? In the captain's bed? Has there ever been a better idea?

We told the old seadog at the wheel to put his foot down and sped back to shore. Once there, the beast from the briny was wrapped in tarpaulin and ferried to the rear of the hotel. While one of us came up with a story to get Athers' room key from reception, the rest took the laundry lift to his corridor (we did consider dressing the shark in an umpire's coat and walking it through the lobby but after some debate concluded that the majority of umpires don't leave a trail). Once in Athers' room, giggling like the schoolboys we essentially were, we removed Athers' duvet, heaved the shark on to his mattress, made the bed back up, and headed to the bar.

There he was! 'All right boys, did you catch anything?' Athers was an angler of no small repute. There was nothing he'd not had on the end of his line – trout, salmon, old iron bedsteads, the lot.

'Nah mate. Nothing doing. Must be the only bit of sea with nothing in it.'

We were desperate for the skipper to go up to his room, and eventually we saw him head for the lift. Trying desperately to stifle our sniggers we sped up the stairs. Peeping round a corner we saw him turn the key in the lock and open the door.

Nothing.

'S***! What if it's got out?'

'Don't be stupid.'

More quiet – and then – 'WHAT THE . . . ?'

We ran to the door. 'Oh my God, Athers. What on Earth's the matter?'

He pointed to the bed. 'A shark! In my bed! A shark!'

'Come off it, Athers, you're seeing things. It's probably just an old towel, or an earwig.'

Thankfully, Athers could take a joke. I do think he might have changed rooms though, possibly in exchange for a gift for the hotel restaurant.

Big Al Mullall. They said with the bat he was toothless. Actually he was a shark.

5 ASHES TESTS

Wickets: 14
Best Bowling: 5–105
Avg: 33.07
Five-wicket Innings: 1
Ten-wicket Matches: 0

Runs: 20
Highest Score: 16
Avg: 2.05

16.

RODNEY MARSH

*Livewire wicketkeeper who famously had a
500–1 punt on England to win the Headingley
Test in 1981.*

*Under the Southern Cross I stand,
A sprig of wattle in my hand,
A native of my native land,
Australia, you f***ing beauty!*

You'd be right in thinking this little poem has never popped
up on the GCSE English syllabus. For some reason that other
one about 'wandering lonely as a cloud' sneaked in above it.
But in certain circles 'Under the Southern Cross I Stand' is
equally revered. I've heard it coming from Aussie dressing

rooms more times than I care to remember. And it's all down to Rodney Marsh.

It was Rodney who, after Australia, and in particular Jeff Thomson, had pummelled England in the first Test at Brisbane in 1974, rose to his feet and delivered the first rendition of what would come to be known as the Aussie team's victory chant. The last line is actually 'Australia, you little beauty', but 1970s Australian cricket, as David Lloyd, fishing his shattered protector from his trouser front, would attest, was no place for poetic niceties.

Rodney is said to have been made aware of the verse, which has military roots, by then Aussie captain Ian Chappell. By reciting it at the Gabba, he started a tradition that lasts to this day, the baton of 'songmaster' being passed on through every incarnation of the Australian team: Allan Border, David Boon, Ian Healy, Ricky Ponting, Justin Langer, Mike Hussey and Nathan Lyon among those who have belted it out down the years.

It does make you wonder why the England cricket team has never had a song. In recent times 'Jerusalem' has been played at the start of home Test matches after being adopted as the official hymn of the England and Wales Cricket Board, and very moving it is too, while in the 1980s then chairman of selectors Ted Dexter did propose 'Onward, Gower's Soldiers', to the tune of 'Onward, Christian Soldiers' (for some reason it never caught on), but in terms of an actual dressing room ditty we're sadly lacking, despite there being some very obvious contenders, not least The Nolans' 'I'm In The Mood For Dancing'.

I can't help feeling that I did once drop a great little number into the suggestion box. To add a bit of showbiz razzmatazz to our one-day international series in New Zealand in 1997, players on both sides were asked which song they'd like to be played as they walked out to bat. While others really had to sit and think about it – someone might have had to point out to Athers the need for something a little more upbeat than Tchaikovsky's 'Piano Concerto Number 1' – I had no hesitation whatsoever. 'Cigarettes & Alcohol', by Oasis. What an absolute belter of a track to walk out to. If that didn't get me fending a short ball down to fine leg, nothing would. Looking back, I regret not seizing a gilt-edged opportunity to push for 'Cigarettes & Alcohol' to be adopted by the team as a whole. I get that attitudes have changed and these days Craven 'A' and Kestrel don't feature quite so prominently in international dressing rooms, but the ECB could have then reverted to Jack Russell's pick for that ODI series, 'How Much Is That Doggie In The Window?'.

While 'Under the Southern Cross I Stand' isn't particularly something you want to hear after being smashed in an Ashes Test, I can't help but admire the fact that the Aussies are always unashamedly who they are. The English character is so often reserved. Lovely bloke, but hard to imagine Mike Brearley stood on a table, swinging his shirt round his head, while leading his teammates in a raucous victory chant. The Aussie attitude to life is 'Give it a go! What's the worst that can happen?'. It was the same when, with the odds at 500–1, Rodney and his old mucker Dennis Lillee chucked a fiver on England winning the Headingley Test in 1981. As far as they were concerned, it would have been stupid NOT to have had a punt on a two-horse race with one of the riders at such a gigantic price. And who can say they were wrong? Even when the Aussies lost, they still won!

When, in England's first innings, Rodney caught Ian Botham off Lillee's bowling, he also became the wicketkeeper with the highest number of dismissals in Test cricket, beating Alan Knott's record of 263. By the time he retired in 1984, that number had risen to 355. While that total would be surpassed by Ian Healy and Adam Gilchrist, 'caught Marsh, bowled Lillee' remains the most lethal Test partnership between wicketkeeper and fast bowler. Some 95 times, Rodney leapt, often both feet off the ground, to snare those bullets from his moustachioed pal. They came as a pair and Dennis, understandably, was heartbroken when his old mate died following a heart attack in 2022. 'I'll keep remembering the good times,' he said. Everyone in cricket echoed the sentiment. Rodney was as tough as they come but he always played the game the right way, famously calling Derek Randall back to the wicket after he was mistakenly given out caught behind in the 1977 Centenary Test, and making his displeasure known – 'No, mate, don't do this!' – when, he realised, horrified, that skipper Greg Chappell had told his brother Trevor to bowl the final delivery of an ODI underarm to prevent the New Zealand batsman hitting a six to tie the game.

More than anything, Rodney made wicketkeeping look exciting. That combination of him and Lillee really did capture my imagination as a schoolboy. Dennis would be sending balls whizzing past people's heads while, halfway back to the boundary, Rodney would be flying around with the seagulls trying to catch them. I can still feel the raw exhilaration that watching them generated.

Give me a moment before we carry on. I really do need to pat down the hairs on the back of my neck.

42 ASHES TESTS

Runs: 1,633
Highest Score: 110 not out
Avg: 27.21
Hundreds: 1
Fifties: 9

Wicketkeeping dismissals: 148

17.

BOB WILLIS

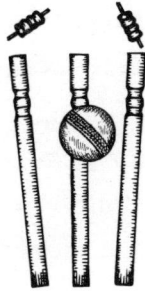

*Terrifying pace and an occasional face like
thunder belied a genuinely lovely bloke whose true
freewheeling nature I experienced early on.*

I had to do a double take. Was that really Bob Willis? Was that really England's former demon fast bowler who'd just leapt, fully clothed, into the swimming pool of the High Commissioner of Barbados?

Whenever I used to bump into Bob Willis in the slightly less rarified atmosphere of various media centres, I'd refer to him as 'Manager', because that's what he was when I first encountered him. Bob was in charge of the England Under-19s on my first trip overseas representing my country, a strenuous sojourn to one of the world's most renowned paradise islands. His role meant he was responsible for maintaining a degree of discipline among the squad. *Good luck with that mate!* I thought as I boarded the plane alongside a load of other teenage lads with one foot already on the beach and the other hanging off a barstool in a rum shack.

Initially, Bob made a vague attempt to maintain a degree of order, reminding us what we were in the Caribbean for, and instilling a curfew, which he'd seek to enforce by remaining in the hotel lobby with a clipboard until everyone was accounted for. However, I'm not sure Bob was cut out for the clipboard life. R. G. D. Willis was, after all, one of cricket's great mavericks, the 'D' in his name added by the man himself to reflect his love of another great free-thinker Bob Dylan, a song of whose I'd heard him singing earlier the same evening. As I watched him hurl himself into the High Commissioner's swimming pool, I think possibly he'd reached the same conclusion. Bob was too passionate a bloke to be wandering around ticking names off a register. He wasn't a soft touch, but he knew that intensity on the field wasn't necessarily dependent on being the same off it, something which, for any young cricketer, is actually a lesson in itself. To survive the pressure of top-level sport, you need a release. You can't be 'on' all the time because physically and mentally it will damage you. It's simply not healthy.

Bob's performance at Headingley in 1981 is the classic example. When he was skittling the Aussies out in their second innings – careering down the hill from the Kirkstall Lane end to take 8–43 in one of the greatest ever bowling displays for England – he genuinely looked like he was in a trance. So focused was he on the job in hand it was as if a hypnotist had put him under. Forget beating the Aussies, he looked like he could have lifted a bus off someone. Even afterwards in the TV interviews he was the same.

When it's happening for you – I mean, really happening for you – that's what it's like. You can't just switch off the minute the game's over. It takes a good while for your system to reboot. There's a picture of me with a towel over my head in The Oval dressing room at the end of the final Ashes Test of 1997, an incredibly nerve-fraying game in which I took 11 wickets as England scraped home by 19 runs having set the tourists just 124 to win. I expect most people would think the minute that last Aussie wicket fell I'd be throwing myself headlong into the celebrations, but actually what I needed was exactly the opposite; just that little bit of time in my own head to absorb what had happened. There are, naturally, a few other pictures of me that day with a fag and a bottle of Champagne, and eventually I did go out that night and have a few pints, but even so it took me a good while to come down.

It's the oddest feeling when you're ticking like that, as if you've got some kind of internal hum that refuses to be silenced. You can be lying in bed eight hours after a game has finished and still feel what's happened in your body. There's an inner warmth, a pulsing, a total physical reaction. You're basically lying there with a big orange glow around you, like the kid from the Ready Brek advert. It doesn't matter what you do, only the passage of time allows you to start coming back to your usual self. It's not on the same scale but I can get a similar sensation now after a stage show, one of my evenings with Aggers or the live version of *A Question of Sport*. I can't just wave cheerio to the crowd and head off to bed. I might be tired but I'm also still Ready Brek-ing! I need a drink or a chat until I get back to normal again.

For fast bowlers, I expect that return to normal is more diffi-cult. For someone like Bob, who was a kind and gentle soul, slipping from full-on aggressive mode to his more usual laid-back and contemplative mode can't have been easy. This was, after all, the bloke who on his first Ashes tour carried a seagull, struck by a drive from an Aussie batsman during the Adelaide Test, to the boundary for treatment. Hardly the act of a man with an unquenchable thirst for blood.

Playing Ashes series Down Under, Bob found a pressure release not just in saving pulverised terns, but in the vineyards of South Australia, to the extent that, following his death in 2019, some of his ashes were scattered in just such a place, in the presence of his great mate Beefy – apt for two blokes who gave England perhaps their greatest Ashes victory of all time, engineered by a captain, Mike Brearley, they both so respected.

I have an image of Brears drawing up battleplans in an apart-ment in Belgravia, pushing little wooden figures around on a felt-topped table. Brears had that kind of Field Marshal Mont-gomery vibe going on. 'Everything will be OK. We know what we're doing. We've done the preparation. The chaps have all been training very hard. Now it's just about putting it all into place. Bob, we'll start with you from the Kirkstall Lane end.'

There must have been something about Brears as a person, because as a captain he actually didn't do anything particularly unusual. Like most skippers, the bulk of the time he had two slips, a gully and a couple of blokes on the boundary. Unlike most skippers, for both county and country, he also had two great bowlers. When you've got Edmonds and Emburey (Middle-sex) or Willis and Botham (England), then you've got more than a fighting chance of getting somewhere. At Headingley, in

1981, however, he still needed one of them to deliver an out-of-this-world performance. And that's exactly what Bob did. I've heard Beefy say it a few times. 'He was like a man possessed.'

Amid all the talk of 1981, it's easy to forget that Bob captained England in the next Ashes, in 1982–83, a series which had its own mad version of the Edgbaston Test of 2005, a finish so nail-biting that I and seemingly half the nation sat up listening to it. Just like at Birmingham, Australia looked dead and buried when their ninth wicket fell still some way short – in this case 74-runs – of their second innings target. Final pairing Allan Border and Jeff Thomson had knocked half of them off as the game nudged into its last day, the MCG throwing open its gates free to a public who poured in to see if the impossible could happen. That looked to be the case when the Aussies whittled the target down to just three runs. Desperate for inspiration, Bob chucked the ball to his old ally Beefy. The man with the golden arm hung a tempter just outside the off stump – and Thommo took the bait. What happened from that point on was like slow motion. The edge arced to second slip where Chris Tavaré looked certain to snaffle the catch – only to misjudge the trajectory slightly and palm the ball upwards. The big chance, gone. Or was it? For there, at first slip, was Geoff Miller. Into his hands the ball bobbled, and that was that. An incredible finish, in some ways even more so than Edgbaston 24 years later. Sadly, however, it wasn't enough to prevent England from losing the series 2–1.

Some observers felt that, as a captain, Bob, who, as we saw at Headingley, could be incredibly focused on his bowling, under-standably didn't have headroom for two such big roles in the team. For sure, the intense focus he showed at Leeds was 100 per cent helped by having Brears doing the thinking around everything else – and that's the image of Bob, swooping in, hawk-like, on his prey that we all hold dear. That was his day. When he did something that felt almost superhuman.

Next time I see Beefy, I need to ask him a question about Headingley '81. Is there, somewhere in Leeds, a swimming pool perhaps, or a boating lake, that Bob hurled himself into to calm himself down afterwards?

---

35 ASHES TESTS

Wickets: 128
Best Bowling: 8–43
Avg: 26.14
Five-wicket Innings: 7
Ten-wicket Matches: 0

Runs: 383
Highest Score: 26
Avg: 10.35

18.

AUSSIE CROWDS

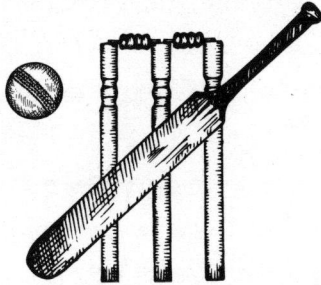

Nothing can ever quite prepare an England cricketer for their first encounter with an Aussie crowd. Not unless they have access to a bearpit.

Some sounds are familiar in sport. A Champagne cork popping at Wimbledon, a galloping hoof at Badminton, a loose rowlock at the Boat Race. Few people, however, have ever attended a cricket match in anticipation of hearing the squeal of a pig. And yet, in a World Series match against Australia in Brisbane in January 1983, this is precisely the noise that ricocheted round the Gabba. A crowd member, one imagines a gentle type who'd spent the game filling in his scorecard while taking the occasional sip of elderflower cordial, had ushered a single swine on to the field with the legend 'BEEFY' daubed crudely on one side and 'EDDIE' on the other. The porcine intruder, intended to emphasise the portliness of England's Ian Botham and Eddie Hemmings, is said to have been smuggled into the ground under anaesthetic in a picnic hamper. Modern-day bag checks make this kind of tomfoolery impossible, although should there be a resemblance to a player, it remains feasible to hide a ferret up the leg of your trousers.

It was with incidents like the Brisbane pig in mind that I ventured to Australia in 1990. At that juncture I hadn't even played a Test for England. My experience of cricket crowds at that point was limited to say the least. People often talk about the one man and his dog being present for a County Championship match at Derby, but in my experience it wasn't even that. Half the time the man didn't turn up.

I could have been forgiven then for being a tad nervous that 26 December in Melbourne, and indeed by the time Goochy went out for the toss I was singularly well-acquainted with the route to the toilets. I was thankful that the skipper did the magic with the coin and chose to bat, allowing me time to settle into the occasion, contributing what *The Times* didn't refer to as a composed nought not out, before the time came to go out and field.

Playing with Mike Gatting at Middlesex I was aware that, on the previous Ashes tour, he'd experienced his own porker moment when another snorter, this time with his name emblazoned on the side, had been released on to the turf at the MCG. Unbelievable that it could happen twice. I mean why not go the whole hog (pun intended) and just give the be-trottered community their own entrance gate and ticketing price? But while I scanned the crowd for livestock, what struck me more than anything wasn't the sheer number of spectators but the intensity of the colour. The blueness of the sky, the lushness of the grass, the rainbow of hats, T-shirts, vests, worn by spectators. It was like going from black and white to colour. As if I'd lived in the dark all my life and someone had suddenly swished back the curtains. That's why Aussies like Steve Waugh have that mean look in their eyes. They can't open them properly because it's so bloody bright.

Of course, this was the Aussie crowd as seen from a distance. At some point I was going to have to get up close. Bear in mind that the MCG was the home to the notorious Bay 13, a section of the ground renowned for unbridled abuse of visiting players, to the extent that a few years later, during an ODI against England, Shane Warne actually donned a helmet while trying to persuade its occupants to calm down. So you can understand my slight trepidation when Goochy dispatched me to field on the fence, at third man, right in front of the infamous area. Initially, as I wandered down there I thought some of them too were wearing helmets. On closer inspection, I realised they were watermelons. Injecting a melon with vodka and pretending it was a quirky bit of headgear was a great way of getting booze into the ground.

I considered my best bet was to show Bay 13 early on that, as Poms go, I was all right. I felt sure I could convince them that, in another life, I could actually be one of them, their mucker, their pal. Walking over I smiled, pulled one or two cheeky faces, even gave a quick nod and a thumbs-up. In times since I've seen numerous TV explorers state that the worst thing you can do when faced with a predator is look it in the eye. I, however, had been raised on *Animal Magic*. There, Johnny Morris, masquerading as a zookeeper, would converse pleasantly with everything from elephants to tigers, all of which seemed to enjoy his engagement tremendously. From the reaction of Bay 13, however, I quickly came to realise that what Morris had presented to the children of Great Britain was mere fantasy. In reality, lions don't want to talk about the weather, or offer their views on local seafood restaurants, they want to have your arm off, and that's the end of it. I mean, spin it all you like, but a thousand people calling you a 'useless Pommie bastard' can never be classed as bonhomie.

So steeped in the art of player harassment was Bay 13 that, even when it appeared they'd had enough and slipped into a beer-drenched torpor, they were secretly plotting their next assault upon your person. The bread trick was a case in point. While you congratulated yourself on taming the hordes, behind your back they'd be quietly throwing lumps of white sliced on to the field. Next thing you knew, the entire gull population of Victoria was descending on your head. Great brutes of things with beaks like fabric scissors squawking and screeching round your face. That previous generation who got the pig treatment never knew how lucky they were.

Other times, they'd find more subtle ways to knock you off kilter, to make you lose that little bit of focus. Down on the boundary at the MCG once I heard a bloke behind me. 'Tuffers! Goochy's shouting at you! He says move 20 yards to your left!' I raised my hand slightly by way of an 'Ah right, cheers!' Only when I arrived at my new spot – and saw a bemused Gooch signalling for me to get back to where I'd just been – did I realise I'd been on the end of another hilarious wind-up. Give me some slack here – the noise in the MCG is so ridiculously loud that it isn't unusual for your captain's instructions to be lost amid the bedlam. Actually, not just the MCG. At Brisbane, it was tinnies not terns that filled the sky. A highlight of the spectator experience down there was the daily battle where hundreds of booze-sodden blokes would hurl beer cans between the bays.

However, my most excruciating Aussie crowd moment came not at Melbourne or 'Brizzy' but the SCG after I fumbled the simplest of run outs during a day/night ODI. At 82–4 we had the Aussies on the ropes. It was then that Steve Waugh called for a single off me to Eddie Hemmings. His brother Mark didn't fancy it and sent Steve back. Mark's call was a little late. So late in fact that Steve was actually stood with him at the striker's end. He actually began to remove his gloves for the walk back to the pavilion. Trouble was, as Eddie's throw came to me, for the slightest millisecond I took my eye off the ball. Next thing I knew it had ricocheted off my hand and rolled a couple of feet from the stumps. By now, I couldn't help noticing that Steve had set off back, and it was perhaps this that sparked an element of panic. Instead of calmly picking up the ball and whipping off the bails, I appeared to have been mentally transported to a coconut shy. I hurled the ball at the stumps, missed them by several inches, and watched, consumed by a tidal wave of nausea, as Steve arrived calmly back in his crease. He couldn't resist adding insult to injury. 'In!' he said as he grounded his bat. Funnily enough, even among 40,000 jeering Australians I could still hear my skipper, Graham Gooch. 'F*** me.' It was the worst I've ever felt on a cricket field. Mess something up in normal life, smash a teacup, put a pair of red underpants in with a white wash, and there's no witnesses. At the SCG, there were 40,000, including those on 'The Hill', a vast grassy bank which was essentially Sydney's version of Bay 13. It's been bulldozered now, a reminder of its past immortalised in the bronze statue of 'Yabba', an old-school heckler revered for a voice that could be heard in the stands at the MCG let alone at Sydney. His most famous bellow came during the 'Bodyline' series. Spotting England's despised captain Douglas Jardine swatting away some insects, he roared, 'Leave our flies alone, Jardine! They're the only friends you've got here.' That was old Dougie told. What Yabba would have made of my embarrassment I'm not sure, but, heading off down to fine leg at the end of the over, everyone I could see was laughing so hard that momentarily they'd even stopped drinking.

Games come thick and fast in those ODI series Down Under. *Soon be forgotten,* I thought of the SCG incident. And then, blow me, if I didn't walk out at the next match to spot a 30-foot long banner with 'THE TUFNELL FIELDING ACADEMY' writ large upon it. At first I was like, *Oh, for f***'s sake!* But then I began thinking of it a different way. *It's cricket. It's not people trying to be nasty. It's just them having a bit of fun.* Rather than feel humiliated, or upset, the banner acted as a reminder that taking yourself too seriously is rarely a good idea. And actually that was what the Aussie crowds liked about me. I didn't behave like a robot. I was never anything less than myself. Having someone go to the trouble of fashioning a 30-foot banner with my name all over it was testament to that fact. It was the others who didn't have 30-foot banners that should have been disappointed! I really should have asked its creators if I could keep it. It would have looked great on the fence at the back of my house. Better than that other one I saw round about the same time – 'PHIL TUFNEL IS A W*****!' I mean, they could at least have spelt my name right.

Occasionally in Australia, crowd members, generally unclothed, would seek to join the players in the middle. Occurring more regularly than in England, possibly because streakers at Old Trafford ran the risk of frostbitten extremities, Aussie streakers tended to be fast and athletic. Were streaking to be allowed at the Olympics they'd be a shoo-in for the gold medal. My favourite streaker – a feature that really should be introduced in *Wisden* – was a chap who made it the not inconsiderable distance to the wicket at the MCG. I was bowling at the time and was just set to avert my gaze as he did the traditional Sally Gunnell-esque leg-cocked leap of the stumps, when he launched himself across the width of the pitch, taking care, considerately, not to step on a length. Mid-air he turned to me. 'How's it going Tuffers?' I wished him well in his chosen task, and, on landing, he disappeared in the direction of the opposite boundary pursued by several burly stewards. They didn't have a chance of catching him, reinforcing my view that major cricket grounds should have a crack team of streaker-ready stewards available at all times.

While there are some sights that are hard to forget, no matter how much you try, for me the most memorable part of cricket Down Under was playing under floodlights. Today, this stuff is just part of cricket across the world – T20, the IPL, it's all about spectacle and noise. Back then, however, the one-day revolution was in its infancy, especially in a country like England where the authorities were still coming to terms with the sleeveless jumper. Floodlit cricket was *so* exciting, like being allowed to stay up late as a kid. The Aussie stadiums, those great bowls, with their beautiful architectural stands, looked incredible, the colours that leapt out in the day now made even more brilliant under the lights.

And you were part of that collage, whites exchanged for 'pyjamas', each team in the Tri-Series of the time having its own strip. Every game was another *'Wow!'* moment. Endlessly, mouth open, often swallowing a moth, I'd peer skywards and see the most magnificent stars, before looking back down at myself, part of something that as a kid I could only ever dream about. There was something else I rather liked about floodlit cricket. No need to go back to the hotel before enjoying a night out. Or before 7 a.m. for that matter (again see chapter entitled 'Graham Gooch').

There are times as a cricketer when you realise you're living your best life. The crowds, and the grounds, in Australia delivered that feeling all of the time. The best place ever to play cricket. We've got some great arenas in England but the grounds Down Under are incredible places to play the game. When you tour Australia for the first time and all you know of these places is their names, heard in the middle of the night as a kid listening to *TMS*, it's as if they have a mythical status – the MCG, the WACA, the Gabba, the Adelaide Oval, the SCG. In fact, so much have you built them up in your imagination, there's a risk that when you actually clap eyes on them they'll be something of a letdown. Far from it. Each ground, same as each city, had its own character. The delicate beauty of the Adelaide Oval, for instance, with its white picket boundary fences and giant ornate old scoreboard couldn't have been further removed from the towering concrete grandstands of the MCG. As someone who soaked up atmosphere, one way or another, I loved them all. And nine times out of ten they were sunny! And you knew when you left them at the end of each day's play you were going to have a bloody good time.

Bay 13, by the way, has been gentrified. These days they summon the gulls with sourdough.

19.

ANGUS FRASER

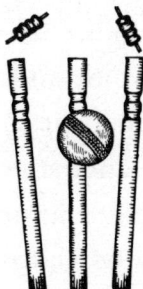

*Wise and wily, Frase taught me the value of
playing – and staying – at the top.*

When I walked out on to the field at the MCG on Boxing Day, 1990, everything was new to me. Except one thing. It was six-foot-six with a huge backside and size-13 feet. Its name? Angus Fraser.

In another life, Frase would have been a shire horse, pulling a brewery dray, or hauling coal wagons round a pit. But in this one he was a fast-medium bowler with a big heart and nagging accuracy. He was also a familiar face from Middlesex, whose socks I'd got to know intimately as we always sat next to each other in the Lord's dressing room, and a great help and comfort to have around when making my England debut. I challenge any cricketer not to feel a little overwhelmed when trotting out on to the MCG for their first international appearance. It's like being in a band and playing your first gig at Wembley Stadium. I needed someone to lean on a little, someone I could gaze up at and ask, 'Excuse me mate, what the hell is going on here?', and Frase filled that role perfectly.

Making his own bow only a year earlier, Frase had already been involved in home series against Australia and India and been on tour to the West Indies. In so doing, he'd accrued a wider perspective on what it meant to play for England, which he was keen to pass on to me. Early on in that Ashes trip he'd knocked on my hotel room door after training. 'Fancy going up the gym on the top floor before dinner, Phil?'

'Well,' I contemplated, 'I don't know. Is that what people do when they play for England?'

I think he could see what was going through my mind – a vision of hell involving treadmills, medicine balls and weights.

'Nothing too strenuous,' he reassured me. 'I just thought it would be nice to make use of the facilities.'

I was only sat in my room watching *Tom and Jerry* so I grabbed my shorts and a string vest and off we went. As Frase ploughed away on an exercise bike, I worked hard to maintain a comfortable position in the hot tub. To be fair, I was exhausted after carrying a bottle of wine in an ice-bucket up three flights of stairs. Eventually, Frase came over and joined me, and we sat there gazing across the South Australian capital with its lovely old buildings and avenues.

'Just look at that, Phil,' he said. 'This is what it's all about. This is what we've worked hard for, and so now we're here we should make sure we enjoy it.'

I couldn't help but think he was right. This was the top of the tree, and I wanted to stay in its upper boughs as long as possible. It was a moment when I really did start to think more about the future rather than just be amazed that I was waking up in Australia every day as an England cricketer.

Now here we were at Melbourne. I got changed next to Frase as news filtered into the dressing room that Graham Gooch had won the toss and we were batting first. The MCG's an odd experience at the best of times, not least because the changing room is basically a bunker in the bowels of a vast concrete expanse. If you want actually to watch the game there's a separate viewing area upstairs. I had a quick look but soon retreated to the 'Batcave' as we came to call it. Again and again during my England career I found that watching from the balcony was a sensory overload. Too much involvement, too much anxiety, too much mental energy. Your stomach's churning, you're feeling a bit sick, which is why I preferred to close my eyes and put myself out of the way until it was my turn to go have a go. Occasionally I might have a little sleep on the physio's bench, which didn't always go down well with Athers if he and Stewie were fending off 90 mph bouncers out in the middle. He felt, understandably, that if a teammate was sniffing the leather, the least I could do was be awake while they were doing it.

Taking the field after my short sojourn with the bat, it was then that I saw for the first time what an incredible player Frase truly was. That Melbourne Test match was notable for an extremely hot wind blowing across the ground, like holding a hairdryer six inches from your face. Somehow, in the baking heat, Frase, a big unit remember, ran in and bowled 39 overs in that Australian first innings. Within minutes he was soaked to the skin, shirt stuck to his back, sweat dripping off the end of his nose. He ran in like a human sprinkler system to take 6–82. By the time the innings was wrapped up he was absolutely shattered, although the funny thing about Frase was he always somehow looked as knackered at the start of a spell as he did at the end. He just had one of those faces.

Certainly, smiling wasn't Frase's forté. While some people find a laugh and a joke gets them in the mood, Frase seemed to perform better the more pissed off he was. To see him at his best, you needed to tap him on the shoulder at the end of his run and tell him you'd just seen a gull empty itself on his windscreen in the car-park. The difference between now and Frase's day is that back then pretty much all the rest of us were grumpy too. The modern Bazball era might be all about going out and enjoying yourself, but when it came to England in my day, the grumpier we were the better we performed. We'd have to remind each other that we could be working in the salt mines of Siberia to put a smile on our faces, although even then someone would say at least in the salt mines of Siberia they got to have a snowball fight every once in a while.

When the 1994–95 Ashes tour came round, Frase was left at home. It was around that time that people started saying he'd 'lost his nip'. It's funny how a label attaches itself to cricketers. Batsmen wake up one morning and out of nowhere discover the overriding opinion is they can't face the short ball. With Frase it was his nip. His big mate Athers would say to him, 'They're all saying you've lost your nip, Gus.' And Frase would be barking back, 'I haven't lost my nip! Will everyone please stop saying I've lost my nip? What even is my nip?' If his nip really had gone, it was probably due to the hip injury that, as a big chap bowling hundreds of overs a season, inevitably came his way. Typical of Frase that he fought back from two years out of the Test team to record a man-of-the-match eight-wicket haul against the Aussies in his comeback Test at The Oval in 1993, England's first Ashes win in 18 attempts and six-and-a-half years. When within minutes he'd got Mark Waugh caught behind off a lifter, England could see precisely what they'd been missing.

Frase was the first bowler on everyone's list to head Down Under in 1994 – everyone's list that is except England supremo Ray Illingworth who instead plumped for the raw pace of Martin McCague, Joey Benjamin and Devon Malcolm. When McCague disappeared to all corners of the ground in the first Test at Brisbane, the selection looked somewhat flawed. With Benjamin and Malcolm then coming down with chickenpox, the England management were fortunate that Frase's reaction to missing out on selection had been to secure himself a spot playing Grade cricket for Western Suburbs in Sydney. In doing so, Frase, knowing how often fast bowlers, especially England fast bowlers, break down in Australia, had effectively selected himself.

Frase proceeded to take 15 wickets in the remaining three Tests. His six-fer at Sydney included probably the best catch of my career. Openers Michael Slater and Mark Taylor had put on 208 for the first wicket when Athers, in desperation, called a team huddle. It was an unusual initiative, but one that I was up for. In blistering heat a huddle offered a chance to lean on someone. Slater, explained the skipper, was a man who didn't hold back on his shots. The plan was to bounce him and get him caught on the hook. Seemed a good idea to me. In fact I said as much as I turned to head back to my fielding position at mid-on. What followed was a classic 'Where do you think you're going?' moment. Athers wanted me – ME! – to go down to deep backward square leg for the catch. I was just about to say I'd left my glasses in the dressing room when I remembered I didn't wear any. Off I went, imagining nothing but total disaster, complete humiliation, were Slater to sky the ball my way. It would be the perfect 'What happened next?' moment as the ball bounced off my head and over the boundary for six.

A few deliveries later, Slater top-edged a short one from Gus and it was heading my way at warp speed. I've watched that catch back and still don't quite know how it ended up in my grasp. The missile came over my shoulder and, with a hoppity-skip, I reached out and there it was. 'Jesus Christ, it's in my hands!' I chucked it in the air and awaited the congratulations of my teammates. Any second now I'd be engulfed, like when someone scores a last-minute winner in a cup final. And then I heard it. 'F*** me, Phil, you caught it!' There followed nine other variations on the theme. I felt like saying, 'Excuse me boys, but aren't I meant to be under a pile of screaming, celebrating bodies? Shouldn't I be signing my name on the TV camera with a felt tip?' Frase did give me a sharp pat on the back. I returned the gesture, and immediately wished I hadn't. There was an unpleasant squelch and then sweat exploded everywhere.

I actually won a KFC Colonel's Privilege Card for that catch (forget man-of-the-match awards – now you're talking!) which meant free chicken at any of the old chap's outlets. It got a bit of hammer that card, I can tell you. I don't think they knew who they were dealing with. The privilege, I soon realised, was the chicken, not the service. I was called a 'Pommie bastard' roughly three times for every leg I was given.

Big-hearted and brave, Frase was a great servant of English cricket. In his first Ashes Test, at Edgbaston, he bowled Steve Waugh with the perfect nip-backer. In his last Test he got his brother Mark plumb lbw. That he played only 12 times in five losing Ashes series says more for his hip and less for his nip. Honestly Frase, I never thought it had gone anywhere.

---

12 ASHES TESTS

Wickets: 46
Best Bowling: 6–82
Avg: 30.06
Five-wicket Innings: 3
Ten-wicket Matches: 0

Runs: 176
Highest Score: 29
Avg: 9.77

20.

ASHTON AGAR

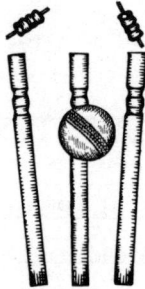

*The Aussie teenager came from nowhere
to play a golden innings that belonged to
a world of fantasy.*

When Glenn McGrath presented Ashton Agar with his baggy green cap before the left-arm spinner made his Test debut in 2013 at Trent Bridge, the legendary paceman told him, 'Never, ever give up.'

Next day, the 19-year-old, the youngest Aussie Ashes debutant for 85 years, walked to the crease with his team's first innings in disarray at 117–9. 'I was thinking we were in a little bit of trouble,' he said later. He wasn't wrong. Australia were the best part of 100 runs behind England's own below-par score.

Two-and-a-bit hours later, Ashton, who just a few weeks earlier had been playing for Henley against North Mymms in the Home Counties Premier League, walked back to the pavilion a history-maker. Blasting 98 off 101 balls, he'd notched the highest score ever by a number 11 batsman in Test cricket. When finally he was caught on the boundary by Graeme Swann off Stuart Broad, it's the only time I can ever remember an England Ashes crowd greeting an Aussie dismissal with total silence. Everyone, me included, was desperate for him to get those last two runs. But once that minor disappointment had subsided, the entire stadium was up on its feet giving the lad a standing ovation.

Not only had Ashton etched his own name in the record books but he'd been part of the highest ever tenth-wicket Test partnership (beaten a year later on the same ground when Joe Root and Jimmy Anderson added 198 against India). Down the other end Phillip Hughes had taken a back seat while quietly accruing 81 not out. Together they'd done the impossible – taken their team from a 98-run deficit when they came together to a 65-run lead. And that against a not-inconsiderable attack of Anderson, Broad, Swann and Steven Finn. No disrespect, but I suspect that's moderately better than the one put out by North Mymms. His achievement even drew praise from then Australian Prime Minister, Kevin Rudd. 'Stunning' and 'gutsy' he called it. I think that's Aussie PM speak for 'Bonzer!'

The beautiful thing about Ashton's innings is that he played the whole thing with the broadest of smiles on his face. Right then and there that young lad was 100 per cent living out his fantasy, the same one every cricket fan has when they're growing up – of being out in the middle smacking the ball to all corners, playing for their country. I think that, more than anything, was what consumed the rest of us. For those couple of hours we were all Ashton Agar. We saw everything through that prism of pure innocence. Forget who you support, where you're from; for every cricket fan, everywhere, it was like an out of body experience.

The nearest I'd ever seen to Ashton's innings was when England fast bowler Alex Tudor, aged just 21, made 99 not out as nightwatchman against New Zealand at Edgbaston in 1999 to help England home in a tricky run chase. Eddie Hemmings was a little older when he made 95, also as nightwatchman, in a superb rearguard action to help England save the Sydney Test in 1983. I'm told Harold Larwood made 98 at Sydney on the 'Bodyline' tour in 1933 but that's a little before my time.

My own highest score in an Ashes Test was eight, at the WACA in 1991. Not bad actually in a second innings where only four England players made double figures. In fact, I was the highest of the single-figure scores. And I had the joint highest strike rate. Actually, the more I think about it, where was my standing ovation and the tribute from the despatch box by John Major?

Sadly, Ashton's feats with the ball didn't quite match those with the bat – plus he had serious competition in Nathan Lyon – and so he only ever played four more Tests. But does it really matter when he has a memory like that to hold on to? Wherever he is in life, he'll always be able to close his eyes and be instantly transported to those two remarkable hours in Nottingham.

A fantasy innings for every Ashes dreamer.

2 ASHES TESTS (TO OCT 2025)

Wickets: 2
Best Bowling: 2–82
Avg: 124.00

Runs: 130
Highest Score: 98
Avg: 32.5
Hundreds: 0
Fifties: 1

21.

STEVE HARMISON

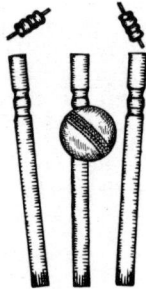

The embodiment of the new aggressive England of 2005, cricket's fickle finger of fate was pointing Harmy's way for the return series Down Under.

I was on commentary when Steve Harmison bowled the first ball of the 2006–07 Ashes series. I'd been chatting with Aggers in the build-up. 'Isn't it funny, Aggers,' I mused, 'how the first ball of the Ashes dictates what's going to happen with the rest of the series?'

'Oh yes,' Aggers replied. 'I remember when Michael Slater smashed Phil DeFreitas to the boundary in 1994.' I remembered that too. I was a member of the England team which watched the ball scream across the turf into the advertising hoardings.

'But then again, Aggers,' I opined, 'surely in reality one ball can't encompass an entire series.'

We were having this to and fro, and then . . . 'What the . . ?' Harmy had only gone and bowled it straight to Fred at second slip. We might as well have all gone home there and then. 'Right, cancel the rest of the series, we're doomed.'

So wide was the delivery that it actually took me about five seconds to compute what had happened. It needed that much time to sink in. At the same time I couldn't help but laugh. Fred's reaction was epic. If it had been me standing at second slip I'd have been wetting myself. Fred? Total nonchalance. He simply caught the ball and tossed it to cover as if this kind of thing was an everyday occurrence in international cricket. In fact, so blasé was Fred's reaction that me and Aggers actually began doubting the evidence of our eyes. 'What . . . er . . . did that really just happen?' In the Sky box next door, meanwhile, David Lloyd's reaction was a classic. 'That's strange,' he noted, in his familiar East Lancashire burr, 'usually when it goes to second slip it's followed by an appeal.'

Fred, of course, was doing his best to normalise the situation. It's like when you slip on a bit of ice and fall flat on your arse. 'Get up quick enough,' you tell yourself, 'and no-one will notice.' But you know inside that everyone's staring at you. The man at the other end, Justin Langer, certainly took note. 'It set the scene for the summer,' he said. 'It was as if England were deflated and almost unable to come back from the disappointment throughout the remainder of the Test.'

Slater's square-cut in 1994 was similar. 'When Michael Slater hit the first ball for four,' then Aussie skipper Steve Waugh recalled, 'it was like, "Righto boys, here we go, we've got them already."' We didn't show it, but the funny thing is we pretty much felt exactly the same. I mean, it wasn't even a bad ball – decent length with just a little bit of width – and it had been completely mullered. An England player would have let that ball go. The Aussies? No way. 'Right, let's get this party started.' If that doesn't tell you what's going to happen over the next two months, what will? 'Disheartening' doesn't even begin to describe it. For weeks, we'd been raring to go. We'd done all the preparation, all the team talks. We'd imagined ourselves dismantling the Australians; dreamed of just how brilliant it would be to win the Ashes. And then with one ball – *WALLOP!* – the balloon was burst and we came plummeting back down to earth. Slater went on to smash 176, we were hammered in the first Test, and lost the Ashes 3–1. We might as well have got back on the plane after Daffy's first ball and saved everyone the pain. Amazing how things like that sit in the mind. Slater probably left the next two, but that's not what you remember. It's the piledriver that's lodged itself in your brain.

It happens again and again. In 2021, Rory Burns was bowled behind his legs by Mitchell Starc. England lost the series 4–0. Two years later, at Edgbaston, Zac Crawley belted Pat Cummins through the covers for four off the first ball of the 2023 Ashes precisely because he wanted to lay down the same kind of marker. It didn't matter what Cummins bowled, he was going to do his level best to thrash it for four. Straightaway, the Aussies knew England were going to come at them hell for leather all summer.

I felt for Harmy that morning in Brisbane. As a batsman you play a bad shot and disappear from the scene. You can hide in the pavilion for several hours out of view of everybody. Harmy had gone haywire with the very first ball. No hiding place for him. He was going to be out there all day, stewing on it, in front of thousands of very unforgiving people. But anyone can have a nightmare. While the 'Brisbane ball' has inevitably followed Harmy around, he can look back with immense pride at his role in the Ashes win of 2005.

Harmy had shown how devastating he could be when England toured the West Indies in 2004. There were times in the Caribbean when he was virtually unplayable. At that point, England knew they'd found precisely the kind of bowler – fast, awkward, dangerous, aggressive – that they'd been lacking. At six-foot-four, he was a nightmare to face, capable of getting right in under your armpit with one delivery and moving it at pace off a good length the next. I mean it as only the biggest of compliments when I say Harmy was a genuinely ugly, horrible, bowler. And when you had him and that other genuinely ugly, horrible, bowler, Fred, firing together, England were unstoppable. While outwardly they looked like pretty normal blokes, once they began their run-ups they were transformed into a dust storm with arms and legs sticking out at all angles. They'd wind themselves up into some awful shape and then 'Urrggggh!', the ball would fly out, some poor devil playing a forward defensive with their ribcage.

England had been used to fielding pitch-it-up swing bowlers, little seamers and hoping for the best. Now we had a pair of absolute brutes who could hurl it down, with skill, and unsettle the best batsmen in the world . . . and the worst. I faced Harmy on a spicy green wicket at Lord's. He wasn't holding back, giving me a few bumpers. I thought I'd deal with this in my usual manner, by retreating to the legside. Unfortunately, he followed me. At one point I was so far down the legside that I cut the ball, middled it, and, instead of it going out towards gully or point it actually went behind the stumps. So ridiculous was the shot that Harmy remembers it to this day. Me? I wish I could forget the entire experience. Even Harmy's pitched-up deliveries were hideous. No matter where he bowled, the ball shot up at you. He was the sort of bowler you ended up playing with both feet off the floor. At the point of contact you'd make an involuntary yelp – 'Aaggghh!' Sometimes I'd do it before the ball had even arrived. 'Ooh! Ow! Stop!'

Ricky Ponting had slightly more decorum, and skill, than to be hopping around making little whelps when facing Harmy, but on the first morning at Lord's in 2005 he knew he was in one hell of a battle when the Durham quick beat him for pace and struck him on the side of the helmet. The impact cut Ricky's cheek. Blood was seeping from the wound. When none of the England boys rushed over to check Ricky out, Justin Langer was beside himself. 'Is this a war?' he shouted over to Andrew Strauss. 'Is this what it's come to?' It wasn't a war, but England wanted to show the Aussies that the days of rolling over were gone. This new 2005 version was hard and uncompromising. A few balls later, Harmy drew Ricky forward and he was caught at slip. Bowling short and hostile and then drawing the man forward with a false shot is a classic paceman's trick. By being aggressive, Harmy was doing precisely what was needed. The result was the Aussie skipper back in the hutch.

It's easy to think of these big fast blokes as one-trick ponies, terrorising batsmen into submission. But Harmy's most important ball of that series was the yorker-length slow ball he conjured up in the next game at Edgbaston right at the end of the third day. Michael Clarke played all over it, leaving

Australia with just that tiny bit too much to do as England crawled over the line by two runs in possibly the greatest ending to a Test match ever the day after.

There's something else that Test produced, one of cricket's most famous ever photos. Fred taking time out from England's wild celebration to console an emotionally shattered Brett Lee has, for two decades, been held up as one of the great examples of sportsmanship. Few people realise, however, that Harmy got there first. Even amid the euphoria of taking that final wicket, winning an Ashes Test match in the craziest of ways, he was aware of Lee's desperation. It's just that nobody clicked the shutter at that time.

That's sport for you – all about timing.

17 ASHES TESTS

Wickets: 45
Best Bowling: 5–43
Avg: 41.91
Five-wicket Innings: 1
Ten-wicket Matches: 0

Runs: 212
Highest Score: 23
Avg: 9.21

22.

JUSTIN LANGER

*A 'baggy green' with legs, JL was the perfect
example of the Aussies' formidable team DNA.*

'G'day Tuffers! Beautiful day to bat. I can't wait to get stuck into
you, mate. I'm feeling good, the sun's shining, I fancy myself to
get a hundred here. I'm looking at a double. Sorry mate, but
this might be the last time you play for England.'

Justin Langer. Nice bloke. Just wished he'd shut up every now
and then. One time I was halfway through my hop and skip run-up
when he piped up, 'Arm ball!' I still had another seven paces to
run. You think you've seen and heard it all and then a batsman
has the actual audacity to predict what you're going to bowl!

But that was JL, a bloke who really could dominate, something I saw up close when he was parachuted into Middlesex in

1998 to deliver a dose of the 'Aussie way' so revered at the time. Counties loved an Aussie overseas player in the 1990s. They hoped their uncompromising nuggetty nature would be contagious in the dressing room. JL definitely brought a bit of Aussie grit to Middlesex. Having played Sheffield Shield cricket for Western Australia, I don't think he could quite believe the rather lax approach of those participating in its English counterpart, where three overs into the morning session conversation at slip would be turning to the best pubs in which to spend the coming evening. Performance was discussed to a degree, but it was generally who was going to get up and do the karaoke.

Through JL's eyes, everything seemed so half-arsed and unprofessional. His disdain for the plates of French fancies and cream horns that littered the average English county dressing room had to be seen to be believed. He was the kind of hard-faced bloke who fed on witchetty grubs and mud. He wasn't interested in custard slices; he gorged on kangaroo entrails.

Thus it was that when, two years later, he was made Middlesex captain JL wasted no time ripping up the tattered county blueprint. In an early Championship match at Lord's he won the toss. Previous skippers wouldn't even have had to tell the players their decision. Win the toss at Lord's and we always batted first. We had a great batting line-up and a decent complement of bowlers, including me and Embers to make the most of the pitch deteriorating over the course of the match. More often than not, we won. The first time JL won the toss, he announced that we were bowling. We couldn't believe what we were hearing. 'Bowling? No, no, Justin! You don't understand pal. That's not what happens here!' It was sheer madness. He couldn't have upset the applecart more if he'd sat down at lunch and poured custard over his roast dinner. By the time the fourth innings came around, set 300-plus to win, we felt totally vindicated. It would take a miracle to get that many. JL, of course, then disappeared through the Long Room and tapped out a century like Lord's was his back garden and he was having a little knockabout. From that point on, win or lose the toss, if we bowled first it never felt like the end of the world. That came directly from his input. Into our midst had been delivered an absolute streetfighter, a man who knew his mind completely and never, ever, gave an inch. Sometimes he'd come back into the pavilion at lunch or tea midway through a knock. 'Well done, mate,' I'd say. 'Fancy a Wagon Wheel?'

'They don't want to bowl to me,' he'd snarl. 'I can see it in their eyes.'

'OK,' I'd say, looking for a table to hide behind.

'One of their bowlers, he's gone mate. I'm telling you, he's f***ing scared.'

I'd remember the opposition had drafted in a little second XI bowler to make up the numbers. *I'll bet he is!* I'd think. *I'm f***ing scared just listening to you!*

JL didn't need to sledge. His mere presence could bring on mental disintegration.

If that was what he was like playing for an English county with which he had no real attachment, imagine what he was like with Australia. When he was given his 'baggy green' in 1993, rumour is he kept it on for a fortnight. He absorbed that cap, slept in it, bathed in it, the works. More than anyone, he made you realise just what the 'baggy green' meant to Australian players. It was something I'd think about a lot – how much more there was to the 'baggy green' than there was to our cap. To them, nothing better exemplified being an Australian cricketer. They'd do anything for that bit of cloth. I felt quite jealous of the relationship they had with it. Whereas we had floppy hats, sunhats, even bucket hats nowadays, to them it was an immovable, unchangeable, object. No way would any of that happen with the Aussies. Can you imagine Ricky Ponting in a bucket hat? To them it's the 'baggy green' or nothing. No wonder Don Bradman's sold for $479,700 in Sydney in 2024. And that's with, as auction house Bonham's put it, 'some insect damage' to the peak. The Aussies got that deep emotional bind to their cap very right. While we were forever scrabbling round for a DNA, they had a brand to attach themselves to.

Consistency of selection helped to build that brand. In the 1989 Ashes, England selected 29 players for six Tests compared to Australia's 12. That's pretty much three teams. They beat three teams of us! The Aussies also put a lot more weight on character in their selection process. They went for people who represented the ethos behind the 'baggy green'. They built a culture and stuck to it whereas for a long time the England selectors just went for whoever was doing OK in county cricket at any particular time.

By 2005, England had come to see that building a team around a core of talented, combative and mentally strong players, unscathed by past Ashes hammerings, was the way forward. They might not have had the 'baggy green' but they definitely had the ruthlessness associated with it. When Ricky Ponting was cut on the cheek by that Steve Harmison bouncer in the first Test at Lord's, JL couldn't hide his shock that the England side weren't all over the Australian captain checking he was all right. He actually asked his old Middlesex colleague

Andrew Strauss, 'Are we in a war or something?' But England's attitude was, 'Why the f*** should we check if he's OK? We're here to beat you, not play doctors and nurses.' That degree of competitiveness comes from within, but it had been added to by a predetermined course of 'F*** 'em! We're England and we look out for ourselves.' In 2005, JL was to discover that even the power of the 'baggy green' wasn't enough. Even though England lost that first Test, and there was a bit of a feeling of 'Here we go again!' in the media, this new England was unblemished. The players didn't have the burden of negative Ashes memories. They could actually look at that game and think, *Well hang on, we did actually have them on the ropes a couple of times there.* That meant they still had confidence going into the next match at Edgbaston. England couldn't allow themselves to be blunted mentally and they didn't.

It took a while, but eventually we beat JL down at Middlesex too. He realised that he alone wasn't going to change the face of county cricket and the way the typical English pro went about it. JL might never have been a fully paid-up member of the chocolate éclair brigade, but by the end he was definitely eyeing up the lemon drizzle.

'I told you JL! I told you!'

21 ASHES TESTS

Runs: 1,658
Highest Score: 250
Avg: 50.24
Hundreds: 5
Fifties: 5

23.

DEVON MALCOLM

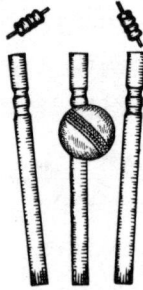

For a bowler the Aussies genuinely feared,
Devon was criminally underused.

For sheer speed, the only English bowler who rivalled Steve Harmison in my playing days was Devon Malcolm. He was lightning fast, so much so that the first ball he bowled in the nets at Derbyshire resulted in the unsuspecting batsman being clattered so hard in the ribs that he had to be ferried to the physio's room on a door.

Devon was another of those who, on his day, could win us a Test match. Which is why it would have helped if he'd been given a few more days. Steve Waugh has said himself that the Aussies were always amazed when Devon's name wasn't on the team sheet, the selectors seemingly preferring players who were consistent rather than matchwinners. As Steve put it, Devon might bowl a great over followed by a terrible one, but most batsmen would take consistency over unpredictability any day of the week. A ball in the throat followed by a 90 mph-plus away swinger is very hard, and indeed uncomfortable, to deal with. Steve knows as well as anyone what Devon was capable of. When we won in Adelaide in 1995, Devon flattened his off peg for a golden duck. It was an absolutely fantastic delivery, just about the quickest I've ever seen. That was the point we really felt we'd opened the door. 'Crikey, we've got a chance here!' Chasing 263, the Aussies slumped to 83–8, but even then refused to be beaten, Ian Healy and Damien Fleming putting on 69 for the ninth wicket before Devon wrapped up proceedings by pinning the leg spinner Peter McIntrye lbw. He ended up with figures of 7–117, and was unlucky not to be named man-of-the-match.

Along the way, Devon provided me with one of the best memories of my Test match career when Michael Slater mistimed a hook and a tricky catch thudded into my hands as I slid on my knees at fine leg. I turned to the crowd to celebrate and was faced with hundreds of England fans leaping around, going absolutely mad, beer all over the place. I can still see them now running towards me, careering down the hill underneath the scoreboard. They clearly had the same feeling as me – that for once the gods were smiling on us. Suddenly there was a feeling the day might actually go our way. Instead of the ball landing just short, or to the left or the right, and Slater going on to get a hundred, I'd actually pouched it.

Devon's own fielding, it has to be said, could be a little hit and miss. There's a clip on YouTube of him misfielding off me three times in a matter of a few balls at the SCG, the ball finding its way to the fence each time. The development of my facial expressions across those three balls is an absolute picture. Frustration. Bemusement. Resignation.

Devon, I should explain, was somewhat shortsighted. Tales of his net-bowling, sending down vicious deliveries unaware that the batsman was in the next one along, are legendary. And yet somehow I have the honour of being one of only two players to have appeared below him in the England batting order. To be fair, I'm in good company. The other is Ian Botham, although disappointingly he is down on the scorecard as 'dnb' (did not bat), being absent hurt at the time.

As a batsman, considering the pacemen who were around at the time – Courtney Walsh, Curtly Ambrose, Allan Donald, Waqar Younis and the like – Devon's shortsightedness was probably to his benefit. A ball flying past your head is like a spider in your bedroom – you're better not knowing it's there. Looking back, I probably should have worn a blindfold. I never mastered even the basics of batting against the quicks. The batsmen who do well against severe pace are those who can override their gut instinct to retreat and get forward. I'd get bowled, on the back foot, convinced the ball had pitched halfway down. My missing off stump would suggest something entirely different. *Well, hang on a minute,* I'd think, *I should have been forward to that.* But these guys are devilishly difficult to get forward to. Even to a half volley it's hard. Picking length is the key to the art of batting, but when you've got a six-foot-eight fella charging in, hurling it into the dirt at 90 mph, the last thing your brain is telling you is *Go on! Press forward! It'll be all right!*

For sure Devon had that kind of worrisome pace. The Aussies' answer was to try to put him off, hit a few boundaries, knock his confidence, until someone a little friendlier came on. But they never took liberties against him. They respected him, which sadly tended to go over the heads of the England hierarchy. For a while chairman of selectors Ted Dexter thought he was called Malcolm Devon! The stats actually bear the Aussies' trepidation out. At The Oval in 1993, Devon removed their top three of Mark Taylor, Michael Slater and David Boon, then followed up with their middle order of the Waugh twins and Allan Border second time round. That's quite a haul and again he can count himself unlucky not to have been handed the man-of-the-match award which instead went to Angus Fraser for his own eight-wicket haul. Having Angus at one end, plugging away, keeping the runs down, while Devon wrought havoc at the other, was a great, and sadly underused, combination for England. Devon had been ignored for the first five Tests of the series. By the time The Oval Test came round, England were 4–0 in arrears.

It wasn't always the selectors halting Devon's charge to the wicket. He almost missed the start on the last day at The Oval after getting stuck in traffic on Vauxhall Bridge, eventually abandoning his car and haring to the ground on foot. At the start of the Ashes tour in 1994–95, meanwhile, both he and fellow paceman Joey Benjamin fell foul (fowl?) of chickenpox. I get that the management didn't want the illness to spread but it was as if they'd disappeared, taken as the rest of us slept. I was constantly asking where they were. I saw a film once where several astronauts discovered the truth about the space landings and were 'vanished' into the desert. I wondered if Joey and Devon had perhaps burst in on Graham Gooch and discovered he was a robot. Days went by without answer. And then one morning I got up and there they were. I've never been so relieved. 'Joey! Devon! Oh, thank goodness! You're back! They let you go!'

Devon's Ashes experience might have started off in the worst possible manner, the Aussies scoring 301–0 on his Test debut at Trent Bridge in 1989, but the fact he climbed back off the canvas to put the frighteners up them for the next eight years says everything about his character. A little rough around the edges he might have been, but Devon was the one England bowler who, during their Ashes domination, the Aussies were genuinely a little bit fearful of, which is precisely why he makes my list.

Just one last thing though, Dev. You should have been batting 11 to my 10. You got 16 ducks in your Test career. Me? Just the 15.

15 ASHES TESTS

Wickets: 42
Best Bowling: 4–39
Avg: 45.14

Runs: 103
Highest Score: 29
Avg: 6.43

24.

ALLAN BORDER

*Hard as nails Aussie skipper who waved goodbye
to the notion that England and Australia
could be pals as well as rivals.*

The first time I met a lot of the Australian team was in a wheelie bin. Well, I was in a wheelie bin. They were on the outfield early on in the 1990–91 tour. I'd hidden in there a few minutes earlier with the purpose of leaping out and surprising my teammates. I know what you're thinking, and you're right, but it really did seem like a very good idea at the time. Unfortunately, as I crouched among various items of rotting vegetation, I didn't realise the Aussie boys were saying a quick hello. And so, when I sprang forth there they all were. 'Phil,' I introduced myself, flicking a tomato off my shoulder. 'Left-arm spinner. Nice to meet you.'

It was a rare expression of bonhomie from the Aussies. Generally speaking, in the ten or so years I played them, if you so much as nodded at one of their players the most you'd get back was a growl. Occasionally, we'd try to reciprocate, but in the 1990s even our growl wasn't as effective as theirs. They were the Dobermann to our Chihuahua.

No-one warned me this was going to happen. They didn't need to. It went with the territory. Even so, as the new kid it can come as a bit of a shock when a bloke you've been watching for years on the telly tells you, 'Listen, you little ****, you're f***ing s***, you shouldn't be here. I've looked at your f***ing statistics and they're f***ing terrible. I'm gonna smash you all over the place.' Especially if all you're doing is taking your jumper off and giving it to the umpire. Martin McCague, the Northern Ireland-born quick who grew up in Australia but played for England on the 1994–95 Ashes tour, was once sledged by the Aussies while bringing out a drink as twelfth man. And Martin's a big bloke, in all directions twice the size of me. Even the Aussie press joined in, describing him as 'a rat who joined a sinking ship'. I mean, the bloke was just having a game of cricket. Mad, but that's how it was.

At least all would be forgotten in the bar at the end of the day – right? Er, no. That might have been the case in the old days but when I encountered the Aussies there was no mixing once the play had finished. It was in the bus and off. Even if we'd wanted to mix, the Aussies were under strict orders not to, an element of snarl instilled by Allan Border. AB had been involved in too many series where the two sides' reaction to one another had been a wagging tail. He'd done it himself, hanging out with and being pals with some of England's biggest names. But after defeats in England in 1985 and Down Under in 1986–87 he'd had enough. He felt too much fraternising with the opposition was affecting the Australians' performance. By the time the 1989 series came round, he'd told his team in no uncertain terms, 'Don't talk to the England players. Don't let them into the dressing room. Don't let them be mates.' He basically portrayed England as the enemy, which meant not only reducing the interplay off the pitch but upping the aggression on it. On one infamous occasion, Robin Smith, batting in the heat, asked AB if it would be OK if he called for a drink.

'What do you think this is,' the Aussie skipper replied, 'a tea party? No, you can't have a glass of water. You can wait like the rest of us.'

I was never out in the middle long enough to warrant such a request. In fact, dropping the teabag into the cup as I went in to bat, and then fishing it out as I came back, usually guaranteed the perfect cup of PG Tips.

AB's win-at-all-costs ethos created an impregnable shield around that Australian team. It wasn't pleasant – far from it – but it worked. Aussie unity had never been stronger. They won as a team, lost as a team, and always stuck together. In the meantime, England were heading in entirely the opposite direction. Players had no stability and even less direction. Building team unity is difficult when the axe is constantly hanging and everyone's playing for their place.

AB was the perfect captain to instil that mindset in the Australians. As a batsman his first rule was never to make a gift of his wicket. He was stubbornness personified and put England through the ringer for 15 years, scoring eight hundreds and 21 fifties along the way. When finally he disappeared, Australia had already found the perfect replacement, first as a batsman, then as a captain, in Steve Waugh, who, if anything, took the cold shoulder to new levels of iciness, never allowing us to see any side to his team other than their game face. It's a policy that only works if you've got the players to back it up. If you're losing every game then you're just going to look silly. But, as the 1980s rolled into the 1990s, the Aussies definitely had the personnel. In fact, that combination of brilliance on the pitch and detached self-confidence off it gave them an aura which they played on to make our task at times seem almost impossible.

While times have moved on, it amazes me that the Aussies have now gone in entirely the opposite direction. With fly-on-the-wall sports documentaries all the rage, they've allowed the TV cameras into their dressing room. I get that it makes for a fascinating watch, but in so doing the aura bubble has well and truly burst. Fragility and vulnerability, which we never saw, is now displayed in front of the TV audience – and the opposition.

I can't see AB ever allowing that to happen. It would have been a brave documentary-maker who stopped him at the dressing room door and asked, 'That sweep off Phil Tufnell, the one that went to Graham Gooch, do you think it was a good idea?'

I can't say I'd have much welcomed it either. 'Day Two at Old Trafford. Shane Warne has just bowled the ball of the century. Meanwhile, Phil Tufnell's pound coin has become wedged in the fag machine in the downstairs bar.'

My exoticism dashed for a bit of throwaway TV? I don't think so.

47 ASHES TESTS

Runs: 3,548
Highest Score: 200 not out
Avg: 56.31
Hundreds: 8
Fifties: 21

Wickets: 4
Best Bowling: 1–16
Avg: 93.50

25

ANDREW FLINTOFF

England's great talisman, Fred produced moments of magic that the rest of us mere mortals can only dream about.

I'm crouched on the wicket, holding Steve Waugh's hand and patting him on the back. 'Hard luck pal. You came so close. No-one deserved to lose that match.' And then the bin lorry pulls up outside and I wake up.

Flintoff-esque commiserating handshakes were in short supply all round when I was playing. The matches weren't quite as close. Fred recognised the Aussies' pain in losing by two runs. We tended to lose by an innings. However, by the time that legendary Edgbaston Test came round in 2005, no longer were we dependent on individual out-of-this-world performances.

England had real competitive strength. If Marcus Trescothick didn't fire at the top of the innings then Andrew Strauss would make a score, or Michael Vaughan, or Kevin Pietersen. Similarly, if Steve Harmison's pace couldn't prise the Aussies out, then up stepped the lightning-fast Simon Jones or the wily Matthew Hoggard. But, like all great teams, England needed someone to hold it all together; to turn 11 men into 12. That summer, Freddie Flintoff was the ultimate Test kingpin, that rarest of cricketers who, seemingly on a whim, can smash the ball out the ground or bowl an unplayable over. A once-in-a-generation character who carried not just a team but a nation with him as England sought finally to end the Aussies' Ashes domination.

The nearest we'd ever had to Fred was Ian Botham, a legend I was lucky enough to share dressing room space with at the end of his England career. I did the same with Fred at the beginning of his own international sojourn as we toured South Africa in 1999–2000. He was still a little raw at that point. In fact, if I'm honest, when, earlier in the 1990s, I played a couple of county games against Fred, I'd never have guessed the Lancastrian would turn out to be such a devastating bowler. He just didn't look right. Stuttering into the wicket, he nearly fell over his own feet. Us Middlesex boys saw him as a number six batsman trying to bowl a bit. But then obviously someone got working on him, and he got working on himself. Once he gained a little bit of confidence he discovered some real bowling acumen. All of a sudden he was a real danger, reaching his absolute peak in that summer of 2005. The Aussies hated facing him, and I can understand why. He was a horrible bowler. Look at other quicks, like Michael Holding, Allan Donald and Brett Lee, and they floated into the crease and unleashed balls that were lightning fast through the air. Fred hobbled up to the wicket and bowled a heavy ball that hit the pitch hard and was on to the batsman before they knew it. He's never mentioned in a list of the quickest bowlers to grace the game but more than a few batsmen have said he's one of the fastest they faced. Look at what Fred did with the ball in 2005. His over at Edgbaston that removed Justin Langer and Ricky Ponting was absolutely top notch – devastatingly accurate and aggressive 90 mph reverse swing. Ricky has described it as the 'best over I ever faced'. That's coming from an all-time great who played no less than 168 Test matches.

England really were on the ropes in Birmingham. It was only Fred's second innings heroics with the bat, when he smashed a quickfire 73, including two sixes in one over from Brett Lee that kept them in the contest, dragging them from 75–6 to 182 all out. The Aussies, chasing a very gettable 282, had then progressed untroubled to 47–0 before Michael Vaughan chucked the ball to Fred, who, in the way that only these real greats can do, reached deep within himself and found something truly special. His second delivery bowled Langer off his elbow. Ricky then survived an lbw appeal, an edge that fell short of gully, and another lbw shout. By this point I'm sure he must have been praying for the over to end. Fred, however, prolonged it with a no-ball (if I was him I'd have claimed this was a deliberate ploy) before getting one to move away at speed. Ricky nicked it, and it thudded into Geraint Jones' gloves. In a flash 47–0 had become 47–2. Considering how tight that game was, England would never have got near without Fred's all-rounder masterclass – 141 runs and seven wickets. In perhaps the greatest Test series ever, Fred ended up second highest wicket-taker with 24, and third highest run-scorer with 402.

As a batsman it had also taken him time to mature. For a while it felt like he was just enjoying being out there swinging the willow, and nothing wrong with that. By 2005, however, he was someone who could combine destructiveness with the knowhow of how to build an innings. Understanding his true capabilities freed him up to back his talent in pressure situations. Which is exactly what he did in that epic two-run win at Edgbaston, and then again in the fourth Test at Trent Bridge when he scored a fantastic first-innings century and then a vital 26 in that excruciating run chase when England stumbled their way to a victory target of 129.

Shane Warne's reaction when Fred got out after that Trent Bridge hundred, running after him to congratulate him on his knock, says so much about the kind of players, and people, that Aussies respect. They recognise a certain freedom of spirit, something that sits above and beyond simply trying to win. Every player wants to come out on top, but occasionally someone comes along who has that something extra, be it flair, cheekiness, or whatever. They just can't help being their true selves. That's why it was so sad to see Fred's lifeforce crushed out of him by the captaincy on the following tour Down Under. Like Beefy before him, people forget that your best captain isn't necessarily your best player. On the other hand, if the chance comes their way they're not going to say no. It's like being asked to be Prime Minister. You might not be the best choice, but you're not going to turn it down. With Fred in Australia, his carefree attitude got clogged up in the clutter of responsibility; the burden of thinking it was down to him to turn round a relentless tide of defeats. When it comes to free spirits, you should never put too much in front of them. In the end, all it does is negate the part of their character that made them successful in the first place.

I was in Australia commentating on that 2006–07 series. I'd known Fred for the best part of a decade by that point. I was used to seeing him relaxing in a bar, heading out on a boat trip (not a pedalo), doing handstands in a swimming pool, and now that side of him had gone. Instead he was in meetings trying to reverse the downward slide of results, and when he wasn't in meetings he had to be a role model. He was constantly 'a captain'. He couldn't escape it. The shackles were on. That's why opening bats so often make very good captains. They're methodical. They're analytical in the way they play. For a maverick, on the other hand, hitting a ball for six isn't a process, it's just something that happens. As a captain, there are things you have to do. On the opening day of a Test match, for example, you have to be there, clad in blazer and cap, ten minutes before the toss. At that point, Beefy, Fred, people like that, are usually lying on the physio's bed with a bacon sand-wich and a cup of tea. They can leave the captain to get dolled up and go out and flip the coin – unless they *are* the captain. For these people, captaincy is personality-crushing because so much of the time they have to be someone they aren't. Instead of doing what they normally do – try their best, hope it's their day, and then if it isn't go back to their hotel, have a little think about how to perform better next time, and switch off – now they're sat in their room stewing over every tiny thing that went wrong, questioning, blaming themselves. They're under siege, from themselves, and the outside world. Once the rot sets in, there's not a time when the press isn't laser-focused on them. I challenge anyone not to feel self-conscious with the eyes of the media boring into them every time they step out of their hotel room.

I felt a lot for Fred on that trip, especially when he was then hung out to dry by the management at the World Cup that followed straight after. After a few beachside drinks, Fred hopped into a pedalo in search of a nightcap with Beefy, who happened to be on a yacht on the bay in St Lucia where the team was staying (I love that Beefy was involved in the shenanigans without even trying!) The pedalo capsized, the press got hold of the story, and Fred was dropped and stripped of the vice-captaincy. He was also made to explain himself at a press conference. From the outside it felt like a schoolboy-esque humiliation, as if you misbehaved in the classroom and the teacher made you ring home to tell your parents. Fred was a grown man. He'd had a few drinks and was mucking about on the way back to the hotel. Don't get me wrong, no-one should be pedalo-ing in the middle of the night. It could have been quite dangerous. But it wasn't the end of the world. To then hang him out to dry in front of the world's press can only have crushed him even more.

Fred did, thankfully, have one more punt at the Ashes with which to redeem himself. By the time the fifth and final Test came round in 2009 he was practically falling apart. His back had gone, as had his knees, and various other body parts, and then all of a sudden he found himself at mid-on, away from his usual position in the slips, pretty much stood on one leg. Chasing an albeit very unlikely 546 to win, Michael Hussey and Ricky Ponting were just getting Australia back into the game. As I'd seen happen so many times when I was playing in Ashes series, England had the Aussies by the short and curlies only for them to crawl back up off the canvas and start counterpunching. A partnership was developing, they were ticking off the runs. Suddenly, it really did feel like they might reach this crazy target. It's the mark of a truly great player that they can somehow conjure up something that the rest of us can only dream about. Hussey clipped the ball in Fred's direction and set off for a quick single. In one swooping action, the creaking Fred grabbed the leather and slung in the perfect throw. Ricky was short of his ground by a foot. At that point, you just sit there and go, 'Wow!' People will say, 'What a bit of luck'. But then is it luck? He meant to do it, and it happened.

That's the thing with these characters. Because they enjoy life so much, cricket isn't on their mind every minute of every day. But once the boots go on, everything changes. With the ball, they run in and slam it into the dirt as hard as they can. With the bat, they ain't leaving anything outside off stump. And in the field they pull off the most audacious run outs and catches.

More often than not, they're also blessed with an essence of absolute generosity, which is why Fred, in that moment of victory at Edgbaston, when he could have been forgiven for collapsing to the floor, or leaping on to the backs of his teammates, made a beeline for Brett Lee, whose unbeaten 43 had taken his side so close to a win that would surely have secured the series. It's a gesture that in some ways eclipsed the drama that had come before. And one which, in its own way, confirmed that the wheel, finally, after so many years of hurt, was turning England's way.

Magnificent moment. Even more magnificent bloke.

15 ASHES TESTS

Wickets: 50
Best Bowling: 5–78
Avg: 33.20
Five-wicket Innings: 1
Ten-wicket Matches: 0

Runs: 906
Highest Score: 102
Avg: 33.55
Hundreds: 1
Fifties: 6

26.

NATHAN LYON

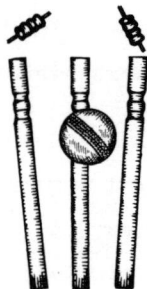

*Never say die off-spinner whose one-legged
heroics added to his Ashes legend.*

At Lord's in 2023, Nathan Lyon hobbled down the steps from
the Lord's pavilion and somehow deposited himself on to the
field. He'd started his journey in the Long Room. Had he done
so from the Australian dressing room he'd have long been
timed out by the time he reached the middle.

Nathan had suffered the kind of calf strain that for any other
Aussie would entail several days' feet-up watching *Neighbours*. I'd
seen him earlier that day on crutches. But Nathan's not any
other Aussie. He's a ball of determination and belligerence that
never knows it's beaten. In fact, when the ninth wicket fell in the
Australian second innings, not-out batsman Mitchell Starc was

already heading back to the pavilion to get ready to bowl when the wreck of his team's off-spinner somehow propelled itself on to the field. The England team were as shocked as Starc. Lyon tells a great story about Jimmy Anderson putting his arm round him and asking, 'Are you stupid?' Lyon didn't need to think twice. 'Yes!' he replied. I'd have to agree. In the same position, I'd have had to be strapped to a stretcher and physically carried out to the middle kicking and screaming. Or alternatively thrown from the balcony.

Thinking about it, when England collapsed in the second innings of the Adelaide Test in 1991, I was actually removed from a drip after being hospitalised with dehydration and ferried back to the ground. 'Remember Eddie Paynter!' they kept telling me, referencing the plucky Lancashire batsman who, stricken with tonsillitis, had crawled from his hospital bed at Brisbane during the 1932–33 'Bodyline' tour and promptly racked up 83 in England's first innings before winning the match with a six second time round. 'Eddie f***ing Paynter!' I kept saying. 'Eddie f***ing Paynter!' Who do you think I am? Just because down the years other players have crawled to the middle with syphilis and dengue fever, or scored a quickfire 35 with a broken tibia, doesn't mean that I have to do it.' I mean, what sort of sport unhooks someone off a drip and makes them go out and play? I expect if push came to shove they'd have had me batting with a bag of saline hooked up at silly mid-on. I'd have been out there in a backless gown and surgical tights. Thankfully, Daffy and Robin Smith managed to hang around to force the draw and my services weren't needed.

The same thing happened during a World Cup match at the SCG in 1992. I'd become badly dehydrated in the field and, when we batted, was again in a hospital with a tube in my arm. On that occasion I'd actually have quite happily gone out to face Bruce Reid and Craig McDermott to escape the abuse spewing forth from the other patients. 'Ya lazy bastard, Tufnell. Typical bloody Pom, lying around in bed all day.'

Back at Lord's, batting on one leg, face etched with pain, Nathan survived 13 balls and actually belted a cracking pull shot to the boundary as he and Starc added 15 runs for the last wicket. At that point, spectators could have been forgiven for being confused by his teammates shouting, 'Go on Garry!' from their dressing room balcony. Former Aussie wicketkeeper Matthew Wade is to thank for this particular piece of confusion. He renamed his teammate in reference to the Aussie Rules footballer Garry Lyon. Whether Garry Lyon now answers to Nathan, I'm unsure.

Considering Ben Stokes nearly dragged England over the line with his pyrotechnic 155, Nathan's heroics were significant in placing the Aussies tantalisingly out of reach. More than that, his innings captured perfectly a bloke who, right from the beginning, has fought tooth and nail for everything he's achieved in the game. Make no mistake, Nathan's journey to the top of his trade is an unusual one. A fringe second XI player for South Australia, he was on the ground staff at the Adelaide Oval, first coming to notice when England toured Down Under in 2010–11 and the Aussie Test team needed an off-spinner to practise against in preparation for facing Graeme Swann. Within a year he was right there alongside his peers.

But no way was Nathan going to go into that Test team with a 'Well, I'll give it a go' kind of attitude. Right from the get-go he wanted to make that spinner's slot his own. He wanted to build his own legacy – and has been writing his own scripts ever since. He took a wicket with his first ball on his way to a five-fer, and between the third Ashes Test in 2013 and his unfortunate injury at Lord's ten years later, played in 100 consecutive Tests, the first specialist bowler to do so, his bald head becoming progressively shinier along the way. I can't overstate what an achievement that is (the Tests not the head), especially considering the footsteps in which he was treading. It was an unenviable task to take over where the late great Shane Warne left off, and like many an Aussie spinner, Nathan had to live with the comparison. Warney, with his zooters, toppies and countless other little tricks was the best there ever was. He also had a personality the size of the MCG. Lyon, on the other hand, is an unprepossessing off-spinner. He must have been told countless times, 'You'll never be as good as Shane Warne', but clearly he's never let it bother him, becoming as integral to the attack as any of the Aussie seamers. Nathan could not only give those quick boys a rest but chances were he'd nip himself a couple of wickets while he did so. No two ways about it, in modern times, he's been just as crucial to Australia's success as Mitchell Starc and Pat Cummins. Year after year, he's been the glue that binds that Aussie attack together. In the dressing room, meanwhile, his desire to win is infectious. Nathan, like most spinners, isn't physically intimidating. Instead he's like one of those little dogs that get their teeth into your ankles and won't let go. Or you think you've shaken them off and then 10 minutes later they're back ripping the seat out of your trousers.

With more than 500 Test wickets to his name, Nathan ranks as one of the all-time great spin bowlers. He's reached that mark by being a very tricky customer. He gets that bounce, gets that turn, and wheels away all day. Time and time again he's been a thorn in England's side, and it says everything for his combative character that it's Edgbaston, England's loudest and most intimidating ground, where he's delivered his finest performances. His 9–161 in 2019 allowed Australia to win there for the first time since 2001. Four years later he took eight wickets and, by joining Pat Cummins in a match-winning ninth-wicket stand, finally banished Australian memories of that horrible two-run defeat on the same ground in 2005.

Of course, there is one memory Nathan will find harder to banish, the missed run out of Jack Leach which, had he not fumbled the ball, would have left England one run short of their victory target at Headingley in 2019. 'The thing is,' he reflected, 'we all make mistakes, the big difference is 25 million people or more were watching my mistake over and over and over.' As someone who's had the occasional fumble myself, his words resonated with me. At Headingley, for poor Nathan the agony only got worse when, the very next ball, he had England's matchwinner Ben Stokes plumb lbw only for umpire Joel Wilson to turn down his appeal. With no decision reviews left, Nathan was left doing a dying fly impression in the middle of the wicket.

There's something else about Nathan. While he might bowl at half the speed, he's very much become the new Glenn McGrath, routinely issuing pre-Ashes predictions that Australia will hand down a thorough 5–0 hammering. I'll have to take a look at his footwear next time we meet. I'm assuming he wears Blundstones 24 hours a day too.

30 ASHES TESTS (TO OCT 2025)

Wickets: 110
Best Bowling: 6–49
Avg: 29.41
Five-wicket Innings: 2
Ten-wicket Matches: 0

Runs: 340
Highest Score: 31
Avg: 16.19

27.

MARK BUTCHER

Like every other England batsman of his era, Butch played in the shadow of Aussie domination. When his day in the sun finally came he seized the chance to reel off one of the greatest Ashes innings of the last 50 years.

As an England cricketer, when the day comes and it's your name written in the stars, you really do hope it's against the Aussies. For Mark Butcher, at Headingley in 2001, that's exactly what happened. Gutsy, forceful and incredibly skillful, Butch, in the form of his life, grabbed his chance to show the world just what an amazing batsman he was.

It was an opportunity which seemed to have slipped away when, in typical England style, the Surrey man was on the verge of being dropped after a late night at the previous Test at Trent

Bridge. Like me, Butch wasn't one to be sat in his room with a packet of Digestives and a cup of tea. Not even a chocolate Hobnob would keep him behind that door. But that didn't make him a bad cricketer. Fact is, there are some players who are much better off going out for a couple of drinks than staring at the wall until 2 a.m. overthinking the next day's play. Thankfully, senior players like Athers and Alec Stewart knew Butch's value even if others didn't. They argued for him to be kept in the side. The result was a display of batting brilliance which will live long in the memory of every England fan.

What a day for Butch that was. I wasn't playing at Headingley, rarely a spinner's paradise, but I was yelling him on as he powered England towards a most unlikely victory. This was, after all, the fourth match of a series in which Australia had gone 3–0 up and retained the Ashes in just ten days. When Adam Gilchrist, covering for injured Aussie skipper Steve Waugh, set England 315 to win it seemed to all and sundry just another stepping stone on their march to an inevitable whitewash. Of all the English Test venues, Headingley, with its often cloudy overhead conditions and none-too friendly pitches, isn't the one where you'd envisage a testing run chase coming off, especially against a salivating attack of Glenn McGrath, Brett Lee, Shane Warne and Jason Gillespie. Subsequently, at 33–2, with Athers and Marcus Trescothick back in the hutch, everyone expected this particular storyline to pan out in a manner even more predictable than the Christmas Day episode of *EastEnders*. England were massive underdogs, although, noticeably, one person didn't seem to think so. At the end of the fourth day, as England set out on their mission-virtually-impossible, Butch was interviewed by Mark Nicholas on Channel 4.

'What do you think your chances are tomorrow?' enquired Mark.

'If somebody plays well and gets a big one,' replied Butch, 'we win the game.'

It was a sneak preview of the sort of cricketing nous that would later see Butch much in demand for punditry work, something that didn't surprise me. While he was seen by some solely as a person who liked to play a bit of guitar and have a few drinks, those of us who knew him understood he was an absolute fount of cricketing knowledge. I tell you, if Butch were to pick 'inclement batting conditions' as his specialist subject he'd be a shoo-in for the title on *Celebrity Mastermind*.

Even so, the sky was as gloomy as England's prospects when Butch set out on his mammoth task that fifth morning. The ball was either going round corners or bouncing over the wicket-keeper's head. Thankfully, mirroring Butch's innings, the sun shone in the afternoon as he put the Aussies to the sword, one of the few batsmen ever to knock McGrath out of the Australian attack with a series of bludgeoning cuts and pulls. I'd urge any England cricket fan to save the footage to their YouTube playlist. There are very few better ways to liven up a slow day.

Even Warney took a bit of stick as Butch played several stonking drives back past him down the ground. In fact, Warney, a man who knew a class act when he saw it, actually high-fived Butch when he completed the winning run off his bowling. By then he'd racked up a blistering 173 not out. Back in the pavilion he stuck a wet towel on his head and tried to come to terms with the magnitude of his achievement. Watching on TV, I might have done the same myself. I couldn't have been happier for my England colleague. I always got on very well with Butch, and so finally to see someone smashing the Aussies around, and for it to be him, was an incredible thing. Thanks to his skill and determination it was the Australian bowling attack getting walloped; it was their tactics, their philosophy on the game, unravelling before their eyes. For once, they were experiencing exactly how we'd felt on so many occasions. Warney would run in, bowl one just short of a length, and Butch would step back, cut it past the despairing dive of the man at cover point and – *BANG!* – into the hoardings for four. All Warney could do was kick the ground and swear. Meanwhile, I was sat there shouting, 'Welcome to my world!'

Butch's 173 not out is one of the great sliding doors moments of English cricket. Had he been dropped it would never have happened and the likelihood is he'd have played his last Test for England. Instead he carried on for another three years, and, as with Graham Thorpe, would have more than deserved to have been part of that team of 2005 which finally clawed back the Ashes. That particular swansong wasn't to be. He can, however, look back, with that broad Butch smile, to one of *the* great days in modern Ashes history.

I don't know why, but Headingley seems to have that effect on Ashes cricket. It's a place where magic happens. There's that little frisson of something in the air which means you just never quite know what's round the corner. The only shame is the guy selling the *Yorkshire Post* is there no more. The backing track to many a drama was the old chap's cry of 'POST!'. Monday, 20 August 2001, was perhaps the only day nobody heard him.

Butch, me old mate, your fireworks drowned him out.

20 ASHES TESTS

Runs: 1,287
Highest Score: 173 not out
Avg: 33.00
Hundreds: 3
Fifties: 4

Wickets: 4
Best Bowling: 4–42
Avg: 45.25

28.

PETER TAYLOR

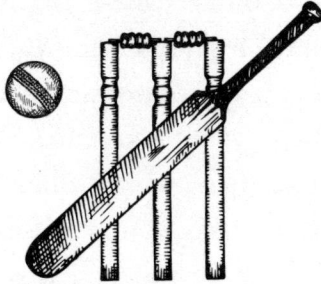

*He turned up, turned us over, and might
not have even been the right bloke.*

'Peter Who?'

I don't think I've ever been picked by mistake. When it came to England, I found it hard enough to get chosen on purpose let alone by accident. Peter Taylor was different. To this day, no-one seems to know if he really was the bloke who the Australian selectors meant to pick for the fifth Test at Sydney in 1987. Whether he was or not, one thing is undeniable, he bowled Australia to victory.

These days, when England pick players who've had a couple of games for their school, or have found a cricket ball in the bushes in the park, it doesn't seem quite so unlikely that a player barely anyone has heard of could be selected for international duty. But in 1987, things were different. Cricketers weren't seemingly plucked from thin air and told to rock up at the next Test match with a couple of pairs of trousers and a freshly laundered jockstrap. And yet this is pretty much what happened to Peter Taylor. He found out he was in the team because his farmer brother-in-law was up early and heard the announcement on the news – a bloke called Taylor, from New South Wales, was going to make his debut. But when his brother-in-law rang to tell Peter, his first reaction wasn't celebration, it was the same as everyone else's. 'Nah! Can't be! They must have the wrong bloke.' Thing is, there was another Taylor in that New South Wales team, an exciting young batsman by the name of Mark. People were saying he was nailed on for a great international career. And that's exactly what happened. Two years later, Mark Taylor made the first of his 104 Test-match appearances. Surely the selectors, looking for new talent after another dismal Ashes campaign, had seen the last Test of the series as a chance to hand a debut to a promising prospect for the future. That must be the case. After all, Peter was 30 and hadn't even played in New South Wales' two previous Sheffield Shield matches.

I remember the whole 'Peter Who' thing well. Mainly because it made me laugh so much. I could just imagine the interview on the Channel Nine news.

'Where did you get the call Peter?'

'Well, I was playing in a second-eleven Shield game in the middle of nowhere, surrounded by 'roos and having a beetroot sandwich for my lunch, when they phoned me up and asked if I fancied coming down to the SCG for a bit of a game. So I got on the next bus from Mount Wongannooey and turned up in the Big Smoke. Never been there before in my life.'

It wasn't quite as bad as that, but a lot of people genuinely did think the Aussies had picked a bloke from nowhere. The TV news shows spent the day trying to find out exactly who this Peter Taylor was. And then – wouldn't you know it? – he came in with his off-spin and blew England away with 6–78 on a turning pitch, snaffling the key wickets of Lamb, Gower and Botham, as well as chipping in a handy second-innings 42 to put the run chase just out of reach. When it came to the man-of-the-match award there was only one choice. If the selectors had made a mistake, they certainly weren't going to admit it after that display. They were going to sit there and lap up the plaudits. Out of nowhere they'd made a choice that, no two ways about it, appeared to be absolute genius. They picked Peter Taylor again, for 12 more Tests and two World Cups.

You could actually say Peter's was the selection that saved Australian cricket. Buoyed by the victory, from that point on, the Aussies never looked back. Trusting in a core group of players, they dominated the next eight Ashes series. In retirement, Peter Taylor played his role in that continued success as a selector.

Word is he never got a name wrong.

2 ASHES TESTS

Wickets: 12
Best Bowling: 6–78
Avg: 19.83
Five-wicket Innings: 1
Ten-wicket Matches: 0

Runs: 73
Highest Score: 42
Avg: 24.33

29.

SIR IAN BOTHAM

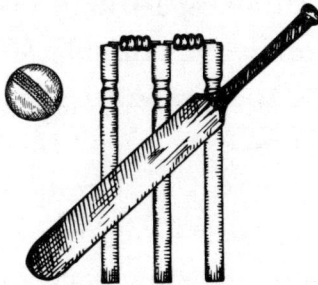

*Beefy had a reputation for enjoying whisky
and ice-cream by the jug – he was always going
to be a man I'd follow.*

It was obvious why Ian Botham loved Australia. Wine, fishing, beaches, hot weather. Taunton has got some of those things but not all of them. Even Beefy, however, couldn't beat the Aussies solely on a bottle of Barossa Valley Shiraz and a big cigar.

While I never travelled on an Ashes tour with Beefy, I did have the remarkable experience of playing alongside him Down Under in the 1992 World Cup. By this point, 16 years into his England career, as far as the sporting world was concerned Beefy wasn't so much over the hill as halfway across the valley on the other side. To be fair, the bloke had just finished a very successful season. Trouble was, it was in *Jack and the Beanstalk* at the Bournemouth Pavilion. But it only took a sniff of Aussie blood to get this giant of English cricket fired up and producing miracles.

When we met the old enemy in the early stages of the competition in front of 40,000 fans at the SCG, Beefy took four wickets in seven balls, including their skipper Allan Border. He celebrated skittling the Aussie captain with the most remarkable, albeit slightly uncoordinated, hip wiggle. Think inebriated Hawaiian hula girl and you'll be in the general ballpark. Where he pulled that little move from I don't know. Physically, he was running on fumes. His back had gone, his legs had gone, everything had gone. In fact, our nickname for him during that tournament was Skippy the Bush Kangaroo, because all he could manage was a little hoppity-skip to the crease where he'd send down these little gentle seamers and swingers. If I'd have bowled like that I'd have been whacked out the ground, but that game showed me up-close just how big an effect Ian Botham, the person, had on the Australians. Obviously, there were a couple of good deliveries in there as well, but it was the first time I'd ever seen a team, en masse, play the man and not the ball. It was like the Aussies only had to lay eyes on Ian Botham to lose control of their faculties. Minds, limbs, feet, were all scrambled in a way I'd very soon see mirrored in English batsmen when faced with Shane Warne.

That match was the greatest ever lesson in the power of an individual to impose their will, their aura, on a game. Acting as a pinch-hitter, Beefy followed up his heroics with the ball by promptly scoring a half century as we romped to an easy win. It really was something very special, which is why I count that match as one of the best I ever played in. His performance amazed me then and it still does now. Just sensational, to the extent it felt like it was written in the stars above the SCG that he was going to win the World Cup for us. Unfortunately, in a parallel universe, it was written that Imran Khan was going to do the same for Pakistan.

Watching Beefy that day, I totally got how Border and his boys felt – because I was awestruck too. This was the bloke I'd idolised when watching the Ashes as a kid. As far back as I can remember I'd sat there, chewing on an Opal Fruit, watching him win this Test and that Test, including, naturally, his most incredible display of all, when, just days after stepping down as captain, he smashed 149 not out to give England a sniff of the most unlikely of victories at Headingley in 1981 (by then I was off Opal Fruits and on to Lambert & Butlers).

Anyone of a certain age will remember Beefy's final moments as England skipper. In the second Test at Lord's, with England already 1–0 down in that six-match 1981 Ashes series, he was bowled behind his legs by Aussie spinner Ray Bright for a first-ball duck, thereby bagging a pair. He walked back into the Lord's pavilion to the silence of the MCC members, most of whom were suddenly so engrossed in their *Daily Telegraph* that they couldn't even look him in the eye. His own form seemingly suffering under the weight of the captaincy, Beefy resigned the position and the selectors – I'm assuming via a messenger on a white charger – sent for Mike Brearley. Beefy's predecessor already had a decent record against the old foe. In 1977, England had cruised to a 3–0 victory, before heading Down Under in 1978–79 and smashing the Aussies 5–1. Australia were, however, underpowered during those series, several key players

191

having jumped ship to enjoy the riches of Kerry Packer's World Series Cricket. By 1981, however, Australian Test cricket had recovered. Even with Brears at the helm, wrestling control of the series away from an Aussie team brimming in confidence looked virtually impossible. And yet three Tests later England had an unassailable 3–1 lead and everyone was wondering just what all the fuss was about.

Key to that recovery was Brears' relationship with Beefy. While they were very different people, one an intellectual, the other a larger-than-life, heart-on-the-sleeve, all-rounder, the two had always clicked. Beefy appreciated Brears' cricketing knowhow, while, for his part, the Middlesex man knew what buttons to push to make Beefy tick. If he wanted him to run uphill into the wind, for example, he might say, 'You'll not be wanting to bowl from that end, will you Ian?' Beefy would have the ball off him in a nanosecond. Same if Brears wanted him to bowl a longer spell. 'I'll give you a rest in a minute, Ian. I can see you're tired.' Cue five more overs at full pelt. I was similar in some ways, except often I'd create my own mind-games, getting a bit of needle going with a batsman perhaps, or grumbling at an umpire. I didn't want to be out there just going through the motions. I always performed better when I had a little something to get me going. But there was more to Beefy and Brears than just psychology. Between them was an underlying trust, a knowledge that, whatever the situation, they'd work 100 per cent to help one another. In 1981, that meant match-winning efforts by Beefy at Headingley, Edgbaston (5–11), and Old Trafford (118). Would any of it have happened under another captain? I suppose we'll never know, but somehow it seems unlikely.

Having, like pretty much every other kid, worshipped Beefy, imagine how I felt when we were both given a call-up for the final Test against the West Indies at The Oval in 1991. Beefy turned up for that match in a cowboy hat smoking a cigar. I wouldn't have wanted it any other way. He'd have gone out to bat like that if it had been up to me. Straightaway, I understood why he was so gifted at carrying people with him. He wasn't bothered that England had been heavily beaten in the previous two Tests. He wasn't interested in the machinations of the dressing room, little bits of internal politics, people looking to save their own spot. His attitude was simple. 'I'm back! Let's get out there, enjoy ourselves, and beat them!' In an instant, he burst the tension. It was as if people had forgotten that playing for England should be, above everything else, bloody great fun.

For me especially, as someone who recoiled at the then England hierarchy's view that constant training and exercise was the key to success, Beefy was a huge dose of fresh air – the ultimate in showing that you don't have to be that person running 50 laps of the ground in the rain to make a difference. In the heat of the action, he could rely on skill and experience to read situations and react. He did still work on his game, but it was his sheer enthusiasm for life and cricket that made him an unstoppable force. His contribution to that Oval Test – 35 runs and three wickets – wasn't his greatest, but he did so much to give everyone in that team a mentality that allowed them to win and salvage a draw from the series.

A few months later, the 1992 World Cup might have been Beefy's swansong, but he still had that unbelievable presence. Every ground he entered he did so with a certain stride. Everyone in the vicinity stopped talking and just watched. Beefy didn't need to walk round anyone, the way just parted for him. The doorman would greet him with a reverential 'Mr Botham' and in he'd go. When the rest of us climbed off the bus any degree of reverence had totally vanished. 'You need me to hold the door? Hold it yourself, ya Pommie bastard!' Beefy, in every way, was on another level. Just look at his hair. What a barnet that was, a proper big flowing mullet. And then the 'tache as well. Wow! Mullet and 'tache is rarely a marriage made in heaven but he pulled the combination off with aplomb. I've never been a 'tache man but I had long hair a few times and it never looked anywhere near as good as Beefy's. Then again, there was no planning involved with mine. Other than what had happened to it when pressed against my pillow for several hours, it was rarely what you might call 'styled'. It just sort of happened, which, in many ways, really should be the title of my autobiography.

Himself no stranger to the mullet, Jeff Thomson once opined that Beefy would make a great Aussie, and he was absolutely right. Aussies respect people who do well against them – so long as they're of a certain larrikin nature. Beefy's the perfect example. They looked at him at Headingley, blithely smashing Terry Alderman, as Richie Benaud put it, 'into the confectionery stall and out again', and thought, 'He does what he wants! He's basically one of us!' That was unlikely to be their attitude to, say, the legendarily snail-paced Chris Tavare, when, at Perth in 1982, he made nine runs in two hours and seven minutes. I think Beefy saw a bit of himself in the Aussies too. He was the staunchest of competitors on the pitch but loved nothing more than having a few beers with the big characters he so admired, like Dennis Lillee, Allan Border and big Merv. While Beefy and I indubitably share the same larrikin DNA, drinking with the opposition was something I never quite got the hang of. No matter how much I tried I could never bring myself to forget the fact that these blokes now offering me a Castlemaine XXXX had been calling me a Pommie **** and trying to knock my head off for the past five days.

I'm so pleased I managed to play with Beefy; so pleased I managed to experience what it was to be in his orbit and be swept along by his sheer love of life. To go from sitting there on the sofa as a kid, little dreams of being a cricketer spinning round in my head – 'I wouldn't mind being like Botham!' – to starting out in cricket, and then wondering if I might one day play for England alongside the great man himself, and then it actually happening, was pretty special. The biggest box, well and truly ticked.

'Don't look back. Don't have regrets.' That was Beefy's big thing. Which is precisely why, finding myself alone in the dressing room when we played our only other Test together, against Sri Lanka, at Lord's, I spotted an unmissable opportunity to cut the toes off his socks. Playing a prank on one of my all-time idols – who'd have thought? I watched as he emerged from the shower, took a sock, silk I seem to remember, fresh from the worm, and pulled it over his freshly-talced foot. And there it went – straight up his leg. Lovely work Tuffers.

I didn't laugh. He'd have had me off the balcony.

36 ASHES TESTS

Wickets: 148
Best Bowling: 6–78
Avg: 27.65
Five-wicket Innings: 9
Ten-wicket Matches: 2

Runs: 1,673
Highest Score: 149 not out
Avg: 29.35
Hundreds: 4
Fifties: 6

30

MITCHELL JOHNSON

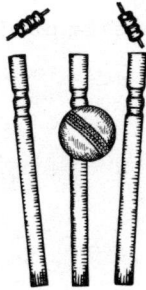

With one of the greatest comebacks in Ashes cricket, Mitchell Johnson left his detractors eating their words.

'He bowls to the left, he bowls to the right, that Mitchell Johnson, his bowling is s****.' It's the Abba lyric that never was. Rather this was the ditty that rang around English cricket grounds in 2009. Sports fans don't hold back sometimes. I should know. The very first time I fielded at the MCG a kindly soul enquired, 'Heh, Tufnell! Any chance you could lend me your brain, I'm building an idiot.' How far down the line he's got with that project in the subsequent 35 years I'm unsure. Maybe he's a contender for the 'View From The Boundary' interview on *TMS*.

Aussie paceman Mitchell was subject to endless jeers on that 2009 tour, his first experience of Ashes cricket. By his own admission he'd lost his radar. Ashes crowds can be unforgiving. As a bowler especially there's no hiding place. Play a terrible shot as a batsman and you're back in the pavilion. For a bowler, you can fire a ball down the legside for four wides, be struck by panic, and still have five more deliveries to get through. And then you've got to collect your cap off the ump and go and field on the fence. While cricket grounds have introduced family sections, party areas, that kind of thing, they have yet to designate a stand for the sympathetic. And so, there you stand, a human coconut shy. But don't worry, there might only be four more Tests.

As a cricketer, when external factors start affecting your game, it's tough. Very late in my career – in fact so late for it to be as bemusing as it was ridiculous – I lost my run-up. I don't mean overstepped a couple of times. I mean totally forgot something that had been absolute second nature to me for the best part of 20 years. Did I take 10 paces? Twelve? Thirteen? Which foot did I set off on? I had no earthly idea. Desperately, I tried to get it back. Derek Randall used to wear his pads around the house to get them match-ready. I'd be hopping and skipping from the bedroom to the bathroom and back again. I'll be honest, it was a factor in me giving up. Losing my run-up felt like a very good hint that my brain was crying out for a rest from constantly thinking about projecting a ball 22 yards towards a bloke who wanted nothing more than to smash me out the ground. In the end I went and sat in a jungle and ate a few witchetty grubs instead.

As an ex-player, you never take pleasure in a cricketer having a rough trot. Like any pro, Mitchell Johnson would have worked hard for years to get his seat on the plane. As he left the ground at Sydney it would have been with dreams of becoming an Ashes hero. It's a horrible feeling when the wheel turns the opposite way. While in the following series Down Under, Mitchell gave a glimpse of his potential with nine wickets in a man-of-the-match performance at the WACA, he didn't make the Ashes tour in 2013. However, things were stirring in the six-foot-two-inch Queenslander, not least on his top lip where a bushy growth eerily reminiscent of Dennis Lillee had taken root, appropriately enough since it was Dennis who'd first identified Mitchell's promise as a teenager. Of course, if simply adopting the facial hair of past greats was a shortcut to glory, we'd all be doing it. In my time, half the batting line-up would have walked out to the wicket with the whiskers of WG Grace. But, when England returned to Australia, Mitchell really did seem to possess all the predatory brilliance of his old fan. An abiding image of that series is England's batsmen desperately weaving out of the way of some seriously hostile stuff. At times virtually unplayable, Mitchell grabbed 37 wickets in a 5–0 whitewash. He was man-of-the-match three times and overall man-of-the-series. Finally, putting to bed that Ashes nightmare in 2009, he was then at the heart of both the Aussies' victories, at Lord's and The Oval, in 2015.

Over time, rather than let 2009 defeat him, Mitchell used the experience to push himself forward and become one of the most genuinely fearsome fast bowlers Australia have ever produced. He came to see the stick he got as a compliment, recognition that he was a threat. It just took him a few years to understand what he was all about, get his game in order and turn threat into something more concrete. In the end, the terrace chant that followed him round in 2009 was rendered obsolete. I'm pleased. I spent a little time in Mitchell's company and, like most fearsome fast bowlers, off the field he's a highly pleasant and sensitive bloke.

Strangely, these days I find myself slightly envious of him for having a song, a form of abuse that was never aimed at myself. Should any close harmony singers think of anything that rhymes with 'Tufnell', do please send a cassette.

19 ASHES TESTS

Wickets: 87
Best Bowling: 7–40
Avg: 25.81
Five-wicket Innings: 5
Ten-wicket Matches: 0

Runs: 533
Highest Score: 77
Avg: 19.74
Hundreds: 0
Fifties: 5

31

JONATHAN AGNEW

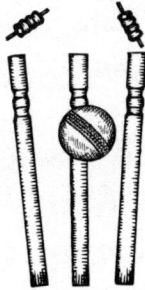

*Aggers might have played only one Ashes Test,
but he's been an epic contributor to countless
series down the years.*

It's the first day of the 2023 Ashes. I spring out of bed – not something that happens a lot – full of anticipation. I open the hotel curtains. Sunny, but not too hot. Perfect. I head down for a spot of breakfast. That's the great thing about being a commentator rather than a player. You don't feel sick when the alarm goes off because it's day three and the opposition are 600–4. I eat my breakfast lovely nowadays. I couldn't get anything down when I played. Back up to my room, comb the old barnet, and I'm out of the hotel quickly. I stop on the steps. *It's half past nine on a weekday and I'm more excited than*

I've ever been! Parking up at Edgbaston, there are people everywhere.

Some are asking questions: 'All right Tuffers? What do you think's going to happen? What do you think the team will be? Do we have a chance?' Others are simply buzzing, really up for it. 'Come on, Phil! We can do this!' I find myself joining in. 'You're right! We can! Come on!!!' I'm not a cricket geek by any means but I can't get enough of this great Ashes morning. It's like I'm actually playing. I have to remind myself to go to the media centre and not the pavilion.

I walk in and there he is – Aggers. The man who brings the Ashes to life. When it comes to *Test Match Special*'s crew of commentators and summarisers he's basically our leader. There's no-one better suited to encapsulate the fever-pitch excitement we're experiencing in the ground and broadcast it down the microphone so that the listeners really can imagine they're here.

The programme goes on air half an hour before the start of play. As ever, on the first morning of an Ashes series, the discussion is all about who'll be the key players, how the series will unfold. But this time there's an added edge. We're in the sparkling new era of Bazball. No-one really knows if this super-aggressive form of cricket is right for a contest as huge and competitive as the Ashes.

England win the toss and elect to bat. Aggers interviews the captains and makes his way back to the commentary box. He takes his position at the mic and I shuffle in alongside him. We watch Pat Cummins prepare to bowl to Zak Crawley.

'Here we go,' says Aggers, 'the first ball of the Ashes . . . AND HE'S HIT IT THROUGH EXTRA COVER FOR FOUR!' The place goes absolutely wild. The noise is unbelievable. Like everyone else in the stadium I erupt from my seat. I've seen a lot of cricket. I played for a long time and have commentated for even longer. But this is absolutely electrifying. And because of the man in the seat next to me, every single listener feels like they too have been plugged in at the mains.

That first ball at Edgbaston will forever be up there with my all-time favourite *TMS* moments. I'll go further – my favourite moment in cricket full-stop. And every time I think of it, Aggers' bellow, fuelled by his own unbridled enthusiasm, his own genuine love of the game, comes to mind. Just the best commentary. Seeing Zac Crawley smack Pat Cummins for four off the opening delivery of an Ashes series is one thing – to put the thrill of it into words and get that across to everyone at home before the ball has even hit the boundary rope is entirely another. Aggers is unparalleled on an occasion like that. He always gets the right tone. I wasn't working on the Headingley Test in 2019 when Ben Stokes dragged England back from the brink with one of the greatest innings of all time, but when Pat Cummins came running in to the all-rounder with one run needed for the most unlikely of wins, and Aggers went, 'He bowls to Stokes – WHO HAMMERS IT FOR FOUR!' the hairs on the back of my neck were standing up like 500 Post Office Towers. Because it came from the heart. As a commentator, you watch a Test match intently. You see it ebb and flow for as long as five days. So when those big moments come you do feel properly invested in them. For Aggers, his own tension was released along with everyone else's.

Everyone at *TMS* feels a responsibility to communicate the magnitude of what they've witnessed. You can't just go, 'And that's it, Stokes hits a boundary, he goes to 135, and England have won the game. Cheerio.' But I imagine truly great commentators like Aggers form a picture in their mind's eye. When a milestone is approaching, there must be an element of knowing what to say and how to say it. Aggers' brilliance is that, when the landmark arrives, he can combine his own deep knowledge with a genuine sense of respect and wonder. It's like he has bullet points in his head which he can pluck out and weave into the excitement. It's a very tricky thing and yet he makes it look, and sound, so easy. I've occasionally found myself having to do a bit of ball-by-ball stuff and it's not as easy as you think. Yes, there's that bit where the bowler runs in and the batsman tries to hit it, but then what? I've found myself sat there thinking *S***! What now?* But Aggers fills every void like it's second nature to him.

So natural does he make it look that it's easy to forget the true complexity of what he's doing. His commentary of England winning the World Cup Final in 2019 is the ultimate example of his brilliance. There was so much going on, not only on the pitch in terms of one of the greatest one-day games ever, but, with the match tied after 50 overs, off the pitch as well, with a whole host of bizarre rules and regulations concerning super overs and boundaries scored and what have you. Anyone else would have been reduced to a blubbering mess. Aggers not only took the whole thing in his stride but also managed to transform the total bedlam of those final few balls into a picture of absolute clarity for everyone listening at home. I was either hopping around like a deranged toad or curled up in a corner barely able to watch. And there was my old pal – a portrait of serenity. Well, OK, if you looked closely you might have seen the odd twitch of the knee but nothing else.

I honestly don't think there's a cricketing scenario that could faze Aggers. With a single run needed for England to win the Ashes, and the bowler in his delivery stride, a gang of pigeons could swoop in, remove the square leg umpire, and still Aggers would remain in his seat calmly explaining all to dumbfounded listeners across the globe.

Even in rather less unusual circumstances, like Crawley's blistering boundary at Edgbaston in 2023, if it was me in Aggers' shoes no-one would know what the hell was going on. It'd just be a series of shrieks and 'Bloody hell!' Fortunately, while it's his job to describe the big moments, mine is to react to them, to add a bit of colour to proceedings. Even so I was nervous when I started out, but Aggers very quickly put me at ease. He provides a great base upon which us pundits can build our own reflections. That's what I love about *TMS*. As a player you're so focused, so intent on keeping a cool head, that at times it takes away the enjoyment. But as a summariser you turn up as a free spirit. Yes, there's pressure to be good, to get your thoughts across clearly to the listener, to find that line between being yourself and informing people about what's going on, but at the same time all you're doing is watching a game of cricket with a microphone.

It's no exaggeration to say I feel honoured to be part of *TMS*. The sound of those voices – the likes of John Arlott, Brian Johnston, Fred Trueman – coming out of the car radio was essentially the first time I encountered cricket. My family had *TMS* on all summer. It was the backdrop to my childhood. We'd be on a day trip to the seaside. I'd be sat there sliding around on the leather car seats in my shorts, nursing my bucket and spade and rubber ring, and in the background would be these wonderful voices talking about this strange game. I was almost transfixed by it, and I know I'm far from alone in feeling like that. Many people have told me how the *TMS* commentary on the Ashes in Australia is one of their favourite childhood memories – snuggled under the covers, middle of winter, with a little transistor radio, signal coming and going, listening to what's happening all those thousands of miles away. Some actually wish *TMS* was still on longwave so they could indulge in the nostalgia of the reception going crackly and fuzzy every now and then.

Covid was a particular reminder of just how much *TMS* means to people. Loads of listeners would email in, thanking us for bringing just that little bit of normality into what felt like a very unpredictable world. Easy to forget how alone some felt at that time. They'd tell us how listening to the cricket, having these friendly voices they knew so well come into their homes, made them feel so emotional that they'd actually cry.

Other times, people have revealed how they've been sat with a loved-one during their last moments in hospital only for them to ask for the cricket to be put on the radio. There's a comfort in *TMS* that should never be underestimated. We just turn up on a glorious sunny day at Trent Bridge or wherever, mucking about, having fun, but then you hear people's stories about what *TMS* means to them and you realise that actually you're doing a little bit more than that. *TMS* has saved marriages. We've been at weddings, funerals, everywhere. There are people who find what we do an absolute lifeline. We are in some small way affecting people's lives. Reflect on that and it makes you feel very humble.

I'm very lucky at *TMS* to work with people who I like but who are also so, so good at what they do. When your career ends you wonder whether that's going to be it for cricketing memories, and yet I've had another two decades' worth and counting. Aggers has been at the epicentre of so many of those incredible moments, no more so than during some epic Ashes Tests. Sat next to him as he describes those events has given me goose-bumps more times than I care to mention. In fact, just writing about it is making them stand up again!

It's a real privilege to be with Aggers in that commentary box, and everyone on *TMS* feels the same.

What he does is a gift. An absolute gift. And we're all incredibly lucky to be on the receiving end.

'AND HE'S HIT IT THROUGH EXTRA COVER FOR FOUR!' Love it!

1 ASHES TEST

Wickets: 0
Best Bowling: 0–99

Runs: 2
Highest Score: 2 not out

32.

STEVE SMITH

He's a Bradman for the modern era, but Steve Smith's fidgety energy has occasionally had me wishing my seat in the commentary box faced the other way.

Steve Smith is just . . . just . . . so . . . so . . . Aussie. His trousers are flappy, his pads don't quite fit, the baggy green is a bit faded (and worn at a jaunty angle). And that's exactly how he likes it. The reason why the bloke's got a slightly weathered appearance about him is because of the hours he's spent out in the middle making runs. Steve Smith is one of those cricketers who you just know revels in the discomfort of a long innings. He enjoys the graft, getting hot, sweat filling his helmet, great streams of it running down his back. One suspects that nothing would give this fella greater pleasure than to get so dehydrated, so mentally fatigued, that he vomited at the wicket. For a bloke whose entire raison d'être is occupancy of the crease, crushing the opposition beneath the weight of relentless run accrual, it would be a whole new level of Ashes exultation.

Let's be honest, as an England supporter, your heart sinks when Smithy emerges, already dishevelled, from the pavilion. In 2019, it really did feel that every time he strode to the wicket he was going to get a ton. That's because he pretty much did. In the first Test, at Edgbaston, he made 144 and 142. In the second, at Lord's, he accrued 92, missing the second innings and the next match after being struck by a bouncer from Jofra Archer. Back in style for the fourth Test, at Manchester, he knocked up a mammoth 211 and 82, before making 80 and, shockingly, a mere 23, at The Oval.

Perhaps the pain of Smithy's presence would be lessened were he a little more pleasing on the eye. I've got a lot of admiration for the bloke as a run-scorer, but watching him accrue hour after hour, with all his little twitches, touching his pads, his shoulder, his head, his arms, added on to his batting ticks, the exaggerated leaves, isn't necessarily how you want to spend six hours in the commentary box. With Smithy, it's rare that you get to salivate over a gloriously executed cover drive. Instead you find yourself searching for adjectives to describe his craft, his determination, his mental tightness, his never-ending willingness to wear an opposition down. I'm just so glad he wasn't around when I was playing. He'd have driven me mad as a bowler. Give me Brian Lara any day of the week. At least he looked good while he was killing you. Smithy, on the other hand, inflicts pain in the ugliest of ways. I often think bowling at him must be like being stabbed to death with a spoon. I'd be pleading for the dagger. 'Please, Smithy, just do it! Put me out of my misery!'

For sheer unorthodoxy that works, Smithy would bring to mind my old Middlesex colleague John Carr. At the crease, Carrsy (we're sportspeople, we're good at inane nicknames) would actually stand facing point with both feet positioned towards the bowler. To the casual observer it looked like he was playing French, not first-class, cricket. And yet he was hugely destructive, hitting the best bowlers through midwicket with a straight bat. When coaches tell batters to play the ball in the 'V', they mean mid-on to mid-off. Carrsy's 'V' was mid-on to square leg. Once he got in, he could smoke disorientated bowlers all over the place. In fact, in 1994, he had a run of seven scores, including two fifties, three tons and one double century, which saw him finish above Brian Lara in the averages despite that being the season when Brian scored 501 not out.

The success of Carrsy and Smithy just goes to show how these sorts of players – tricky, unconventional, virtual one-offs – are incredibly difficult to play against. But, like a quirky old car you might tinker with in the garage, they're also prone to the occasional malfunction. The problem is it only takes one cog to go just a little awry for the whole machine to start to misfire, which is why the vast majority of batters go for something a little more reliable. A Ford Mondeo rather than an E-Type Jag. Thankfully for Smithy, and unfortunately for England, while he has started nicking off a bit, or walking across his stumps and getting hit on the pad, he's yet to find himself at the side of the A1 on the phone to the RAC. I've never looked under his bonnet, but his pistons, cylinder head and big end all seem in pretty good condition. One assumes he drinks Castrol GTX rather than Foster's.

In 2019 especially, all those moving parts, those twitches, those flicks of the shoulder, those touches of the collar, were in perfect sync. England quite literally had no idea how to get him out. Not a chink in that armour. Nothing. Again and again he dismantled the bowling attack. And that's the thing – when these highly unusual players get it right, all you can really do as a skipper is scratch your head. Your plan's in action, your field's set right, the bowler's sending down good balls, but none of it seems to apply to this nightmare of a bloke who's stood there repelling everything you've got. That's tricky. Very tricky indeed.

It says everything that Smithy is considered the best Australian batsman since Don Bradman. His Test record, averaging a ton pretty much every three games is simply ridiculous. Naturally, the majority of those have come against England.

Smithy, could you leave it out, mate, please. Or at least, if I'm going to have to spend multiple more hours watching you batting, pretty things up a little bit. You're clearly a bloke who can adapt to any situation. How about spending the twilight years of your career pretending to be David Gower?

37 ASHES TESTS (TO OCT 2025)

Runs: 3,417
Highest Score: 239
Avg: 56.01
Hundreds: 12
Fifties: 13

Wickets: 7
Best Bowling: 3–18
Avg: 53.85

33.

STUART BROAD

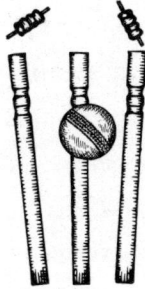

A supreme entertainer, the ultimate twinkle-in-the-eye cricketer, Broady's given me some of my most treasured Ashes moments.

Stuart Broad was destined for Ashes greatness from the get-go. While most kids were watching *Postman Pat*, he was sat in front of *On Top Down Under* (be careful when you Google that) and *The Ashes: Victory in Australia* videos which told the tale of England's wonder tour of 1986–87. This might sound a bit random until you remember Stuart's dad Chris reigned supreme on that trip, scoring tons in three successive Tests.

Chris would probably have played more for England had he not smashed his stumps to the ground in the wake of being bowled by Steve Waugh after another century in the Bicentenary

Test at Sydney in 1988. This sort of thing was much frowned upon by the English powers-that-be and, presumably to the relief of Australians everywhere, Chris's Test career ended soon after. However, if Aussies thought that was it for uncompromising Poms named Broad, they were much mistaken. Chewing on his rusk back in Nottingham was a new nemesis. And it didn't take long for Stuart to become the man the Aussies loved to hate. If winding up Australians was an Olympic sport then Stuart Broad would need a medal table all of his own. Trent Bridge, in the first Test of 2013, is a classic example. It was here that Stuart edged a delivery from slow left-arm spinner Ashton Agar via wicketkeeper Brad Haddin's gloves into the hands of Australian captain Michael Clarke at first slip. In the whole of Nottingham-shire, only umpire Aleem Dar hadn't seen the deflection and the Aussies, having used up all their reviews, could do nothing but seethe. Stuart made the most of his great escape by adding another 28 runs. When England eventually won the Test by a super-tight margin of 14 runs, his decision to stay put at the crease was dressed up by a rabid Aussie press as him cheating the tourists out of a victory. Because, of course, Australians are well known for their penchant for walking!

To solve the problem of the Ashes cycle clashing constantly with the World Cup, the subsequent series in Australia was brought forward a year. That meant ten Tests in a row. And when England headed south in the autumn, the Aussies could taste blood. Stuart Broad's blood. Traditionally, the first Test Down Under is staged in Brisbane, and it was there that the city's news-paper, the *Courier-Mail*, declared, by way of retribution for Stuart, as they put it, 'sullying the gentlemen's game', that they would deny his existence by blanking him out of photographs and referring to him not by name but as the '27-year-old English medium pace bowler' or, alternatively, 'Stuart Fraud'. With England in the field, Stuart was faced with banks of Aussie fans sporting T-shirts bearing the legend, 'Stuart Broad is a Sh*t Bloke' and bellowing very uncomplimentary songs. If they thought any of this was going to remotely bother Stuart, they were very sadly mistaken. Stuart was made for the drama of Ashes cricket. At the end of the first day's play at the Gabba he marched into the press conference with a five-fer under his belt and a copy of the *Courier-Mail* under his arm. One of the great off-field Ashes moments, it was a fantastic way of puncturing a situation which was all a bit silly and showing that he was going to take any gyp that came his way with a smile. He even reckoned he'd been singing along with crowd renditions of 'Broad is a W*****,' whistling the tune at the end of his mark.

Now he's retired, I bump into Stuart a lot in the media centre and totally get that slightly mischievous element of his character. He's a really funny chap. Dry as anything. I also know he'd have seen having the Australian nation on his back only as the biggest of compliments, the clearest indication that he was doing a good job. He was never going to shy away from it, which in any case would have been impossible. All England players have to get used to getting stick wherever they go in Australia, but for Stuart that stick was 100 times worse, and was actually stirred up by the Aussie coach Darren Lehmann who, after Trent Bridge, declared that he hoped 'the Australian public give it to him for the whole summer' when the Ashes moved Down Under. It was an incredible outburst. People couldn't believe what Lehmann was saying. 'Hang on. What? He's put a hit out on Stuart Broad?' You have to be a particular sort of character to deal with that sort of thing. But then only Stuart could edge the ball to slip off a spinner and then stand it out. 'What? Nick it? No, don't think so. I'm going nowhere pal.' Only he could carry that off. Plenty of other people would have just melted in that situation. Not Stuart.

Thankfully, I was never stood at the other end when Stuart was firing them down, but nevertheless he very nearly caused my demise at the next Trent Bridge Ashes Test in 2015. I barely had time to draw breath when he took five wickets in 19 balls, part of a spell of 8–15 in 9.3 overs as the Aussies were sent packing for 60 in just 111 balls. Nothing can prepare you for that sort of craziness. I was on commentary with Blowers, whose excitement appeared to travel from his brain, down through his body, and straight into his right leg which was suddenly acting like it was plugged in to the mains, going like the clappers thumping against the desk. What you need in a situation like that is a supremely ordered mind. I'm not entirely sure Blowers or myself qualify for that description. Confusion reigned. 'What's happening now? Who's coming in next? What day is it? Who am I? What's my name?' It was like Piccadilly Circus out there. Blowers' usual conversational topics – buses and pigeons – didn't get a look-in. He just kept saying the same thing over and over again. 'And he's gone!' It was the quickest half hour of my life. I aged 10 years in 30 minutes. Trent Bridge was absolutely jumping. The reason it was like that was because it was the Aussies. And then on top of that it was Stuart Broad! I mean, 8–15! For crying out loud! You don't get 8–15 against the Aussies on your own ground, in front of your own fans – and your dad. It's outrageous! There's a great photo of Stuart after one of his wickets where he's got his hands in front of his mouth, eyes wide, like he simply can't believe what's happening. In that moment, he's basically having an out-of-body experience. It's his day of all days and it's happening against the Aussies in his own backyard.

Stuart was an incredible player, a contestant for any all-time Ashes eleven, one because of his skill and two because of just how much he loved the fight. A player for the biggest of the big occasions, it says everything for his ability to make things happen that, at The Oval in 2023, he not only hit his final delivery in Test cricket for six but took a wicket with his last ball to win the match. The chances of that happening are infinitesimally tiny, and yet, weird as it sounds, because it was Stuart it felt like the most natural thing possible. Sometimes when you're commentating, you get a feeling that something unusual is going to happen. The opposite of the commentators' curse, whereby you make a statement or prediction only for it to immediately collapse around your ears, there are times when you'd put your house on a certain eventuality. You've seen so much cricket over such a long time that it almost feels like you're directing proceedings. I'm not saying we're up there in the *TMS* box pushing chess pieces around like Greek gods in some old film. We're not Zeus, not even Aggers. But you can definitely get a strong inkling that something remarkable is about to happen.

That hunch was compounded, one by it being Ashes cricket, two by it being Stuart Broad, and three by it being his final game. More than once in that commentary box someone said, 'I bet he gets the last wicket,' or 'I bet he does something silly with the bat.' Nothing qualified as 'unbelievable'. It's why Stuart is one of my favourite-ever England cricketers. When he was around there was always something happening, a combination of phenomenal talent and arch devilment. I loved it that whenever he was left out of the team he'd make his unhappiness known. He didn't just sit back and take it. He had too much individuality, too much spark, to be media trained, to meekly toe the line. He's always had something to say, and if it pricked the Aussies then all the better. After England lost 4–0 in Australia in 2021–22, Stuart declared that the result didn't count as Covid restrictions meant the series wasn't real. 'I've written it off as a void series,' he opined. Once again, the Aussies were left spluttering in their Foster's.

It was a shame for Stuart that he got walloped in the gob, top-edging a bouncer from India paceman Varun Aaron through the grille of his helmet at Old Trafford in 2014, leaving him with a damaged nose and two black eyes. The mental scars were slow to heal, but even so he'd go out and give it a good clout. When Jonny Bairstow was controversially stumped by Alex Carey at Lord's, Stuart was the perfect bloke to have in next. He absolutely thrived on a bit of confrontation. The first thing he did when he got to the wicket was look Carey square in the eye and tell him, 'That's all you'll ever be remembered for.' Then, whenever he left his crease, he engaged in some supremely over-the-top placement of his bat back over the line to announce to the Aussies that he was very definitely 'in'. I loved all that – because I'd have done exactly the same, if not more. Stuart thought it was bang out of order what the Aussies had done, and, being an emotional bloke, was going to let them know. He couldn't match Ben Stokes with the bat but he could match him all the way in his determination to stick it back to the Aussies. Together they added 108 runs and took England tantalisingly near what would surely have been the most satisfying Ashes win of all time.

The beauty of Stuart was that he understood that sport is theatre. He had a real sense of occasion. You'd see him, at the end of his mark, waving his hands, whipping up the crowd. Spectators pay a lot of money to watch Test cricket and Stuart was brilliant at making them feel part of the action. He was our version of Warney, always making something happen. Look at what he did with the switching of the bails during the fifth Test of 2023 when the Aussie first innings had stagnated, Marnus Labuschagne taking root with just nine runs off 81 balls. Before the fifth ball of a Mark Wood over he approached Labuschagne's end and swapped the bails round. Next ball, Labuschagne nicked off and was caught at first slip. OK, swapping bails round can't in itself materially affect a Test match, but maybe it interrupted Labuschagne's thought process, twisted his melon just enough, to make that tiny bit of difference. When Stuart did the same trick at the bowler's end immediately before having Todd Murphy caught behind, so ending a frustrating partnership holding up England's victory charge, people were talking of him like he had mystical powers. Perhaps this was why he was retiring – he'd succumbed to a new career in soothsaying. Mystic Stuart, reading palms and predicting Saturday night's Lotto balls.

I'm not sure Stuart expected much from his bail-swapping, but you're in the field a long time and so anything that keeps your mind active is worth thinking about. The bail-swap was a great way of sparking energy in the team, a prod of the fire when the embers were just starting to die. I've been part of teams which used codewords to reinvigorate the team in the field. You'd just be dozing off at long leg when someone would shout 'Onions!'. It worked as well, sometimes for upwards of 10 seconds. On my first Ashes tour I recall David Gower offering a similar solution to our habit of losing a bit of oomph in the field when the Aussies were on top for long periods. It might have gone down better with the skipper, Graham Gooch, had David not suggested a cry of the word 'Shovel!'. Possibly this was to suggest an element of 'digging in', but by then Gooch and Gower's relationship had soured to the point that I expect the only shovel Gooch was interested in was one which he could clunk David on the head with.

The bail-switching was all good fun but Stuart didn't need to resort to tricks to trouble the Aussies. Over the course of 40 Ashes Tests, he took 153 wickets at an average of 28.96 with eight five-fers and one ten-fer. His top three 'bunnies' in Test cricket are all Aussies – and great ones at that. He snared Michael Clarke and Steve Smith 11 times each, and had David Warner on a string, dismissing him 17 times. During Warner's final Ashes in 2023, even he admitted he was singing the Barmy Army chant 'Broady's going to get you!' in his head.

Stuart Broad – from the heart mate, thanks for the entertainment.

40 ASHES TESTS

Wickets: 153
Best Bowling: 8–15
Avg: 28.96
Five-wicket Innings: 8
Ten-wicket Matches: 1

Runs: 1,019
Highest Score: 65
Avg: 18.87
Hundreds: 0
Fifties: 4

34.

MARK WAUGH

*Mark was stylish, but every now and again
I'd rock up and ruffle his feathers.*

Mark Waugh was my bunny. I got him out seven times in Ashes Tests, including for 99 at Lord's. Even if I say so myself, that's not a bad tally against a batsman widely considered one of the best to have played the game. Really, I should have kept him in a hutch, although given the chance he'd definitely have had my finger off.

There was a bit of niggle between me and Mark, based, I think, more around county than country. Mark was Essex's overseas player for a while. It didn't take him long to cotton on to the rivalry with us boys down the road at Middlesex and so inevitably we had a good few tussles in the Championship. Lurking in the background, however, were our Ashes encounters, a slight element of needle dating back to the time I got him out – or he got himself out – playing a terrible reverse sweep, dragging the ball on to his stumps, at Brisbane in 1994. After that, the more we played the more I could see that I narked him. It happens – no matter who you are or how good you are there's always someone who gets under your skin. Mark was a fabulous player of spin but never quite fathomed me going over the wicket to him. It was like I'd found this little route into his psyche, this way to keep him quiet, and he didn't like it. When I got him out twice at The Oval in 1997, I really could see how pissed off he was. Before the game he'd spouted off in the papers about how he was going to give me a bit of a hiding. As it turned out he scored the grand total of 20 runs. He never said it, but the words, 'You bastard!' were written all over his face. But I wasn't there to serve it up so he could hit me around, although, in the interests of fairness, I should point out that he did get more than a few runs off me throughout his career. I should also point out that I do get on very well with him now. Fellow broadcasters, we've left our Ashes competitiveness behind. We don't saw through each other's chair legs or anything.

I'm glad me and Mark are OK, because he did once save me from the ignominy of collapsing on the pitch. I was in Dhaka after being asked to represent a Rest of the World team in a one-day game against an Asian XI. I was going along OK, actually bagging Sachin Tendulkar and Sourav Ganguly, when suddenly I was totally sideswiped by the climatic conditions. I'm not saying it was warm in Bangladesh but had a pigeon entered the stadium it would have been ready to eat in five seconds. By the time my spell was coming to an end I wasn't so much skipping as wobbling to the wicket. By rights I should have been as red as the ball, but I was actually as white as a sheet. It was at this point that Mark, captaining the Rest of the World, put all thoughts of battles past to the back of his mind and intervened.

'You OK, Tuffers?' I was mumbling incoherently, something about seeing multicoloured animals floating around. Smouldering beneath my skull, it was as if my brain had unilaterally decided to place me in an episode of *The Magic Roundabout.*

'You'd better go and have a sit down, mate,' Mark advised. I was dragged, scarecrow-esque, from the field, spending the next few hours under a cold shower before being placed on the flight home. In times since, I've always had great sympathy for those beached whales you see being sprayed by rescue workers before they re-enter the sea and head back to their pod.

By the time of that one-off game in April 2000, both Mark and I were reaching the end of the line. As with Athers, me and him shared a final Ashes Test at The Oval in 2001. He made 120 as the Aussies racked up 641–4 and we lost by an innings. Essentially, they won the match having lost just 20 per cent of their wickets. It's a mad statistic that should really be a once-in-a-career freak. Sadly not. In that Lord's Test where I snaffled Mark for 99, the Aussies racked up 632–4 in another huge innings win. Chris Lewis and I shared those dismissals. We were both dropped for the next match. Which in its own way says everything about what times were like back then.

Thinking about it, 1993 was the only time I played the Aussies at Lord's. While it would have been nice to have gone back and created some happier memories, I did at least get to say hello to the Queen who came along to meet the teams on the fifth day. I was tempted to ask her for a little advice, whether she thought

I was bowling a little too wide perhaps, or if there was something I could do with the flight. The Queen had, after all, seen a lot of Ashes cricket, often with England in a bit of trouble. In fact, I couldn't help but admire her optimism in scheduling her visit for the fifth day

Mark's appearance in our Oval Ashes farewell gave birth to one of the legendary cricket sledges. When England's Jimmy Ormond arrived at the wicket for his debut innings, Mark's alleged to have asked him, 'Mate, what are you doing out here? There's no way you're good enough to play for England.'

Jimmy's reply? 'Maybe not, but at least I'm the best player in my own family.'

The stats bear Jimmy out. Steve Waugh averaged a full 10 runs more than Mark over the course of his Test career, but really to compare the two is like comparing chalk and cheese. Steve was a grinder. Mark, on the other hand, was one of the most elegant players the Ashes has ever seen.

As players, we might have grated a little, but as a batsman I always knew he was a class act.

He just needed to perfect that reverse sweep.

29 ASHES TESTS

Runs: 2,204
Highest Score: 140
Avg: 50.09
Hundreds: 6
Fifties: 11

Wickets: 14
Best Bowling: 5–40
Avg: 37.07
Five-wicket Innings: 1
Ten-wicket Matches: 0

35.

GRAHAM THORPE

The most talented batsman of his generation,
but more than that the best friend a bloke
could ever have.

People would sometimes ask me a question – 'Who would you
rather have batting for your mortgage, David Gower or Graham
Thorpe?'

Well, if you look at their stats there's actually very little
between them. Their Test career averages and those against
Australia are virtually the same. I think, though, for me, if I'm
honest, Graham's fighting spirit would have me putting my
house on him every time. He was the man for the big occasion.
Which meant he especially relished taking on the Aussies. Yes,
as a Test player you try your best whoever the opposition, but

when it came to Thorpey and Australia, his steeliness was always just that little bit more apparent.

A lot of nuggety players aren't that great to watch, but Thorpey was different. I'll be honest, when I first came up against him in county cricket I thought he was a bit of a grinder. But it didn't take me long to realise he was actually a very intelligent batsman. Every minute he was out there he was working things out, thinking strategically and then backing up his ideas with incredible ability. He'd been like that from the minute he picked up a bat. If my memory serves me correctly he actually started off right-handed before switching round to bamboozle his brothers when they played in the garden. He then told his coach he was sticking with the stance because left-handers have more success!

While that version of events might seem a little unlikely, it sounds about right for Graham because he never stopped thinking about how he could improve himself. From an early age he wanted to play Test-match cricket for England and very quickly realised that if he was going to fulfil that dream he'd need to be able to play a full array of shots, the pull and cut especially. He was incredibly astute in putting a Test-match game together. For him, batting was never going to be 100 per cent natural and flowing and so, very cleverly, he developed a way of becoming the best player he could possibly be. In so doing, he gave England someone who could negotiate any bowler anywhere, be it Shane Warne at Edgbaston or Glenn McGrath at Perth. Such was his class from an early age that no-one was hugely surprised when he began his Test career in 1993 with an Ashes century at Trent Bridge.

While we've become accustomed to players coming into the England ranks and making an immediate impact, back then

Graham was the first to score a hundred on debut in two decades. From that point on he was England's main man. Mark Ramprakash, Nasser Hussain and Graeme Hick were all excellent players, but Thorpey was the one who you always felt was going to get the score, was going to be the glue to hold everything together. Even the selectors felt so. To play 100 Test matches in a time of constant chop and change was unbelievable.

Graham spent his entire Ashes career battling, and often succeeding, against a ruthless Aussie bowling machine. A player of his class didn't deserve constantly to be on the losing side and it was a real shame that he didn't quite manage to hang on until the 2005 Ashes, his final, and 100th Test coming against Bangladesh that same summer. It was a mark of the man that it took a player of Kevin Pietersen's ability to replace him, but even then there was a bit of 'Should we, shouldn't we?' from the selectors. Graham was 35 at that point but still playing well. If anyone could perform against the Aussies it was him. He had the mental resilience not to carry the scars of past defeats.

Graham was a fabulous cricketer, 100 per cent one of the very best I ever played with. He was tough, a fighter, nuggety, which is probably why not just England fans, but Australians, both players and public, had so much time for him. For us tailenders, his ability to fend off the most hostile of attacks meant he was like our defensive line in American Football. 'Keep them out, Thorpey! Protect me! Don't let them get to me!'

But more than anything he achieved as a cricketer, Graham was just a truly wonderful chap. It was utterly devastating in 2024 to hear of his death. Actually, beyond devastating, because I really did love Graham. We roomed together a lot and I counted him as a true and trusted friend, brilliant fun to be around, a great wingman to have on tours. We had some incredible laughs, but at the same time there were occasions I couldn't help but notice a slightly detached look in his eye. I'd be up and down with my mood on tour, as would other players, but with Graham it was slightly different. At times he'd just go off and stare out the window. From time to time, there'd be an element of not quite knowing what was going on in his head, a sort of slight separation that could just pop up out of the blue. It's an absolute tragedy for all who cared so deeply about him that he's no longer around. Difficult to believe and so desperately, desperately, sad.

I count myself fortunate to have so many good memories of my old friend to look back on. I was thinking the other day about how he'd be there almost from the minute the alarm went off. I'd take a bit of waking up most days on tour and I'd need him almost to tell me what was going on. I'd be sat bleary-eyed at the back of the bus. 'So what's happening today, mate?' And he'd be there, 'Well, Cat, we're playing the Aussies so I expect either you'll be having a little bowl or I'll be having a little bat. Or probably, knowing us, a bit of both!' Sounds mad, but touring with England in those days was such a maelstrom, so unpredictable, that it was easy to lose touch with where you were and what was happening. Graham was a calming influence on us all from that point of view. Within minutes, we'd be sat on that bus talking, laughing, about the previous night. Just the best of times with a brilliant, brilliant mate.

That's how it is for everyone who knew Graham. Both as a great, great cricketer and an even better man, he lives on through so many vivid memories. Graham, my old friend, you will never, ever, be forgotten.

16 ASHES TESTS

Runs: 1,235
Highest Score: 138
Avg: 45.74
Hundreds: 3
Fifties: 8

36.

ADAM GILCHRIST

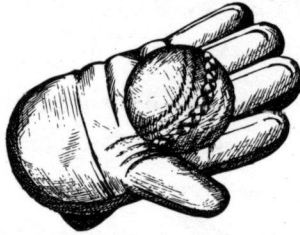

*The whirlwind gloveman was one of the first
players to make the world sit up and see that
Test cricket could be played in a totally different way.*

Revolutions have happened throughout history. Regimes have
been toppled, people cast into the wilderness and heads
removed. And that's just at Yorkshire County Cricket Club.

But has anyone ever ripped up the rulebook quite like Adam
Gilchrist? With his explosive batting, the Aussie wicketkeeper
redefined what Test cricket could be. He was playing Bazball
before the idea was so much as a glint in Brendon McCullum's
eye. One minute the opposition would be sailing serenely along,
everything under control, the next they'd be stood dumbstruck
watching Gilly smash them out of the game. They could be

forgiven for walking straight off the field and directly on to the psychiatrist's couch.

For a long time, wicketkeepers were picked predominantly for their ability with the gloves. If they could snaffle a few runs down the order, all to the good. That began to change through the 1970s and '80s when keepers would more regularly make significant contributions, the likes of Alan Knott and Jack Russell digging England out of holes on many an occasion. But no-one had ever seen a gloveman as pyrotechnic as Gilly. Forget the state of the match, he went out there, got on top and then just kept going. He didn't so much rip up the rulebook as incinerate it. Opposition skippers had never encountered such a player. They didn't know what to do. But I always felt the best way to combat Gilly was to lose by an innings. That way you didn't have to suffer him twice. I lined up against Gilly at The Oval in 2001 and that's exactly what happened. A tactical masterclass by Nasser Hussain, I thought.

By the time of the Perth Test in December 2006, I'm glad to say I was well into retirement, because that was one game where being an ex-England player rather than a current one was very much the preferred position. It was there at the WACA that, coming to the wicket in an admittedly comfortable position, with his team 365–5 in their second innings, Gilly went ballistic in a manner completely unrivalled in the Ashes annals. If England thought the Aussie keeper was motoring when he lamped a half century off just 40 balls, nothing could prepare them for what happened next. Just 17 deliveries later Gilly was raising his bat having battered the fastest ever Ashes century, and the second quickest in Test history, missing West Indies master-blaster Viv Richards' 56-ball record by just one delivery.

As anyone who's played the game will tell you, cricket is fickle. What's often forgotten about Gilly's achievement that day is that, after a first-innings duck, the latest in a pretty rough trot of scores, he was actually so downhearted that he was considering quitting. As so often happens, it was going out second time round with a *Sod it! What have I got to lose?* attitude that freed him up mentally to do what he did.

As much as I admired Gilly's firepower, I couldn't help but feel for the England boys. The temperature that day was almost 40 degrees. To stand there, baking in that heat, being absolutely destroyed, on a Tour which had already been hugely punishing, must have been so, so demoralising. When a batter's really firing it's like being a passenger stuck on a train careering down the tracks out of control. Amid the panic and confusion, all you can hope is that somewhere out of sight someone's inching along the roof intent on dropping into the driver's compartment and pulling on the brake. In this case, England had a helping hand from Ricky Ponting who, once Gilly had reached three figures, promptly declared. Even so, there was no way back. The pummelling had killed off any chance of England winning or saving the game. A day later the Ashes were back in Australian hands. A 5–0 whitewash awaited.

I recall something England coach Duncan Fletcher said about Adam Gilchrist at the end of that Perth encounter. 'He can take the game away from you in an hour, and he had two good hours there.'

Two hours which took the game forward 20 years. Vive la revolution!'

20 ASHES TESTS

Runs: 1,083
Highest Score: 152
Avg: 45.12
Hundreds: 3
Fifties: 6

Wicketkeeping dismissals: 96

37.

NASSER HUSSAIN

*An innovator who used lessons learned
from his own Ashes defeats to ensure future
generations could compete on a level playing field.*

In county cricket you can always tell when an Ashes Test is happening elsewhere. Forget what's going on outside. Everyone in the dressing room is watching TV.

That only happens with the Australians. Any other touring side and it's a quick glance up at the telly before wandering off to see who's in the bar. Nasser's double ton at Edgbaston in 1997 is the perfect example. When those big moments happen in the Ashes, it doesn't matter where you are, it's spellbinding. I didn't play in that game, but in the Middlesex dressing room nobody moved a muscle. People were shouting at the TV, 'Come on Nass!' and I was one of them. Even the disappointment of being dropped from the England set-up didn't change that, because I knew how much it took to beat that Australian side. England had bowled the visitors out for 118 in their first innings, before, thanks to Nasser's 207 and Graham Thorpe's 138, racking up a mammoth 478–9 declared. That was a lead of 360. And still the Aussies wouldn't go away! Any other team would have capitulated under that weight of scoreboard pressure. Not them. Mark Taylor and Greg Blewett both made centuries as the Australians wiped out two-thirds of the deficit with only one wicket down. Forget losing, they were building a platform for the win. In the end, even with their last nine wickets falling for 150, they managed to set England a tricky little victory target of 118. Thankfully, the home side carried their first innings momentum into the second and knocked off the runs for the loss of just one wicket. There's that great moment which every England fan of a certain age will remember when Alec Stewart smacks Shane Warne through cover for four to notch up the winning runs and the crowd spills over the hoardings, a moment of unbridled celebration enhanced by the fact that the victory at Edgbaston came not in a dead rubber, but at the start of a series when the Ashes was still up for grabs.

For the first time in an age – England hadn't led in an Ashes series since 1987 – it felt like we had a genuine chance of securing the urn. Naturally, that wave of optimism didn't last. By the time I was recalled to the side for the sixth and final Test we'd been well and truly hammered, 3–1 down in the series. But that in no way detracts from what Nasser achieved that day in Birmingham. I couldn't have been more delighted for him, and less surprised. Nasser was a real fighter. I'm sure he had the same thoughts as everyone else – *We keep coming up against these boys and it's always so, so hard* – but he was desperate to lay down a marker, to say to the rest of the boys, 'Come on! We can get rid of this scar tissue. It doesn't have to be like this.' And, momentarily at least, he managed to do just that. What a day that was for him. A beautiful sunny Edgbaston. Crowd rocking. Batting with his close mate Thorpey.

There was a time I never really understood the whole 'scarring' theory; this idea that players could subconsciously be nagged at, gnawed at, by the wounds of past defeats. And then I got older and realised I'd got more scars than a wildebeest in a scrap with a cheetah. Part of my initial dubiousness came from the fact I'd always seen every new game as a blank canvas. It didn't matter who we were playing, I'd genuinely start every Test match believing I was going to get a ten-fer and we'd come out on top. But then, thinking about it, I realised that by day two, with the Aussies once again rampant, I was scarred from head to foot. Other players might have been different. Perhaps they carried their scars right from the toss – *Oh s***! It's McGrath!* (Athers) or *Oh s***! It's Slater!* (Andy Caddick) – but for me only once the reality of another dominant Aussie performance had set in would I be overwhelmed by feelings of déja-vu.

The Aussies were seasoned pros when it came to opening up scars. They never let us start well. If they were batting, they had rock solid openers. It felt like they were always 100–1 and never 35–3. If they were bowling, they could chuck the ball to two of the best in the world and one of our boys would be back in the pavilion before we'd got 20 runs on the board. Whoever was number three would then be under pressure, and so on, and so on. Very rarely could we get any impetus at the start of a game.

It always seemed like we were coming from behind, forever trying to work ourselves back into the game. Inevitably, that feeling of being second in the race gets under your skin.

Nasser worked as hard as anyone to rid England of their scar tissue. He helped to build a system, with central contracts at its core, that allowed England to compete. Add in a new wave of players such as Marcus Trescothick, Andrew Strauss, Michael Vaughan, Andrew Flintoff, Matthew Hoggard, Simon Jones and Steve Harmison, all of whom came in with a fresh outlook, and the foundations were set for what happened in 2005. By which time, of course, Nasser himself had gone. Those players who, like him, had suffered in the 1990s would have loved to have had central contracts, to have played with security, not constantly waiting for page 340 to roll round on Ceefax to see if they were in the team. Nasser's desire for change, to create an England team that could compete with the very best, saved future generations that indignity.

It didn't surprise me that Nasser was at the heart of the England revolution. He was always a free thinker. He invited people into his world, welcomed their input, rather than keeping them at arm's length, and understood the value of having different types of personalities in his team. In my case he was happy to go against the grain and say that I was a good tourist, and not just because I kept things interesting off the pitch. It wasn't uncommon for him to ask my opinion on cricketing matters too. If he could find me, I was more than happy to share my thoughts.

I get this does all sound a little like a Nasser love-in, so I'll leave you with one final recollection of the Essex man. During one Ashes Test, Steve Waugh asked a fielder to get in close, right under Nasser's nose. It was then that Ian Healy piped up from behind the stumps. 'Jeez, skip,' he noted, 'that could be anywhere within a three-mile radius.'

Big conk. Great bloke.

23 ASHES TESTS

Runs: 1,581
Highest Score: 207
Avg: 38.56
Hundreds: 2
Fifties: 11

38.

PAT CUMMINS

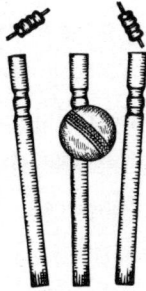

An incredible competitor, Pat hauled his team through the aftermath of 'Sandpapergate' before revealing his own true grit.

Sandpaper isn't a great thing to mention to Aussies. They tend to assume you're referencing the scandal that swamped their national cricket team rather than ascertaining which grade is best suited to taking a layer of varnish off a bedside table.

It was March 2018 when, during the Cape Town Test against South Africa, Cameron Bancroft was spotted by an eagle-eyed TV camera operator rubbing the DIY favourite on the ball. Roughing the leather would help cause deviation in flight. It's strictly against the rules. Hence why you don't see bowlers setting up lathes when they're marking out their run-up.

The upshot of this unseemly incident was the suspension of then captain Steve Smith and vice-captain David Warner, while coach Darren Lehmann announced he'd step down. All in all, 'Sandpapergate' sparked huge outrage. Malcolm Turnbull, Australia's Prime Minister at the time, described it as a 'shocking disappointment'. What Mrs Thatcher thought of England's use of four skippers during the capitulation to Australia in the home series of 1989 is unclear.

While wicketkeeper Tim Paine initially took on the captaincy, overseeing a period of rebuilding and reassessment for Australian cricket, since 2021 it's fallen to Pat Cummins, initially Paine's vice-captain, to really take the team forward and re-establish the baggy green's place at the pinnacle of the global game. I admire him greatly for what he's achieved. I can only imagine how delicate a balance he's had to find between eradicating his side's previous win-at-all-costs shortcomings while still encouraging them to be ruthlessly competitive.

Essentially, after 'Sandpapergate', Pat had to create a friendlier face of Australian cricket, but one which maintained a nuggety edge. There was a time when I thought such a far-reaching rebrand might open up a chink in the Aussies' armour, but I've come to see that's far from the case. They've exhibited time and again, against all the top sides, not just England, that they're still up for a battle. And Pat has led from the front, showing his team that just because he's not sledging the opposition, getting in people's faces, it doesn't mean he's not a strong character. That includes in the dressing room. Finding himself in charge of a team of big personalities, not least Smith and Warner, it has, I'm sure, taken strength and courage for Pat to impose his way. While alongside Mitchell Starc, Josh Hazlewood and Nathan Lyon, Pat had already revealed himself an absolute bedrock of Australia's bowling success, he's shown himself to have steel as a leader as well. I can't praise the bloke enough for what he's done to resurrect that shattered Australian side and bring them all together.

The late great Shane Warne once said to me, 'Pat Cummins will be one of the best there's ever been.' He's been proven exactly right in so many ways. While Pat's a fantastic bowler, another of those very nice chaps who steams in at 90 mph and tries to knock your head off, he's so much more than that. From his position at the top of the Australian game he's shown that you can be a good guy in your own right without it being to the detriment of your competitiveness as a cricketer. Initially I thought the New South Wales man a bit of a defensive captain, again an antidote to the aggression of previous eras, but actually he's stood toe to toe with other teams and pushed a really positive style of cricket.

The bloke's definitely got bottle. He must have known the furore it would cause when he encouraged Alex Carey to have a shy at the stumps when Jonny Bairstow was out of his ground at Lord's. But he was happy – actually, more than that – he wanted – to be in the thick of it for his team. As the previous Test at Edgbaston drew to a close, Australia appeared doomed to defeat, 55 runs short of their target with just two wickets remaining. And then Pat clubbed two sixes in a desperately-needed 44 not out. The photo of him chucking his bat in the air after hitting the winning boundary is one of the great Ashes images. That's someone who knows what it's like to be on the wrong end of a close finish. Pat had, after all, watched helplessly as Ben Stokes smashed him to the boundary to grab England the most unlikely of victories at Headingley on his previous Ashes tour.

When questioned about the revenge factor, his response was the excellent, 'No idea what you're talking about mate!' Saying everything while saying nothing. Like it.

Without Pat's inventiveness and effort, you really do have to question whether, after those first two Tests of the 2023 series, Australia would have found themselves 2–0 down rather than 2–0 up. And all with barely a hair out of place. I have to say, Pat's such a very good-looking chap. I don't know what's in the water in the Blue Mountains where he grew up but he's the very antithesis of the gnarled old Aussie skippers who I played against. If ever he wants to double-up for some modelling work he knows where to find me. When's the next Screwfix catalogue out?

19 ASHES TESTS (TO OCT 2025)

Wickets: 91
Best Bowling: 6–91
Avg: 24.10
Five-wicket Innings: 2
Ten-wicket Matches: 0

Runs: 471
Highest Score: 44 not out
Avg: 20.47

39.

BEN STOKES

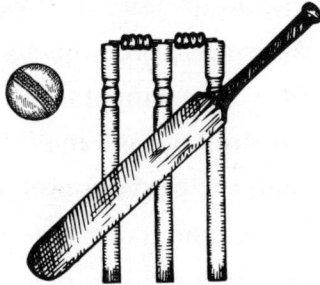

*Light the fuse and stand well back! Ben Stokes
has been responsible for the dynamite moments
of recent Ashes encounters.*

Ben Stokes is an absolute one-off, best remembered for the
jaw-dropping innings he played at Headingley in 2019, slowly
dragging England off the floor and then accelerating and accelerating to the point where somehow he managed to pull off
perhaps the most audacious victory in the history of English Test
cricket. Ben's 135 not out is perhaps the greatest knock most of
us will ever see. I say 'perhaps' because personally I'd put his
155 at Lord's in 2023 right up there alongside it. There's plenty
of people who'd like to do something like that – 'Right, you've
just run my mate Jonny out, I'm going to make you regret it in a

way you never thought possible!' – but only a tiny handful who might actually be able to do it. Most batsmen would have a few swings and then one would go straight up in the air and that would be that. But Ben kept precision hitting again and again and again. Ultimately, it didn't quite come off. But the fact he can bat like that as part of a narrative, be it sticking one to the opposition or guiding England to the most ridiculous of wins, makes Ben Stokes the rarest of cricketers. Think about it. Within all that anger swirling round Lord's he had to find the inner calmness to execute the most ridiculous skills. He wasn't slogging, he was playing very, very good cricket shots. He was selecting the right ball, utilising his talent, and writing a story all at the same time. Is that sheer mental strength? Or is it the ability, amid the madness, to wipe everything from your mind and focus microscopically on just one thing?

The first glimmer of Ben's never-say-die attitude came with the hundred he made at Perth in 2013, a window into the mindset of a man who didn't believe in the concept of the losing cause. With England subsiding meekly to another defeat, chasing an admittedly extremely unlikely 504, here was a young bloke, just 22 years old, happy to stand up and say, 'You know what, I've had enough of this. I'm going to punch back here.' The bloke clearly had the potential to be explosive with the bat in his hand, a fact no better confirmed than by the 258, with the small matter of 11 sixes, he blasted in the Cape Town Test against South Africa three years later. It was as if he was reinventing the game. Things like that just didn't happen. And that was without the other supersonic elements to his game, the amazing catching and the genius bowling. The swing, the seam, the bounce. This was a bloke who'd work all day for his team on one leg. And he'd run through umpteen walls and leap several canyons on the way.

What then happened is, he found the perfect coach in Baz McCullum. Together they made England absolute box office. You couldn't take your eyes off them. They totally redefined the way cricket can be played. Some say Bazball is about smashing the ball out of the ground. And there's more than a few spectators who've ended up with a cricket ball in their pint of lager who'd agree. But there's a lot more to it than just that. What Bazball is really about is the messaging around belief and self-expression that goes on in the dressing room. It's like a positivity brainwash. Negativity is not allowed. Look at Tom Hartley. The Lancashire left-arm spinner had his first ball in Test cricket belted over the ropes for six. In days gone by, that would have been the cue for a complete collapse in confidence. And yet he ended that Hydera-bad Test with 9–193, the best figures for an English spinner on debut since the 1930s. Ben and Baz knew that, with his height, on that pitch, he was the best man for the job, and they backed him all the way to do it. It's the same with the bat. When England needed 399 to win the next Test, Jimmy Anderson stated that England had been ready to chase down 600 if necessary. In the end, they fell 107 runs short, but the point was they had positive intent.

England's mindset now is one of zero fear. 'Forget the opposi-tion – we play our own game.' Very much 'Don't play the man, play the ball.' I compare that to my own time. We definitely played the men too much. Instead of playing the delivery, we played Shane Warne, Merv Hughes, Allan Border and all the rest of them. In our defence, 'Play the ball, not the man' is easier said than done when the bloke delivering it has got hundreds of wickets, a track record of knocking you over and is being roared on by tens of thousands of feverish Aussies in an arena that's part stadium part cauldron.

The Aussies were tough characters and it felt like they could see the chinks in our armour. We were all capable of scoring runs and taking wickets but they just knew that in a dogfight one of us would nick off and four wickets would go down quickly. Nine times out of ten they'd get past us. We, on the other hand, would have to be totally at the top of our game to have any chance. I'm honest enough with myself to know that Allan Border didn't lose any sleep batting against me. He was way too gritty to do that. His attitude to pretty much any England bowler was 'F*** you, mate.' I'm pretty sure, however, that a fair few of our boys lost sleep about batting against Shane Warne. When added up, those differences meant Australia were always, with a very occasional blip, in the ascendancy. We couldn't escape the fact that they were better than us. We couldn't get that out of our brains. I can only compare it to a football team coming up against that great Liverpool side of the 1980s or that dominant Arsenal team of the 1990s. I've talked to a few professional footballers who played for lesser clubs and they've told me that, quite honestly, they'd be sat on the coach on the way to Anfield or Highbury openly saying to one another, 'Let's try and get out of this five-nil.' There was no point anyone denying the fact that they could very well be totally mugged off for 90 minutes and come out on the end of a cricket score. That's the difference between what a fan might be thinking – 'You never know, we might have a chance here!' – and a player – 'F*** me, we're going to get absolutely tonked!'

I don't think there's any denying the Aussie team of the 1990s was stronger than it's ever been since. For us, reversing the pressure and putting it back on the Aussies was a Herculean effort. But that doesn't in any way detract from what Ben and Baz have done with England. The situation in that England dressing room is clear. Ben Stokes will do anything for his teammates and his teammates will do anything for him.

Baz once said to me, 'If you can get everyone facing the same way on the bus you're more than halfway there.' And that's exactly what's happened. Under Ben and Baz players feel appreciated. Instead of constantly worrying about personal performance, they feel safe, empowered to hand themselves over to a bigger goal. Zak Crawley is a case in point. At times in his England career he's struggled for runs. But he doesn't have to worry. He can trust that the captain and management believe in him. It's as if he's been told, 'Look, go out and score us a match-winning 150 every fifth Test and that's all we want.' Back in the 1990s, he'd have been dropped 10 times. But Ben and Baz have a model of how they want to play and, with the odd variation, have stuck to it. Look at the players who are getting picked. Paceman Gus Atkinson was barely known outside Surrey, as was wicketkeeper Jamie Smith, well down the pecking order when it came to wearing the gloves at The Oval. Shoaib Bashir had taken all of 10 first-class wickets when he was included in the squad for the tour of India in 2024. Brydon Carse was basically a white-ball cricketer for Northern Superchargers when he started ripping up trees as a fast bowler in Test cricket. Jacob Bethell was batting number three for England without even having a first-class ton under his belt. It's like overnight England became the best talent-spotters in the world. Which does make you wonder a little bit why it couldn't have been like that before. Where was the understanding that worrying about performance stifles performance? I'd have loved someone to have put their arm round me and told me not to worry; that all I needed to do was allow the talent to come out of myself. Especially since I was a person who had the talent but possibly never quite believed it.

When that lift door opened in Australia in 1990 what I really needed to see instead of Peter Lush, Graham Gooch and Micky Stewart, was Rob Key, Ben Stokes and Baz McCullum. With them behind me I'd have worked harder on my fielding, would have tried to bat better. I'd have wanted to go down to the gym with Ben and Baz and trained with a smile on my face rather than an arm up my back. Instead I carried a feeling of not being valued. When people in a team feel appreciated, the sky's the limit.

Ben's obviously got a great affinity with the boys. He can clearly be a very tough character but at the same time has an enormous amount of empathy. He's a fighter who understands his teammates not just as players but as humans. A man who doesn't just talk but listens. Everyone in that dressing room loves Ben. That's not just me imagining it, you can see it, in the way they respond to him, believe in him. Sometimes there are people who are made for the job. Simple as that. Ben is one of those people, same as Michael Vaughan was one before him.

Baz is exactly the same. The players love his normality, same as they love his desire for everyone to succeed. Baz is a great man. A few years ago I was fortunate enough to travel round New Zealand with him for a TV programme called *This Could Go Anywhere* in which he showed me his beautiful country while I took on various challenges, some pleasant, like a round of golf, some less so, like a bungee jump. Right from the start, I saw how singularly well-equipped Baz is at putting people at ease. I got off the plane after a mammoth journey feeling a little bit nervous, same as anyone when they're meeting someone new. There was Baz waiting for me.

'Hi Cat, great to meet you!'

'Hello Brendon. How are you?'

'It's not Brendon, mate, call me Baz. Are you a hugger?'

'Well, not really Baz.'

'Give us a hug!'

I gave him a little hug and he picked my bags up. 'I've got the motor outside.'

I don't think I've met anyone better at engendering calm. I sat in that car and it was like I'd known him for 40 years. Baz is astute, a deep thinker, but with such a human element to the way he goes about things. He was more than happy, for instance, to stop the car and let me be sick on the way to the bungee jump.

Whatever happens in the 2025–26 Ashes, Ben and Baz will go down as one of *the* great cricket partnerships. At the point Ben was made captain, people wondered who exactly he was. He'd missed the 2017–18 Ashes tour because he was caught up in a court case, eventually found not guilty of affray. But if everyone thought he was going to lead through feistiness or bullishness or whatever, they were very much mistaken. There's an incredibly subtle side to Ben. The result is one of the best captains England have ever had. A joy to watch, he's brave, innovative, and on every level able to lead from the front – easy to forget, for instance, about the bowling he did the day before his heroic innings at Headingley to get his side into a position to be able to win that game. Baz's presence, meanwhile, has allowed Ben to express himself fully through his own talents and those of his players. Years from now, I genuinely believe we'll still be talking about his feats in the same way we do about Beefy's.

Just such a pity you got out at Lord's, Ben. Next time, eh mate?

---

24 ASHES TESTS (TO OCT 2025)

Runs: 1,562
Highest Score: 155
Avg: 36.32
Hundreds: 4
Fifties: 8

Wickets: 41
Best Bowling: 6–36
Avg: 38.95
Five-wicket Innings: 2
Ten-wicket Matches: 0

40.

TERRY ALDERMAN

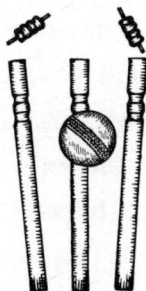

The classic smiling assassin, Terry would creep up, pigeon-toed, and have half the England team lbw before they even knew what had hit them.

Terry Alderman wasn't a frightening bloke. While Merv Hughes could justifiably have had his own Hollywood horror franchise – *The moustache is back, and it's coming for you!* – and Craig McDermott too could, when he wished, be moderately unpleasant, once enquiring as to my views on hospital food (I quite like spotted dick and jam roly-poly, so not bothered since you ask), Terry inflicted his pain more subtly. As Craig and Merv sent balls past batsmen's noses, at the other end Terry would calmly ply his trade, swinging it round corners, floating it up on the wind, and getting the Poms lbw for fun. In many ways he epitomised the

Aussie bowler of the period. Gone was the express pace of Thommo and Lillee to be replaced by a bunch of blokes – Bruce Reid being another – who weren't necessarily the fastest guys in the world but could be relied on to get the job done.

Thankfully, by the time I was starting out for England, Terry was coming to the end of his career, but on my debut at Melbourne in 1990 I saw straightaway why for a decade he'd been England's nemesis, trapping Graham Gooch leg before wicket, a dismissal which very much illustrated the Western Australian's modus operandi. During the previous summer's Ashes in England, of his 41 wickets, 19 were lbw. Bowling wicket to wicket he could zero the ball in on a batsman's pads like no other bowler before or since. It's said that when someone graffitied 'Thatcher Out!' on a wall in London, someone else came along and added 'lbw Alderman'.

The bloke just loved playing against England, and especially in England. In the 1981 series, he'd taken a ridiculous 42 wickets – and that in a losing cause. In fact, of his 170 Test wickets, 100 came against us. Maybe that's why, disconcertingly, he always seemed to run in with a smile on his face, unusual among the fast-medium boys who generally tended to look about as happy as a carthorse with a nail through the hoof. That would be on a good day in Gus Fraser's case. Possibly Terry's demeanour was due to his starting out as a primary school teacher. After all, you can't walk into a classroom of infants scowling at everyone and using industrial language.

Doubtless Terry would have wreaked more havoc had he not suffered a badly dislocated shoulder while wrestling a pitch invader to the ground during the Perth Test of 1982. Thankfully, I was never subjected to serious injury from a pitch invasion, but it wasn't uncommon, at the end of one-day games in particular, to reach the dressing room looking like a dishevelled shop dummy, with bits of clothing either ripped at the seams or missing entirely. If you were wise, with one run needed, you'd position yourself directly in front of the pavilion, jostling for position with the eight or nine other blokes who'd all had the same idea. I was just going to say that the most notable pitch invasion I was involved in was when Brian Lara broke Sir Garfield Sobers' record Test score of 365 at the Recreation Ground in Antigua in 1994, but actually that particular event went on so long that I think in the end it was the England players invading the West Indies fans' celebration rather than the other way round.

Personally, while pretty much every other England player of the period got out to Terry – including Athers, who was lbw to him for a duck on debut – I never succumbed to his guile. The lbw dismissal wasn't one that tended to trouble me against the faster fellas, generally because by the time the ball reached my end my pads, like the rest of me, were retreating at pace towards the legside. I admire the bloke, though, because in an age when so many Aussie bowlers were all about sledging and aggression, he just quietly got on and did the business. Never once did he cast aspersions on my lineage or ask if I had any particular attachment to the food at the local infirmary.

It's just the smiling I had an issue with. It set a bad example. We're bowlers – we're frustrated, we're irritable, we're angry. It's been that way for eons. It's the way it's meant to be.

Terry, mate, it's cricket, not synchronised swimming.

17 ASHES TESTS

Wickets: 100
Best Bowling: 6–47
Avg: 21.17
Five-wicket Innings: 11
Ten-wicket Matches: 1

Runs: 76
Highest Score: 26
Avg: 9.50

41.

DARREN GOUGH

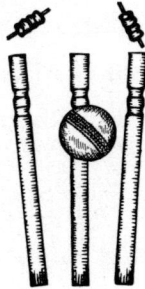

'Why do they call you the Rhino, Darren?'
'Because I'm as strong as an ox.'

Goughy, Dazzler, the Rhino – it doesn't matter what name he was going under at any particular stage of his Ashes career, the Aussie players respected few England cricketers more than Darren Gough. The Yorkshire quick was a wholehearted performer who left everything out there on the field, and that was good enough for our tormentors. It was a bit of a mutual love-in. Darren loved the Aussie way of life, loved the country, the grounds, and the way the Aussies played their cricket. He wanted to get that nod of appreciation from the Australians – as did so many of us. Earning the respect of the Aussies was what we played for in a funny kind of way. That might sound odd, but think about it, as an England player all you ever heard was how great *they* were. And to want to be respected by the best out there is only natural.

It wasn't just the players who liked Darren. He had enough big Ashes moments to cement his position as a favourite in the heart of every cricket fan. On his first tour Down Under in 1994–95 he was being touted as something of an all-rounder after scoring 51 in England's first innings at Sydney and then taking 6–49 to help to skittle the Aussies for just 116. The Test would become better known for the Athers/Hick declaration incident but Goughy's antics with bat and ball won him the man-of-the-match award.

With happy memories in mind, Goughy returned to Sydney four years later and provided England supporters with one of *the* great moments in Ashes history. I'd say a once-in-a-generation event – but actually it hadn't happened for 99 years. When Goughy had Ian Healy caught behind with an awkward riser on off stump, no-one thought too much about it. But he then took Stuart MacGill's middle pole out with a yorker to leave himself on a hat-trick. Out came Colin Miller, otherwise known as the off-spinner, and Goughy repeated the trick only this time with off stump. Goughy was lost in a scrum of his England colleagues as thousands of England fans went insane in the stands. A great, great moment for Goughy, although it happened in the 1990s and so, naturally, wasn't quite enough to prevent England losing the game.

While I didn't make that tour, watching Goughy's hat-trick from home was still a great Ashes moment. There was a perception from some that he liked talking about how many wickets he got a little too much – 'Five for me!' – but I always got on very well with Goughie. I liked the fact that he didn't beat about the bush. Proper Yorkshire. What is it they say up there? 'Don't take any of this and you won't get any of that.' Something like that anyway! The point being (I think!) that if you're straight up with people, you'll get on in life. And that was Goughy, always wore his heart on his sleeve, as both a person and a cricketer. For Nasser, he was his go-to boy. He felt he could always rely on him to give everything he'd got – throw the ball to Goughy and let him do the rest. He always steamed in, always gave 100 per cent. Unfortunately for both of them, Goughy had a lot of injury problems. Hard to believe such a great bowler played only 59 Test matches, but unsurprising that he did most of his damage against the Aussies.

A third of his wickets came in Ashes battles and it was great that he got to have one last crack at them, albeit in the short form of the game, in that golden summer of 2005, a last hoorah which produced a moment which delivered the perfect insight into the mind of Darren Gough. The night before the ODI at Chester-le-Street, the Aussies spent the night at Lumley Castle overlooking the ground. Dating back 600 years, the ancient structure is said to be haunted by the ghost of Lily of Lumley who apparently has a habit of rising from a well in the castle grounds where she was hurled by two priests in times long distant. In 2005, Lily, perhaps seeking advice on how to play a punchy lower order innings, appears to have popped up at the end of Aussie all-rounder Shane Watson's bed in the early hours, traumatising the Queenslander to the extent that he hotfooted it to fast bowler Brett Lee's room and spent the rest of the night on his teammate's floor.

By the next day, word of the spooky goings-on had clearly reached the England dressing room. As Goughy walked past

Shane on the way back to his mark, he couldn't help but deliver the classic arms-in-the-air 'Whooo-oo!' ghost impression. That was Goughy. He believed cricket should be hard-fought, but he was also insistent on it being fun – whether intentionally or not. 'All these sheep here in New Zealand,' he reflected in the dressing room once, 'and you can't get a bacon sandwich anywhere.'

Darren might not have won the Ashes in 2005 but he did win *Strictly Come Dancing*. His quickstep and American smooth were particularly well-received. Not bad for a rhino. Or was it an ox?

17 ASHES TESTS

Wickets: 74
Best Bowling: 6–49
Avg: 30.81
Five-wicket Innings: 4
Ten-wicket Matches: 0

Runs: 240
Highest Score: 51
Avg: 10

42.

DAVID BOON

Destructive limpet who fed mercilessly on England attacks, and, if rumour is to be believed, cans of Victoria Bitter.

Essentially a barrel with a moustache, if there was one Australian batsman you wanted to see the back of early it was David Boon. He had a very nasty habit of making his way to the wicket, annihilating you, and vanishing again. I'm pretty sure in all the games I played against him I never even heard him speak. For several years I was under the impression he was mute. At the same time, reminiscent of a cub scout sat round a campfire being scared stiff by a ghost story, I'd hear tales of him necking 52 tinnies on a flight from Sydney to London. Hmm, I'd think to myself, he does sound a little bit tough.

Boony sits at the centre of one of my best, and several of my worst, Ashes experiences. The memory I draw upon to make the nightmares go away is the ball I bowled him at the Gabba in 1994, the delivery first drifting to leg and then turning violently to hit his off stump. It was an absolute snorter, even if I do say so myself. The back of Boony was always his best side, and watching him disappear, dumbfounded, back to the Brisbane pavilion went some way to heal the wounds inflicted during previous Ashes series. In 1993 I'd spent way too much of the Lord's Test seeing Boony front-on. By the time the Aussies declared their *first* innings on the *third* morning at 632–4, he'd made 164 not out from 378 balls across nearly eight hours. This was on top of 111 and 152 from openers Mark Taylor and Michael Slater. Had I not bowled Mark Waugh for 99, the top four in the Aussie batting line-up would have all made a ton. When Allan Border finally put us out of our misery, having himself made 77, I felt I knew the Australian top order intimately. To this day, I could tell you their feet, waist and inside-leg measurements.

Right from the off, my relationship with Boony had been one of almost relentless frustration. He should, all things being equal, have been my first Test wicket, edging one behind to Jack Russell on my debut at the MCG. I'm not saying the nick was obvious but there were people cracking lobster shells in the fish restaurants of St Kilda who heard it. The only one who didn't was my old mate (see chapter, *The Umps*), the Aussie umpire Peter McConnell.

Boony was a decade-long thorn in England's side, scoring seven tons and eight fifties in that period. Some claim it should be nine fifties in recognition of those 52 'stubbies' the 'keg on legs' is said to have downed on the way to England in 1989. Something of a tradition among the Aussies, Boony was reckoned to have surpassed previous efforts by Doug Walters and Rodney Marsh. His own response to constant questions about the feat is to say the story has been embellished (perhaps it was only 51), but fellow batsman Dean Jones claims there was an actual announcement from the captain as the aircraft approached the runway. That does sound a little unusual. Fair enough telling people to fasten their seatbelts and the temperature on the ground at Heathrow, but informing passengers there's a bloke who's just broken a drinking record? Seems unlikely unless the announcement was accompanied by an appeal for unused sickbags, or for a couple of larger passengers to help him down the steps off the plane. Former Aussie captain Ian Chappell, meanwhile, declared that in his day Boony's tally would have qualified him as a teetotaller. Those old 1970s boys really did like a drink, didn't they?

Whatever the truth of it, Victoria Bitter clearly liked the tale as Boony became a brand ambassador, starring in TV ads. 'A hard-earned thirst needs a big cold beer,' viewers were told, 'and no-one deserves it more than David Boon. No high-fives or jumping around when Boony made a ton, just a tweak of the box and back to business.' Thanks for that.

These days, Boony's better known as a match referee. That's cricket matches, not yard of ale competitions.

Twice I flew the opposite way to Boony, never once tempted to challenge his mythical score. After the Rusty Nail incident in 1990 (see *Introduction*) it didn't seem a particularly good idea to take it on next time I toured in 1994. By then I was dreaming of the Australian vineries awaiting me on arrival. Perhaps I'd visit 52 of them instead.

31 ASHES TESTS

Runs: 2,237
Highest Score: 184 not out
Avg: 45.65
Hundreds: 7
Fifties: 8

43.

MIKE GATTING

*Remembered by many for being on the wrong
end of Warney's 'ball of the century' but remembered
by me for being the very best of man-managers.*

'Who the f*** is Father Christmas?'

Melbourne's annual Test match, starting on Boxing Day, sounds like it should be a festive affair. Spectators kissing one another under mistletoe, umpires wearing reindeer antlers, stumps festooned in tinsel, that kind of thing. But truth is, for us Poms, it never actually feels Christmassy in Australia because it's so bloody hot. Go into town and there's Santa on the high street sweating his nuts off. Everyone's walking around in shorts. The famous tradition is Christmas on the beach. I tried it once. Terrible. The Aussies are all there eating oysters and lobster. That's not right. Where's the turkey and the stuffing? The pudding and the custard? The Harveys Bristol Cream and the After Eight mints? It never sat well with me. Christmas should be at least a little bit chilly. Why can't they have it in June down there so it's cooler? It's like us having Wimbledon in December. It just doesn't feel right. When Yuletide comes round I want to be down the pub sitting by the fire with a coat on and a bobble hat, not running round in 90-degree heat playing cricket.

Unusually, Melbourne's 'Boxing Day Test' of 1994 started on Christmas Eve. If you got a first-baller, the next day was ruined. Thankfully, Australia were batting and we actually had a pretty good day, reducing them to 220–7 as we retired to enjoy the festivities for 24 hours. Well, most of us had a pretty good day. Except perhaps Mike Gatting. Every time he wandered, be-whiskered and portly, down to third man, my old Middlesex skipper was welcomed by the ever-rowdy spectators in Bay 13 as a somewhat puce and sweaty incarnation of Santa Claus.

Gatt might have wished he'd stayed at home for that 1994–95 Ashes tour. By the time the trip came around, he was 37 and had been playing on and off for England for 16 years. A superb middle-order technician, Gatt had seen and done it all, but even he was beginning to find the situation a little awkward. By the mid-1990s a new generation of players was coming into the England side and they weren't afraid of giving someone they saw as a relic of yesteryear a bit of stick. All of a sudden, after a great career, here was Gatt having to fight his corner in the dressing room when the mickey-taking was flying around. As an Ashes-winning captain, to be thrown back into the trenches, alongside a bunch of kids unafraid to poke fun, usually about his weight, was, I think, tricky for Gatt. While I always gave him a huge amount of respect, a few of the others saw his presence among the rank and file as a bit of a licence to rub it in. 'You're back with us lot now, mate.' Gatt didn't quite know where he sat. He was a senior player but with no more status than the youngsters.

Truth was that for both Gatt and his old pal Graham Gooch, now 41, the 1994–95 Ashes was a tour too far. Both had been great servants to English cricket but now found themselves sharing changing space with people with a completely different outlook. For some of those younger blokes it was like having their dad along. Time changes everything and cricket's no different. Dressing room banter moves on, people dress differently. While, in an attempt to make me selectable for England, it was Gatt who'd marched me down Uxbridge high street to get my hair cut, maybe now it was me who should have been finding him a new look!

Gatt and Gooch knew the end was nigh and announced their intention to quit international cricket at the end of the trip. What might have seemed like a positive move, recognising their own limitations, backfired horribly. By revealing their retirement plans all they did was put their heads on the block. When, inevitably, things didn't go to plan on the pitch, they were slaughtered by a media who couldn't fail to notice that, compared to gazelle-like colleagues such as Mark Ramprakash and Chris Lewis, Gatt and Gooch looked more like a pair of gently grazing moose. I didn't want it to end like that for my old mate and was delighted when his first-innings 117 in Adelaide set us up for our only Test victory. More than any other cricketer, I owed my own career, with Middlesex and England, to Gatt. Every year I was on the verge of getting thrown out of

Lord's for various misdemeanours only for him to come to my rescue. He stuck with me through thick and thin, and I'd like to think I repaid him with my performances.

For me, Gatt was the perfect captain, a normal bloke who didn't hold any grudges. You could have a bit of a tear-up after a day's play and by the next morning it was forgotten. The slate could always be wiped clean. He also managed to get something into my head that resonated for a long time. 'I'm here to try to get the best out of you, so stop fighting me. You don't need to – I'm on your side.' As a bit of an anti-establishment youngster, to me everything was a hierarchy. The way I saw it, those with authority just wanted to keep the rest of us down and, therefore, deserved to be confronted. Gatt made me see the world a bit differently. 'Phil, you're a very good player. You've got ability and a chance to get somewhere. If you listen to me, I might be able to help you progress. But if you keep pissing people off that's not going to happen. Stop kicking off every five minutes and together we might actually get somewhere.'

It didn't happen overnight. He actually sent me off the field at Sheffield after I had a massive blow-up when two Yorkshire players were smashing me around the park. At the time I thought that was bang out of order, but I look back now and understand he couldn't have done anything else. It was a learning curve and before long I realised how lucky I was to have Gatt as my captain. He taught me that whatever happened on the cricket field wasn't the end of the world. I compare that attitude to other captains I played under who were unable to separate the game from the rest of life and over time visibly shrank under the weight of the position. They'd take on the job in prime physical condition and three months later be signing autographs as Catweazle.

Gatt saw his prime captaincy role as helping his players be successful. Do that and team success would follow. Until Gatt got hold of me, I'd always had an element of 'Give me the ball, and I'll do it!' But you can't play cricket on your own, you need the help of your teammates. Gatt was the first person who made me think about the concept of team spirit, rather than turning up with a Mohican, earrings and bondage trousers and trying to get a few wickets for myself. John Emburey was the same. He pulled me aside a couple of times. 'Come on, Phil, you can't keep wanting to punch the umpire. You can't stagger in at four in the morning. You've got to grow up. You've got an opportunity here and you need to take it and not mess up.' Between them they got a career out of me. To be honest, I've always wondered if Gatt got up to a few shenanigans himself when he was a youngster. Perhaps his learning curve hadn't been that dissimilar to my own and so he could relate to me. He knew how to get the best out of me, persevered with me and looked after me, for which I'll be forever grateful.

Since Gatt was one of the main reasons I got to play for England, I'd have loved to have had him as my skipper, but by then the baton had passed to the rather more authoritarian Graham Gooch. It was a shame as Gatt knew exactly how to beat the Aussies from the position of underdog. He was in charge on the 1986–87 tour, the one where the *Independent* journalist Martin Johnson famously declared, 'England have only three major problems. They can't bat, they can't bowl and they can't field.' At that point, as a young county player barely out of the blocks, I distinctly remember thinking, *Blimey, well that's going to be a bit tricky then!* And then of course they went and won the series 2–1. I found it all a bit confusing. If a team that's been totally written off can go to Australia and win the Ashes, what did that mean for me as a cricketer? Could you win any game? Lose any game? I mean, if winning doesn't depend on who's the best, then what does it depend on? Whether you've had scrambled eggs for breakfast? Or fried eggs? Or egg and soldiers? What the hell is going on?

Spending the next few years under Gatt at Middlesex, I got to see how he'd done it. Here was a bloke who knew how to get the best out of everyone; to really get a team going. If you can't bat, can't bowl, can't field, then you're going over to Australia with not a lot of pluses. Somehow, though, he brought that band of players together, an impressive feat considering some of the strong and fiery characters on the plane, not least the Nottinghamshire opener Chris Broad, fined for knocking his leg stump out of the ground in the one-off Centennial Test in Sydney in 1988, and my Middlesex spin colleague Phil Edmonds, who during a particularly slow day in the field during a Test match in Kolkata had taken to reading the *Daily Telegraph* at square leg.

But that was Gatt, a supreme man-manager, brilliant at uniting a group in a cause, something which, I expect, he'd learned from playing under Mike Brearley, a bloke who definitely knew how to carry people with him. While he was Cambridge University-educated, studying classics and moral sciences, Aussie paceman Rodney Hogg called it right when, after seeing the bloke's wizardry in getting the best out of players, he opined that what Brears really had was a degree in people. That has to be the case because, purely as a cricketer, Brears couldn't expect devotion. Across a 39-Test career he averaged just 22, with no centuries. While for any normal captain, repeated failure would weaken their position beyond repair,

Brears had a dressing room which would run through walls for him. While my own Middlesex career didn't overlap with his, I would see Brears knocking about round Lord's a little bit. I always found him the most personable of chaps, very softly spoken, his wise words occasionally sidestepping my hearing and disappearing into the oak panelling. But I understood that to have achieved so much as a captain he must have had a real inner steel.

At Middlesex, tales were oft related of the ding-dongs he had with Edmonds, great minds going hell for leather against one another, a real battle of the eggheads. It definitely seemed that, if he believed in something, Brears wasn't afraid of putting people's noses out of joint. And I think Gatt was the same – so, so fiercely protective of his team. When, the following winter in Faisalabad, he blew up at the Pakistani umpire Shakoor Rana, you knew he must have been pushed to the absolute limit. Rana had accused Gatt of cheating, a massive slur on a bloke who was never less than fair and in fact had done well to hold his tongue so long in a country where, at the time, the odds always felt stacked in the home team's favour. Understandable that Gatt finally exploded and gave Shakoor a bit back.

While Gatt was always right there in the thick of it with his players, he was shabbily treated as England captain, sacked in 1988 after an alleged liaison with a barmaid during a Test match at Trent Bridge. It felt like the excuse the England authorities were looking for following the Shakoor incident. Gatt wasn't a posh lad, which, if anything, was held against him a bit in those funny old times. I might be wrong with that, but that was how it felt.

Gatt will admit himself he could have got a few more runs at international level but he finished that 1986–87 Ashes series having scored almost 400 runs with a hundred and three fifties. He remains the last England captain to oversee a win in Brisbane, in 1986, and it would be 2005 before any other England captain got their hands on the Ashes. For a captain of a team that couldn't bat, couldn't bowl, and couldn't field, Mike Gatting really didn't do too badly.

At the end of the 1994–95 Ashes, he also had the perfect rebuttal to the sniggers and smirks from the youngsters on the trip. Only two tourists remained fit and uninjured throughout those four months. One was Gooch. The other was a bloke who, in a certain light, really could be mistaken for Father Christmas.

27 ASHES TESTS

Runs: 1,661
Highest Score: 160
Avg: 37.75
Hundreds: 4
Fifties: 12

44.

JEFF THOMSON

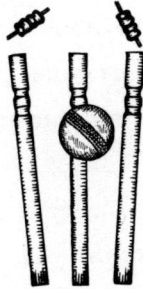

Blond-streaked mullet-wearer who made terrifying Poms look like a stroll in the park.

Jeff Thomson once bowled a ball recorded at 100 miles an hour. His short ball was so venomous that it wasn't unknown for it to bounce off the pitch and slam, still airborne, into the sightscreen 50 yards back. I mean, I know people say W.G. Grace was pretty handy with the bat, but you could argue those Victorian types really were playing an entirely different game. No way would you be wearing wicker pads if Thommo was around. I'm supremely grateful that the only time I faced him was in the *A Question of Sport* studio.

Thommo was able to summon up such incredible pace thanks to a trademark slingshot action. By drawing his spine back and planting his foot on the crease he was essentially half man, half trebuchet. The Australians had basically wheeled a medieval weapon on to the field. Maybe the sight wouldn't have been so bad had Thommo not so ably matched menace with words. Prior to the 1974–75 series in Australia he told one interviewer, 'I enjoy hitting a batsman more than getting him out. I like to see blood on the pitch.' It was as if they'd called up Dracula.

To make matters worse, in 1974 they were still bowling eight-ball overs in Australia. That's Dennis Lillee at one end, Thommo at the other. In my time, I can compare that attack only to the West Indies' Curtly Ambrose and Courtney Walsh. I'd have superglued myself to Michael Atherton rather than go out to face eight balls from either of them.

Thommo is widely considered the fastest bowler the world has ever seen, to the extent that Rodney Marsh used to put raw steaks in his wicketkeeping gloves to cushion the pounding, apt because after half an hour of Thommo, raw steak is exactly what the England batsmen looked like. Derek Underwood would waddle out to face this horrific attack, bat made from match-wood, no helmet, looking absolutely petrified. Sixty seconds later he'd make a vague stab with his willow as something flashed past and his stumps would be spread everywhere. You've really got to admire those old-school fellas. The first Test in Brisbane cost England the broken hands of John Edrich and Dennis Amiss. Who did they send for to see off Thommo in the next game, on perhaps the fastest wicket in the world, at Perth? Colin Cowdrey – who'd made his Test debut in 1954. A bloke who was 41 going on 68. I had visions of him scrambling around for his kit in his attic, blowing the cobwebs off some ancient ivory armguard. Colin, however, was a classic English gentleman. His country needed him and he wasn't going to say no. Indeed, when Thommo stepped up to bowl, Colin offered his hand. 'Good morning, my name's Cowdrey.' It's like being invited into the cage to help the lion-tamer and trying to shake hands with the lion.

To the beautiful, almost Aled Jones-esque, sound of the Aussie fans singing, 'Ashes to Ashes. Dust to dust. If Lillee doesn't get you Thommo must,' Colin performed gamely but nevertheless couldn't stop Thommo adding seven wickets to the nine he'd taken in Brisbane. Leaning on his bat at the other end he also had the best view of one of the most infamous moments in Test cricket when Thommo fired a 90 mph-plus delivery straight into David Lloyd's box. Equipment manufacturers never had Thommo in mind when they were designing these things in the 1970s. The plastic wasn't much different to that used in Tupperware. No modern player would go out to bat in something structurally suited to keeping a sandwich fresh, but back then there was no choice. Bumble's box split and his personage slipped through the gap before it snapped back shut. He still needs to lean on a wall when he talks about it.

Thommo was the only bowler who needed another column in his bowling analysis: Overs – Maidens – Runs – Wickets – Bollocks. By the time he injured his shoulder playing tennis on the rest day during the final Test at Adelaide, he'd claimed 33 wickets and half a dozen testicles. If only England could have got him on court earlier they'd have saved themselves an awful lot of bruises. Mike Denness wore a St Christopher pendant at the crease. On one occasion, after a torrent of short balls, he returned to the pavilion, lifted his shirt, and found it embedded in his chest. St Christopher is, of course, the patron saint of travellers. If that had been me I'd have taken the hint and leapt on the next flight home.

Thankfully, at that point I was still a kid. And growing up in 1970s Britain, where, for some inexplicable reason, brown had been chosen as the go-to colour for everything from wallpaper to soft furnishings and dogs, I loved any sight of Thommo. He and the other Aussie pace boys were colourful and flamboyant. They'd appear on TV in eye-popping suits and vast kipper ties. They were united in their undying love of sunshine and beaches. Thommo had blond streaks for crying out loud. Somehow everyone looked just that little bit more glamorous than Jack Simmons.

Even now I think how great it must have been to have played alongside those fellas, players who were allowed to be themselves, something not always apparent with the England side. Watch the Aussies and everything seemed so natural, like anyone could do it. If one of their boys scored a double hundred down the SCG, you wouldn't have been in the least surprised if afterwards they'd told the TV interviewer, 'Yeah, mate, it was great. Two weeks ago I was playing with my brothers in the back garden and then before I knew it my dad got me a proper bat, my mum was driving me down to Sydney and I'd got myself a double ton against the Poms.' International cricket seemed a lot more accessible, the natural result of a much more relaxed society. While the Aussies just got on and enjoyed themselves, in England we had to progress through various coaching manuals, endless age-group teams, ground staff, seconds, tentative few seasons on the fringes of first-class cricket, and then a few years plugging away in the Championship before we even got near the national team. Part of why the Aussies took to me was that I looked like I'd never done any of that, even though I most definitely had.

In Thommo and Lillee's case it looked like they were having fun while being utterly terrifying at the same time. I could never really do terrifying. It's hard to skip in aggressively, especially when you bowl at 50 mph. Which is why occasionally I reached for a little bit of something else to keep me ticking, a little bit of the old verbals with the batsman perhaps. Not if they doubled as part of the opposition pace attack of course. Had I ever bowled to Thommo, I'd have sent each ball down with a complementary spa weekend.

Only fair – those fast boys work bloody hard.

21 ASHES TESTS

Wickets: 100
Best Bowling: 6–46
Avg: 24.18
Five-wicket Innings: 5
Ten-wicket Matches: 0

Runs: 295
Highest Score: 49
Avg: 14.75

45.

SIR JIMMY ANDERSON

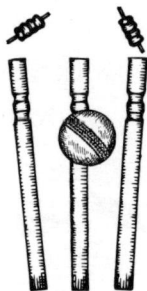

A man who redefines the word 'legend',
England's greatest ever bowler was never more
inspired than in the heat of an Ashes battle.

'Did you hear what he just said about you Phil? He said you're s***. He said he's going to smash you out the ground. He said he's going to make you wish you'd never been born.'

It wasn't uncommon for my England teammates to wind me up before I came on to bowl. They'd do it to get me switched on. Actually, to get my blood boiling. By the time they'd finished I'd be straining at the leash. 'He said f***ing what? Right, I'll f***ing have him.'

I'll let you in on a little secret – us bowlers thrive on being annoyed. Jimmy Anderson never wanted to be making small-talk with the umpires, admiring the cut of the outfield, appreciating passing ladybirds. What he wanted was to be pissed off. Proper, snarling, muttering under his breath, pissed off. I don't think it's going too far to say there's a very good chance that at times during his career he's used the language of the factory floor.

In Jimmy's ideal world, to get him in the mood to cause some mayhem of his own, he'd hear there'd been a burst pipe at home and his TV was under three feet of water. Or a fox had sneaked in and done something unpleasant in his favourite pair of shoes (though Aussie skipper Michael Clarke infamously telling him 'Get ready for a broken f***ing arm' at Brisbane in 2013 might be taking it a bit far). Stuart Broad was the same. On the opening morning of a Test the best thing a colleague could do was hide a wasp in his trousers. When you see bowlers growling away it's not that they're being deliberately difficult, it's just they know the shift they've got to put in and that being in a certain state of mind will help them through it. They need to hate what they do to love what they do.

People sometimes say it would be nice to see more players with smiles on their faces. And actually, these days, possibly due to the environment engendered by Ben Stokes and Brendon McCullum, you do see a lot more of that with England. Once or twice I've mistaken the slip cordon for a toothpaste advertisement. But a lot of players do need something to bite on. Playing against the Aussies in the 1990s I needed every last bit of impetus I could get. Having something to rail against could give me that extra five or 10 per cent. With any luck, on a bowling day, my scrambled eggs would be runny at breakfast, the bus wouldn't turn up at the hotel and my tracksuit would have shrunk in the wash. I needed to feel like I was fighting against the world. On tour especially, I'd wind myself up into such a state that I disliked everything and everyone. It's a good job I was never skipper because it would have made for a very different kind of pre-match interview.

'Lovely day here in Sydney, Phil, you must be looking forward to another great Test match.'

'Listen mate, how about you go and stand in front of the roller?'

Not everyone's like that, but it's definitely how a fair few get themselves into a frame of mind to compete. Before the series Down Under in 2017, David Warner explained how he created his own competitive psyche. 'You try and get into a battle as quick as you can,' he said. 'I try and look in the opposition's eyes and try and work out "How can I dislike this player? How can I get on top of him?" You have to delve and dig deep into yourself, find some hatred about them, to actually get up when you're out there.' He got a lot of criticism for talking about hatred in what is, basically, a sporting contest, but he was only being truthful about how he motivates himself. It's different strokes for different folks. Not everyone can be beaming all the time.

To be fair, there have been occasions when we've seen a smile on Jimmy's face. Like most England bowlers, very little seemed to cheer him up more than seeing an Aussie batsman on his way back to the pavilion. Jimmy's Ashes peak was his ten-fer in a drama-packed Test at Trent Bridge in 2013. This was, remember, the same match when Aussie spinner Ashton Agar made 98 in his team's first innings, a world record for a number 11, while sharing in a last-wicket stand of 163 with Phillip Hughes. It was clearly going to be an epic Test, and with the Aussies chasing an unlikely 311 to win it seemed to be going England's way, especially with the tourists nine wickets down and still 80 runs short. Australia has a long tradition of obstinate wicketkeepers, the sort of blokes who'd be stood on an Outback farmstead, watching a tornado form on the horizon, and calmly shove another stick of gum in their mouth while pulling the next bemused ram on to their lap for shearing. Right now, that man was Brad Haddin. With Agar promoted up the order, James Pattinson was the number 11 stubbornly refusing to yield to England's attack. The pair were just 15 short of their target when Jimmy finally persuaded Haddin to offer an inside-edge to England's own gloveman, Matt Prior. Unfortunately, umpire Aleem Dar didn't see it. Fortunately, DRS did. Now that really did make Jimmy smile. And rightly so. It couldn't have been more appropriate for him to take the match-winning wicket. So often during that topsy-turvy game it had been Jimmy who had popped up with the unplayable delivery to wrestle control back England's way.

Easy to forget that, while England's early 21st century Ashes sides had a lot more success than we did in the 1990s, it was still no mean feat to get one over on the Aussies. Down Under especially remained a fortress. Jimmy himself had been on the end of a whitewash before England finally smashed down the wall in 2010–11. The Lancastrian was central to that victory, his mastery under a cloudy sky perhaps never better illustrated than in his 4–44 as England knocked Australia over for just 98 on the first day at Melbourne, followed up by seven wickets in another innings victory in the following match at Sydney.

But weirdly, for all his brilliance with the ball, one of my greatest Ashes memories of Jimmy is with the bat. At Cardiff in 2009, after the Aussies had piled up 674–6 in their first innings, Jimmy's challenge was to guide England to an unlikely draw by surviving the final few overs with Monty Panesar. Not so much the last chance saloon as the derelict and cobweb-festooned inn that comes a few miles after it. And yet somehow they survived 11.3 overs to deny Australia a victory that had seemed pretty much certain for the previous three days. Odd how a nailbiting draw can be more exciting than a win; how, when the chips are down, seeing Monty Panesar block a good-length ball from Mitchell Johnson is more exhilarating than watching Kevin Pietersen smack one into the stands for six. When Jimmy hit the boundary that finally wiped off England's deficit, Sophia Gardens erupted. In the commentary box, people were screaming down the mic – 'We've made them bat again! That's ten minutes between innings out of the game!' It's times like that when you're reminded what a truly ridiculous sport this is. For England, snatching a draw from defeat was a massive morale booster. The team fed off the momentum to win the next Test at Lord's, and, eventually, another tight series 2–1. In 2009, Jimmy's forward prod was potentially more important than anything he did with the ball.

Of course, an England record 704 wickets at an average of 26.45 against 1,353 runs at 8.96 would suggest that, across Jimmy's entire career, bowling was his superior discipline. The bloke stands as an absolute legend not just of English, but of world cricket. For a fast bowler still to be bagging wickets 21 years after their debut is nothing short of ridiculous. Had England not taken the decision to concentrate on the next generation of fast men, doubtless he'd have been on the plane Down Under in 2025. My guess is there's more than a few Aussie batsmen very glad he wasn't. And surely there can be no greater measure of his brilliance than that.

39 ASHES TESTS

Wickets: 117
Best Bowling: 6–47
Avg: 35.97
Five-wicket Innings: 5
Ten-wicket Matches: 1

Runs: 277
Highest Score: 29
Avg: 7.69

46

IAN CHAPPELL

*No-nonsense Aussie skipper who was always up
for a scrap – and a word about my fielding.*

For a long time, I thought that to be an Australian cricketer you had to be gnarled with a moustache. Not the women's team, obviously, but definitely the blokes, and never more so than in the 1970s and '80s when they all looked like they'd been wrestling with crocodiles. And when they weren't doing that they were having a good punch-up. Or crushing drained tinnies of Victoria Bitter on their foreheads.

Whether the rest of Australian society reflected the cricket team, I'm unsure. But back then I wouldn't have bet against eight big moustachioed blokes slugging it out on their version of *University Challenge. Surely*, I'd think, *there must be fellas like me over there, rather more slight gentlemen, less knobbly, still on their first Bic razor.* But then when I arrived I realised there really were an awful lot of blokes of the gnarled/moustachioed variety in Oz. It was 1990 at that point but still they were apparent, not least in their Ashes line-up – David Boon, Merv Hughes and Allan Border all very much hit the mark. They were intimidating enough in the 1990s, so what must it have been like in the heyday of these kinds of characters? When Dennis Lillee, Rodney Marsh and Ian Chappell were around? Chappell especially. Uncompromising, surly, surely he was the king of the gnarled? It was as if he'd been crafted from bark.

Mike Brearley, a claimant to the title of king of the ungnarled, once opined that going up against an Australian side captained by Ian Chappell was comparable to gang warfare. Thankfully, by the time I ventured Down Under Ian was retired, building a new career as a pundit. I did, however, feel a little of what Brears was referencing when, after I missed a run-out chance, Ian weighed in with the suggestion that Graham Gooch should ensure I was tied up at one end. 'The other advantage England have got when Phil Tufnell's bowling,' he told viewers, 'is that he isn't fielding.' Listeners to *TMS* will know that my own presence in the commentary box is rather less brutal. Why point out someone's frailties when there's a cake to be eaten?

Ian, as Brears noted, was not a man to shirk confrontation. Unsurprising then that he's at the centre of one of the most infamous and long-running feuds in Ashes history, dating back to 1977 when he and a young Ian Botham were drinking in the same Melbourne bar. Accounts differ over what was the catalyst for the dispute but Beefy, a notoriously patriotic character, is said to have tired of listening to Ian being less than complimentary about English cricket, a situation which, after a bit of back and forth between the pair, very nearly resulted in fisticuffs. The animosity simmered until it boiled over again in the car-park at the Adelaide Oval in 2010 where both men were commentating on the Ashes. I'd like to point out that this kind of dispute is rare in the commentary community. Fellow *TMS* broadcaster Glenn McGrath and I played in several Ashes series and have yet to feel the need to get one another in a headlock.

Ian, it seems, was a born fighter who would do anything for his team. He was lucky to have several other born fighters come through the Aussie ranks at the same time, not least Jeff Thomson and Dennis Lillee who helped him reach the glorious height, as skipper, of regaining the Ashes in 1974–75, the series where England's twelfth man was an air ambulance. He once said that he'd rather his team be described as a 'bunch of bastards' on the field than 'a nice bunch of blokes'. But with firepower like that, he was going to win whatever the attitude of his side. There's always talk about sledging and 'psychological warfare' in cricket, but none of it means anything without talent. That's what ultimately wins you games.

And yet it did, for a while at least, seem to help if you were gnarled with a moustache. There's one or two of the Aussie boys favouring a bit of the old fur on the upper lip again these days. I'm issuing a warning. England – you'd better watch out.

30 ASHES TESTS

Runs: 2,138
Highest Score: 192
Avg: 41.11
Hundreds: 4
Fifties: 16

Wickets: 6
Best Bowling: 1–10
Avg: 71.50

47.

ROBIN SMITH

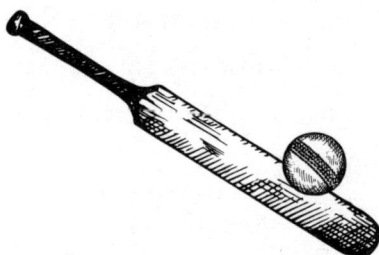

A big-hearted batsman, fearless against the
fastmen, 'The Judge' was the go-to man when
things were getting tough. Which, against the
Aussies, was more often than not.

'Help! Judgey! Can you sort this lot out?'

In 2009, I appeared on *Strictly Come Dancing*, making it to
week nine when, regrettably, my American Smooth let me
down. Had line-dancing been on the agenda I might have fared
slightly better. While no expert in the art, I did at least have
prior experience. Although, like week nine at *Strictly*, it wasn't
entirely positive.

Touring Australia, while the big cities are great, I always liked it
when we found ourselves playing a warm-up game in the middle

of nowhere. I'd look at some of these places and be transported to the westerns I watched as a kid. There'd be a dusty high street with a couple of bars and we'd be the gunslingers riding into town, the sheriff emerging to cast a wary eye over these interlopers. Such places, devoid of regulation nightclubs and bars, and where the spittoon remains very much in fashion, also tend to provide a less predictable night out. Thus it was that on the 1990 tour I found myself in Geraldton, not a particularly memorable place per se, although for some its role in sheep logistics makes it an unmissable stop-off on any visit to Western Australia.

You can imagine that, aside from the occasional duel, nothing much happens in towns such as Geraldton, which means the England cricket team rocking up becomes something of an event. For those few days, you really are the biggest thing in town. In any such conurbation, as an ambassador for my country, I always saw it as my duty to try to educate myself in the local culture. Off I'd head to the library or museum. Of course, this is Australia. It's hot, often uncomfortably hot, and so, for medicinal reasons, I might stop off at the pub on the way. I'm not sure how it happened, but two or three hours after I'd stopped off at the pub in Geraldton I was still there. Not only that but I was line-dancing. Well, I say line-dancing, I was more sort of clapping my hands, tapping my ankles, and doing 360-degree heel pivots while playing a game of human pinball with the regulars. Rather harshly, in my opinion, some of them were of the opinion I was spoiling their fun. They might have asked me to desist, I honestly don't recall, but what I do remember is the right-hander I took full in the chops.

This is where, as a slight bloke, I always found it useful that cricket is a sport that allows for a multitude of body shapes. Big

Devon Malcolm was also out that night, although I couldn't see him in the melee, and, more usefully, Robin Smith. A tough bloke, one of the bravest I've ever seen when it came to taking on the chin music so beloved of the West Indies teams of the era, Robin was having none of it. In a manner honed by walking out to face Curtly Ambrose and Courtney Walsh with England two down for nothing, he waded straight in to sort it out. He didn't need to grapple with anyone. His mere presence put an end there and then to any further unpleasantness. 'The Judge', as he was known, for his tight curls that had the appearance of a horsehair wig more than any involvement with the Old Bailey, had ruled there was to be no more argy-bargy and that was that. It was a measure of the sheer presence of the man, something I'd been very much aware of from the very first time I clapped eyes on him.

Rewinding a few years, it was during a second XI game for Middlesex against Hampshire at Harefield that I first encountered Judgey. I was still making my way in cricket while he'd dropped down to the seconds as he came back from injury. The fact that Judgey, a bona fide England player, a real brute with a bat in his hand, a big bloke who'd smashed international pace attacks around with impunity, was playing caused a bit of a stir in our ranks and, as it turned out, justifiably so. Harefield's a lovely little ground, surrounded by houses with gardens backing on to the field, protected from flying cricket balls by fence panels. Early on, our medium-pacer Graham Rose bowled one wide of off stump and Judgey cut it so hard that it flew across the grass and actually cannonballed an entire fence panel to the ground. We all looked at each other. 'F***ing hell!' The fence had exploded. An elderly woman popped her head through the gap. 'What's going on?'

'Oh, sorry love, that was Smithy's square cut.'

Thankfully, I sent down a beautiful arm ball and managed to bowl him before the old dear felt the need to retreat to her Anderson shelter. But it was a definite eye-opener. If Robin was anything to go by, the first class and Test cricket I aspired to was populated by people well capable of demolishing houses.

After seeing first-hand Judgey's incredible combination of power and skill, it was no surprise to me that he should be one of the few highlights of England's abysmal 1989 Ashes series, topping our batting averages thanks to two great back-against-the-wall centuries, making 143 out of a total 260 in the first innings at Old Trafford, and 101 at Trent Bridge when England, in answer to Australia's epic 602–6 declared, were on the verge of complete humiliation at 2–1. Merv Hughes was on the end of Judgey's destructiveness that day, appropriate enough since the pair traded more than a few insults down the years. 'You can't f***ing bat,' Merv told him during one battle, only for Judgey to dispatch his next ball for four. 'We make a fine pair,' he told Merv. 'I can't f***ing bat and you can't f***ing bowl.'

Judgey's greatest innings against Australia came not in a Test match but in the one-day series in 1993 when he scored 167 not out off 163 balls at Edgbaston, a display of limited-overs batting that even now, when runs come so freely, would be deemed remarkable. It says everything for England in the 1990s that Judgey could turn on that level of pyrotechnics – a record which stood for 23 years – and still end up on the losing side!

He was a hell of a player, someone I'd definitely interrupt a nap on the physio's couch to go out and watch from the balcony. He should have played more than three Ashes series, and 62 Tests, but, while he'd smash the quicks out the ground, he was prone to struggle against the spinners. I could never understand it. Surely he'd got it the wrong way round. The spinners were the only ones who didn't make me shake.

In retirement, he would ace bigger tests with his mental health than could ever be found on a cricket pitch. I couldn't be happier that he navigated his way through those challenges. Judgey was a great tourist and an even better pal. I enjoyed his company immensely. Perhaps never more so than in Geraldton during that most ill-advised of line-dances!

15 ASHES TESTS

Runs: 1,074
Highest Score: 143
Avg: 39.77
Hundreds: 2
Fifties: 7

48.

MATTHEW HAYDEN

*Vast Aussie opener, like bowling to an oak
tree which could tell you to 'F*** off'.*

I always felt Matthew Hayden and his more diminutive Aussie opening partner Justin Langer were like Little and Large. They really did love the big stage. The difference was they very rarely left you with a smile on your face.

In that last Test of mine, at The Oval in 2001, they did what they always did (or at least it seemed that way) and ran-up a century partnership in quick-time. It wasn't a bad England attack – Darren Gough, Andy Caddick and myself included – but we were swatted away with ease. And the horrible thing is, Hayden and Langer knew that was exactly what was going to happen. As they came out to bat, they were actually sledging the England team – 'I don't know why you're bothering! We're going to smash you round the park!' All this kind of thing. Arrogance? Or recognition of reality. After all, they were an integral part of one of the best sides the world had ever seen. Their top seven that day was Hayden, Langer, Ponting, the Waugh twins, Adam Gilchrist and Damien Martyn. By the time they declared ten-and-a-half hours later, three (Langer and the Waughs) had centuries and three others had fifties. Only Gilchrist missed out.

Hayden was particularly – how shall I put this? – combative that day. Skipping in to bowl my first ball to the six-foot-two-inch Queenslander, I couldn't help but notice he was heading straight at me. The bloke was literally on his way down the pitch. I don't mean in a couple of steps kind of way, like a batter might do when looking to mess up a bowler's length and hit them for six, I mean actually walking down the track. A few yards further and we'd have been shaking hands. I was actually stopped in my delivery stride.

'What's going on?'

'Nothing to do with you.'

'But you can't do that!'

'I can do what I want, mate. All you need to do is bowl the ball.'

It was all very disconcerting. I was half expecting the PE teacher to intervene and tell him to play properly. I'd say I had the last laugh by getting him out for 68 but by then I felt so much like a schoolboy that I wasn't far off going to the office with a stomach ache and asking if I could go home early. It was like being on *Grange Hill*, locked in a classroom with Gripper Stebson for half a day.

Hayden was known to his teammates as Haydos. I've thought about this. Possibly it was a cross between Hades, the Greek god of the dead, and Hydros, the Greek god of the primordial waters. I say that because bowling at him all day made you feel like you'd had your head repeatedly shoved down a toilet.

Remarkable then to think how much things had changed by the time Hayden/Haydos returned four years later for the 2005 Ashes. Before the Test series began, there was the little matter of the ODIs. And that's where England laid down a marker. They made sure the Aussies knew, in no uncertain terms, that the days of England being pushed around were over. In the third and final ODI at Edgbaston, England were utterly uncompromising. At one point Simon Jones had a shy at the stumps only to hit Hayden in the ribs. In the bowler's defence, the opener, built like the proverbial brick outhouse, was tricky to miss. While Jones apologised, Hayden wasn't best pleased, and said as much. In meetings past, that would have been that but this new England weren't having it. Paul Collingwood was straight in there challenging Hayden, backed up by Andrew Strauss, Freddie Flintoff and Michael Vaughan. That ODI showed the Aussies that, despite what they might think, England definitely weren't there just to roll out the red carpet. It was a proper case of, 'F*** you lot! Who the f*** are you?' No way were England going to sit back and be bullied. They were on Hayden like a pack of dogs but in this case Jack Russells, not those ones that look like a sausage.

Whereas the England teams I played in would have been a bit timid with the verbals, knowing that soon enough we'd be on the end of an onslaught, forced to swallow our words, the 2005 version could genuinely look Hayden in the eye and tell him, 'Who do you think you are, you big ****?' We could never say something like that. Well we could, but not from the heart, and not without hiding behind the sightscreen. But times had changed so much. These new boys could write those words in big bold letters on a fresh sheet of paper and shove it right up Hayden's nose if they wanted to. That never happened. It would have taken sledging to a whole new level of unseemliness. But even so, England's attitude took Australia by surprise. While their hosts had been successful in the couple of years running up to that Ashes series, I think the tourists assumed there would still be real doubt in the England players' minds as to whether they could really beat the Aussies. Did England, second in a two-man race for so long, genuinely think they could impose themselves on a team which had slain all before them? Did they really think they could get across the line? When they discovered the Poms truly did mean business, it took them by surprise. *Hang on, don't these boys remember four years ago? Don't they remember what happened in the 1990s?* And the answer was no. They were coming into that summer with a totally open mind. The past meant nothing to any of them. Bad memories had been banished, replaced by mental toughness and competitive desire.

It was amazing how, in such a short period of time, the psychological equilibrium of the two teams had changed. At The Oval Test of 1997, the pressure had been on me to bowl the Aussies out in their fourth innings. By the time I took the last wicket, securing a win by just 19 runs, I was exhausted. Beating the Aussies really did take it out of England players. And yet a comparable task didn't appear to affect them in anything like the same way. It felt like they played against us in the manner that I'd play county cricket. If I got a seven-fer against Glamorgan to win the match I'd have a shower and a fag and drive home. It was like falling off a log. Meanwhile, I'd watch one of the Aussies get a five-fer to win a Test match and they'd leave the ground so full of energy I'd have been in no way surprised to pass them on the M25 as they ran down the fast lane back to the hotel. The media narrative at the time only added to the sense of imbalance, constantly referencing this thing called 'the Aussie way' and enquiring why our approach was so rubbish by comparison. As a player it was a little off-putting. I'd be thinking, *Hang on, I've got to go out there and play them. I really don't need to hear how much better their system is and how it produces such vastly superior players!* But there was no denying it was the truth. Occasionally, we'd play the Australia A side. In this supposed second-string would be Michael Bevan, Darren Lehmann, Damien Martyn, Stuart Law and so on. The bowlers would include a few rookies trying to knock your head off to prove a point to the selectors. Australia A was a team that, had it been able to play full Test cricket, would likely have been ranked second in the world.

The Aussies appeared to be superhuman, and no-one exemplified that feeling more than Matthew Hayden, a big man with a huge talent and a massive amount of confidence. The only way to counter the feeling of being in the shadow of extraordinary sportspeople is to chip away at their pedestal. Go into their dressing room for a drink after the game and you might see one of the greats with his head in his hands after a low score, or a bowler sullenly sucking on a bottle of beer after going wicketless in an innings. At that point you realise they're flesh and blood just like you; that they're dealing with their own pressure to perform. Of course, realistically, as I've pointed out, mixing with people who've just rubbed your nose in the dirt isn't always what you want to do. I mean, if Gripper Stebson had spent the day stealing your sandwiches and making you do his homework you wouldn't be massively enthused at the prospect of spending the evening round at his house as well.

I'll be honest, in south London in 2001, after toiling away for five sessions on a flat pitch and then watching us fail to make the Aussies bat again, I wasn't hugely enamoured at the prospect of mixing with my tormentors. I'd tried my variations, my little bits and pieces, but when you've got no rough to play with, no tracks in the wicket, and it's not turning, good players like Matthew Hayden just knock you around.

It was the end of another Ashes summer and I knew inside it was time to say goodbye. Looking back, it was a bit like when I was on *Strictly Come Dancing*. I reached Blackpool, which was great, but at the same time I understood it was the end of the road. Time to head down to the pier and watch Little and Large instead. That's Syd and Eddie not Justin and Matthew. I'd be jumping off the pier if I thought I was going to bump into them.

20 ASHES TESTS

Runs: 1,461
Highest Score: 197
Avg: 45.65
Hundreds: 5
Fifties: 2

49.

KEVIN PIETERSEN

Controversial he might have been, but at The Oval in 2005 KP took the rulebook and smashed it out the ground in one of the most remarkable Ashes innings.

Easy to think of Aussies as somehow superior. Physically they tend to look the part, their climate helping by encouraging them to show large swathes of themselves off. Compare that to your everyday British bloke, wrapped in a vast ribbed sweater or encased in a voluminous anorak. If ever you find yourself in Sydney, go down to Bondi Beach and then consider the last time you were in Cleethorpes. Watch as oiled Aussies effortlessly carry cool-boxes on glistening shoulders. Then think back to yourself, struggling along the promenade, eating a pie with one hand, keeping your hood up with the other, all the time being divebombed by a savage gull. There are some areas of life where Aussies really do just seem better made for the job.

And then along came Kevin Pietersen. With his hedgehog hair and purple streak, KP was like no other England cricketer. Bob Taylor had a great set of locks but it would be a cold day in hell before you found him in the dye aisle at Boots. Wandering round bronzed in a singlet, KP was the perfect man to remove the shackles from English cricket, taking advantage of the platform built by Michael Vaughan. The captain viewed banishing the layers of formality, the idea that to play for England you had to look and behave a certain way, as integral to instilling the forward-looking attitude crucial to eradicate those last few scars of recent Ashes pastings. Added to his own not inconsiderable level of self-belief, playing in such a free and easy atmosphere allowed KP to shine.

KP had come into the 2005 Ashes side after exploding on to the scene with two whirlwind centuries in England's ODI series in his native South Africa the previous winter. The man he replaced was my old mate Graham Thorpe. That in itself would normally have created a bit of pressure. Thorpey was, after all, a class act who'd been performing at the top level, and against the Aussies, for years. But with KP none of it seemed to touch the sides. He made two half-centuries on his debut at Lord's, smashed the Aussie attack around for another at Edgbaston, steadied the second innings at Trent Bridge when England were on the ropes, and then, as the Aussies sensed blood at The Oval, delivered one of the greatest Ashes innings of all time to put the game, and the urn, beyond the tourists and send the country into absolute delirium.

Bear in mind this was KP's first Test series and there he was hooking 90 mph Brett Lee bouncers off his face into the stands for six. Forget doing the textbook thing, rolling the wrists and hitting the ball to the fence for four. It didn't matter who was bowling, KP's attitude was clear – 'I'm going to take him on and hit him over the rope.' Shane Warne, the greatest spinner of all time? Kev didn't try to defend him, knock him around for a few runs here and there; he came down the track and launched him for six. Glenn McGrath? He took a step outside the line of that metronomic off stump ball and whipped it thorough the legside. Nearly five hours and 158 runs later, KP had completely erased any lingering views of how English batsmen should play against the Aussies. His psyche was never to take a step backwards. He showed that it was possible to go out there and get on top of them; that they were human after all.

Even when Kev flashed a chance to Warne at slip when he'd made just 15, his Hampshire colleague dropped it. Finally, the boot was on the other foot. How many times in the past had we given an Aussie batsman a second chance and been punished for it? If you dropped them early on, it felt like they always made you pay. Matthew Elliott is perhaps the most famous example. At Headingley, in 1997, with his side wobbling on 50–3 in their first innings, the opener was dropped on 29 by Graham Thorpe, normally the safest pair of hands, at slip. Elliott went on to make a seven-and-a-half-hour 199 as Australia cantered home by an innings. For too many years England gave Australia too many let-offs. On countless occasions we'd be sat in the dressing room at the end of the day thinking, *For f***'s sake! Why didn't we just catch it?* Especially since, on the rare occasions the Aussies gave us a second chance, we'd seemingly never take it.

KP had never sat in a dressing room like that. He'd never offered a chance and then felt the pressure to rein himself in, to go on the defensive, occupy the crease and drag the game to a draw by using up time. If anything, Warne's drop simply bolstered his belief that this was his day, his moment. From that point on he never looked back. He took the game by the scruff of the neck and blasted his team out of sight. Fifteen fours and seven sixes later, any chance of Australia bowling England out cheaply and mounting a successful run chase had gone. His onslaught has to go down as one of the most extraordinary Ashes innings of all time. The perfect embodiment of what England had been doing all summer, stamping their foot down and saying, 'We're not going to roll over at home anymore. This is our patch and we're going to make life difficult for you.' It had been a long time since an England team had done that. But it worked. England have been very hard to beat on their own turf ever since, nurturing the personnel to ram the advantage home. Swinging and seaming at Trent Bridge? Meet Anderson and Broad. Last-day turner at The Oval? May we introduce Graeme Swann?

The 2005 Ashes was KP's honeymoon. The problem was that as he progressed further into the marriage he began to frustrate. Whereas once he'd dominate attacks in a clinical and clear-headed manner, now he was getting himself into a great position, making 70 or 80, only to play a rash shot and give his wicket away. Against the best sides in the world, that's damaging. More recently we've seen the same issue creep in with Bazball. Gifting wickets to Australia cost us victory in 2023 and could do so again. To beat a team as good as them you need to dominate, but intelligently. If you've reached 75 on a good, true Australian wicket, don't, whatever you do, reverse scoop Pat Cummins and get out because that won't win your team anything. I agree with the ethos of Bazball – taking the attack to the opposition – but silly shots don't beat Australia. Look at how Alastair Cook succeeded in 2010–11 – big innings built on concentration and discipline. You have to grind the Aussies. Because they will grind you. The Australian psyche is never to give it away. Seventy to an Aussie is nothing. 'You got 70? So what? You're a batsman, mate, you're meant to get 70.' Get 190, on the other hand, and you're hurting them. The runs are piling up and you're keeping them out there for hours, putting miles into their legs, grinding them mentally and physically. Seventy doesn't cause a dent; 190 and you're on your way to causing a write-off. In their 1990s pomp, the Aussies sought those big scores every time. Look at that Headingley Test in 1997. England's top scorer in the match was Nasser Hussain with 105. Great effort, but after Matthew Elliott's 199, it didn't touch the sides. Australia won by an innings.

Ultimately, while KP finished his final Ashes series in 2014 – a whitewash Down Under – as top run-scorer, he pressed the self-destruct button on his England career by time and again making poor shot decisions. Being top run-scorer is one thing, but it's meaningless if you're not getting your team into winning positions, if you keep hitting the ball down the opposition's throat. I couldn't help thinking of the players who wouldn't have played those shots, who would have stuck around and built a platform for their side to exploit. I get that mavericks have to be allowed a degree of flexibility, but you have to back up the enigma with the application.

KP will always split opinion. To some he was a one-off and so should have been allowed to play as such. To others, he was a loose cannon, his unwillingness to compromise on the pitch mirroring an inability to mould into a team player off it. But in that summer of 2005 every England cricket fan was united in sheer admiration of a once-in-a-generation player using his undoubted genius to stick it to the Aussies.

Talking of generations, I wonder, had I debuted under Vaughany in 2005, if my barnet too would have been indulged rather than, desperate to make me see the light and give me the best chance of selection for England, my Middlesex skipper Mike Gatting marching me down Uxbridge high street and into the nearest barbers to have my ponytail cut off. Fifteen years later and I'd have been a trendsetter. Everyone would have had one. Freddie, Hoggy, Dickie Bird. Sadly it wasn't to be. Some mavericks will always be lost to the time in which they operated. Still upsets me. It wasn't even purple.

27 ASHES TESTS

Runs: 2,158
Highest Score: 227
Avg: 44.95
Hundreds: 4
Fifties: 13

Wickets: 2
Best Bowling: 1–10
Avg: 158.0

50.

MERV HUGHES

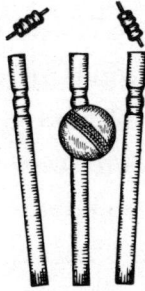

*Generously moustachioed paceman who
didn't give a XXXX what he said to a Pom
if it helped get them out.*

The first time I batted for England, Merv Hughes greeted me in
the middle. 'All right Tuffers?' he asked. *What a pleasant chap,* I
mulled. *How considerate to enquire about my welfare.* He paused to
look me square in the eye. 'I'm going to use you for target practice.' *Ah, right,* I thought, *I might have slightly misjudged this bloke.*

Merv was, shall we say, pretty vocal. 'Turn the bat over, mate,'
he once told Graeme Hick. 'You'll find there's instructions on the
back.' Another time he asked Graham Gooch, 'Would you like
me to bowl a piano and see if you can play that?' These are two of
the mere handful of surviving examples of intelligible sledges

from the vast Aussie paceman. Sadly for cricket historians, everything else was lost in his vast expanse of Merv's moustache. You knew he was giving you the mother of all goings-over but all you'd make out was the occasional word – 'bat', 'arsehole', 'Pommie' and 'bastard' typically audible within the general melange of spluttering and growling. Dickie Bird did actually once ask Merv to stop swearing. And, to be fair to the six-foot-four Victorian, he obliged. For one ball.

In my case, I had no intention of hanging around to be on the end of either Merv's tongue or his bouncer. On one occasion I was gutted to glove a blisteringly unpleasant ball through to Ian Healy behind the stumps only to realise the ump hadn't heard the deflection and was about to give it not out. The repercussions didn't bear thinking about. Merv was bad enough to face when he was in a good mood. Imagine what he'd be like if a nailed-on caught behind was turned down? There was nothing else for it. 'Ahh!' I shouted, holding my thumb and wincing. Up went the umpire's finger. Job done. Safely back in the hutch.

Thing with Merv was, possibly because people were so obsessed with the way he looked – one commentator famously compared his run-up to a wardrobe cartwheeling down a hill – he was hugely underrated as a bowler. Javed Miandad once told him, 'You look like a fat bus conductor.' Merv's send-off to the Pakistan batsman a couple of balls later – 'Tickets please!' – remains a classic of its kind.

His skill with the ball was no better exemplified than at Old Trafford in 1993. While that Test will always be remembered for Warney's incredible delivery that did for Gatt in England's first innings, the yorker from Merv that demolished poor Gatt's stumps second time round was, in its own way, equally as brilliant.

Coming right at the end of the fourth day it was a massive blow to England's chances of batting out the match for a draw.

And yet, at the same time, he was hardly averse to playing up to his larger-than-life image. In the summer of 1989 it seemed every London bus I clapped eyes on had a Merv 'tache smeared in Castlemaine XXXX froth, plastered on the side, complete with the advertising legend *Australians wouldn't give a XXXX for anything else.* By his own admission, Merv made sure he stayed in the sponsor's good books by drinking the stuff every chance he got. Worth remembering though, that it was Merv who, as we watched, hearts in mouths on the Lord's balcony, motored round the boundary and threw the ball in to run Athers out on 99. Supreme fitness in players is one thing, ultimate willpower entirely another. Shane Warne, with 34 wickets, got all the head-lines in that 4–1 Ashes win in 1993, with Merv right behind him on 31. Neither were exactly poster boys for the gym but they performed brilliantly when it mattered.

These days, gazing from the *TMS* box, I see Merv sat in the crowd at Ashes Tests in his modern guise as a tour guide. He'll have 50 Aussies all wearing yellow sat around him, the main surprise being that he hasn't got them on their feet bellowing obscenities at the English batsmen. At least he never went back to his original job, as a menswear salesman. No-one wants to pick a jacket off the rail and be told from six inches distance, 'You're never going to fit in that, you fat bastard.'

Merv was the classic Aussie of his time. A demon on the pitch, something completely different off it. After all, when, as a wannabe cricketer in Melbourne, he'd spotted a young Ian Botham in town and asked him for some advice, Beefy's sugges-tion was that he take up tennis or golf instead. A few years later, after making his Ashes debut in the Brisbane Test of 1986, in which Beefy smashed England to victory with 138, Merv asked what Beefy thought of his advice now. It was a free header for the great all-rounder, especially since he'd taken 22 off a single Merv over. Naturally, he impressed on his inquisitor that clearly he'd been right. And yet, 38 years later, there was Merv plucking Beefy from a shark-infested river. They'd been mates all that time. Says everything for how the Ashes rivalry should operate. Same as if I'd have been there, Merv, and it was you floundering in the depths, I'd have pulled you out.

No, really, pal, I would. Honest.

---

20 ASHES TESTS

Wickets: 75
Best Bowling: 5–92
Avg: 30.25
Five-wicket Innings: 1
Ten-wicket Matches: 0

Runs: 278
Highest Score: 71
Avg: 13.23
Hundreds: 0
Fifties: 1

And me?

---

12 ASHES TESTS

Wickets: 36
Best Bowling: 7–66
Avg: 38.13
Five-wicket Innings: 2
Ten-wicket Matches: 1

Runs: 30
Highest Score: 8
Avg: 2.72

(Look, I wasn't there for my batting was I?)

ACKNOWLEDGEMENTS

Compiling my Ashes heroes hasn't been easy. There are more than a few names that didn't quite end up on the honours board. It's the first time in my life I've had a bit of sympathy for selectors.

I'd like to take this opportunity to thank each and every player, in blue cap or green, who shared my Ashes odyssey. There is pleasure and pain in being an Ashes cricketer, but it is never less than the most remarkable of experiences. Thank you for being part of the most incredible memories a bloke could ever have.

To those I watched growing up, who helped form the idea that I too might one day be part of the greatest sporting contest on Earth, thank you too. It was your character, your spirit, that planted the seed. Even so, getting into the arena was far from easy, and my deep gratitude goes to those cricketers and coaches who supported me and gave me belief that I could make the leap.

I have loved writing this book, but not a word of it would have appeared without the support of my wife, Dawn. For all the time

I've spent squirelling away on this project, thank you. I can lift my head up from the laptop now – at least until the next one! Huge thanks also to Jonathan Taylor at HarperCollins for his support and advice, and John Woodhouse for helping me transfer our many highly enjoyable chats to the page. We did occasionally manage a little bit of work between the laughs.

I suppose more than anyone I should thank a certain Reginald Shirley Walkinshaw Brooks, the young *Sporting Times* journalist, who, after England lost at The Oval, on 29 August, 1882, penned the mock obituary of English cricket that gave birth to this most remarkable of contests. 'The body will be cremated and the Ashes taken to Australia,' he wrote. There were a couple of times playing the Aussies I felt like I'd been cremated too! But seriously, to be witness to such drama, such tradition, first in the field, and then from the commentary box, has never been less than the hugest of treats.

Join me in a sip of something bubbly, preferably from a bottle freshly sabred by David Gower, as I raise my glass and say, 'The Ashes! Thank you, and long may you continue!'